ASSIGNMENT
PENTAGON

Also by Maj. Gen. Perry M. Smith

The Air Force Plans for Peace, 1943–1945 (1970)
*Creating Strategic Vision: Long-Range Planning for
    National Security* (1987) with Jerry Allen, John Stewart,
    and Douglas Whitehouse
Taking Charge: Making the Right Choices (1988)
How CNN Fought the War: A View from the Inside (1991)

ASSIGNMENT: PENTAGON

The Insider's Guide to the Puzzle Palace

Second Edition, Revised

Maj. Gen. Perry M. Smith, USAF (Ret.)

BRASSEY'S
Washington London

Library of Congress Cataloging-in-Publication Data
Smith, Perry M. (Perry McCoy)
    Assignment—Pentagon : the insider's guide to the Potomac puzzle
palace / Perry M. Smith ; foreword by Harold Brown.—2nd ed., rev.
        p.   cm.—(AN AUSA book)
    Includes bibliographical references and index.
    ISBN 0–02–881018–X.—ISBN 0–02–881017–1 (pbk.)
    1. Pentagon (Va.)   2. United States—Armed Forces—Management.
3. United States. Dept. of Defense—Management.   I. Title.
II. Series: AUSA Institute of Land Warfare book.
UA26.A745S55   1993
353.6—dc20   92–41824
                                                           CIP

10 9 8 7 6 5 4 3

Printed in the United States of America

To Connor, McCoy, and Serena
who lifted me up so many times
during those years that I worked in the Pentagon.
Their gentle reminders that what I was doing was important
helped me overcome the setbacks, the down times,
and the frustrations that are part of
everyday life in the Building.

An AUSA Book

The Association of the United States Army (AUSA) was founded in 1950 as a not-for-profit organization dedicated to education concerning the role of the U.S. Army, to providing material for military professional development, and to the promotion of proper recognition and appreciation of the profession of arms. Its constituencies include those who serve in the Army today, including Army National Guard, Army Reserve, and Army civilians, the retirees and veterans who have served in the past, and all their families. A large number of public-minded citizens and business leaders are also an important constituency. The association seeks to educate the public, elected and appointed officials, and leaders of the defense industry on crucial issues involving the adequacy of our national defense, particularly those issues affecting land warfare.

In 1988 the AUSA established within its existing organization a new entity known as the Institute of Land Warfare. Its purpose is to extend the educational work of the AUSA by sponsoring scholarly publications, to include books, monographs, and essays on key defense issues, as well as workshops and symposia. Among the volumes chosen for designation as "An AUSA Institute of Land Warfare Book" are both new texts and reprints of titles of enduring value that are no longer in print. Topics include history, policy issues, strategy, and tactics. Publication as an AUSA book does not necessarily indicate that the Association of the United States Army and the publisher agree with everything in the book, but does suggest that the AUSA and the publisher believe it will stimulate the thinking of AUSA members and others concerned about important issues.

CONTENTS

FOREWORD

In a complex, chaotic, and dangerous world of the post–cold war era, the Department of Defense will remain a major element of the U.S. government. Maintaining foreign and security policy continuity from one administration to the next has proven increasingly difficult—especially in rhetoric, but also in substance—during recent decades. Fortunately, the professional military provides an institutional memory, a tradition of responsibility to past policies and commitments, and an ability to get things done.

In common with most large organizations, the Department of Defense has an elaborate set of rules and regulations, codifying formal procedures and professional relationships. But it also has a sociology, a decades-old, but constantly evolving, informal and often unwritten set of procedures and relationships. A large number of individuals, some long-termers and some short-termers, military and civilian, embody that less visible structure. General Perry Smith's book *Assignment: Pentagon—The Insider's Guide to the Potomac Puzzle Palace* is an outstanding introduction for the newly assigned military person, the fresh civilian, and the interested outsider to this informal set of arrangements, networks, and functions, which operate in the service and joint service world of "ops deps," division heads, action officers, two-hour four-projector briefings, and "woodshed sessions" in preparation for congressional testimony.

Many—not all—of the assignments at the Pentagon involve long hours and demanding intellectual and personal commitment. The strain tells on individuals and on their families. The book assists in these areas by providing advice on sensible management of Pentagon life, whether dealing with when to exercise at the Pentagon Athletic Club, how to avoid Shirley Highway traffic, or which are the best news broadcasts to watch on television. This helpful "how to" information is useful in any new environment. The extensive glossary and the chapter on the "Strange Language of the Potomac Puzzle Palace" will be particularly valuable to outsiders trying to understand what happens in the Pentagon and, with the inclusion of acronyms and jargon that seldom appear in the newspapers, to the newly assigned neophyte civilian or officer fresh from the world of field operations.

But even more important than the jargon, the location of the restrooms, and how the documents flow are issues that have come into sharp relief during the 1990s—issues of command responsibility, of personal and professional ethics, and of behavior that has tarnished both civilian and military reputations. During the next five years, we are likely to see decreasing defense budgets, increasing "jointness" in military planning and operations, more interservice procurements, and a decreasing willingness of senior military and civilian officials to be treated like mushrooms—"kept in the dark and fed on manure." These trends will make attention to matters of ethics and responsibility even more important.

Fortunately, Perry Smith devotes considerable attention to these matters as well. His own service, as military assistant to the deputy secretary of defense, as a wing commander in Germany, as director of Air Force Plans, and as commandant of the National War College, the nation's premier military academic institution, gives him a broad perspective on organizational matters and individual behavior. I am sure that his unique and very useful *Assignment: Pentagon* will find wide interest and application among civilians and members of the military. I also expect that positive feedback to the author from numerous grateful readers will enhance this fine book's many future editions.

HAROLD BROWN
Washington, D.C.

ASSIGNMENT: PENTAGON

1
INTRODUCTION

Work smarter, not harder.
    —RON CARSWELL

The idea for this book came to me when I had just taken over as director of plans for the United States Air Force. I was dictating a welcoming letter for the officers and noncommissioned officers who were headed to Washington to work for me. I wanted to suggest that they read three or four books to help them get ready for the work ahead. One of the books I looked for was a practical guide that covered Pentagon rules of the game and the helpful hints that couldn't be found in a manual or a regulation. There was no such guide. Since there is clearly a need for such a guide or handbook, I thought I would pull my ideas and the ideas of many others together.

This book was designed to help people who are headed for the Pentagon for their very first assignment and who would like to get the kind of informal advice that they might get over a couple of beers at the bar or on a Sunday afternoon with a friend who worked there. But this book is designed to be more than just a practical guide to a strange new environment. It is also written for people who are interested in how that monstrous five-sided-building-on-the-Potomac operates, but who have no expectation of working there. Military people in the field, scholars, members of the media, defense contractors, military attachés, and others may find this guide of use.

3

In our democratic society, it is important that the interaction between those who work in the Pentagon and those who do not be a productive one. So often it is the lack of understanding of the rules of the game in the Pentagon, particularly on the part of those who have never worked there, that makes dialogue and understanding so difficult. Scholars, for instance, do extensive research and interviewing, yet they often miss some important subtleties of the Pentagon. The result is research and analysis that may be 95 percent accurate but misses the key 5 percent that may really make the difference. In football terms, they may have the playbook, but they miss the audibles.

It is my hope that this book will have some value over both the short and the long term and that, with periodic updating, it can be a useful guide for many years to come. With that in mind, I would like to solicit comments, criticism, suggested changes, and additions from those who do me the honor of reading this short book. Feel free to write or phone me. My address is P.O. Box 15666, Augusta, Georgia 30919; telephone (706) 738–9133.

When I was the commandant of the National War College, during the last three years of my military career, it occurred to me that if someone were to write a practical guide to the Pentagon, it should probably be someone who had worked there for many years and who had a broad background in the affairs of the four most significant uniformed services. In this regard, I am indeed most fortunate. I have had the privilege of being closely associated with these four services during much of my lifetime. Born into an Army family at West Point, New York, in the middle of the Great Depression, I left the country for Panama when I was six months old. At age six, I watched the Japanese bomb Pearl Harbor. At age 12, I got caught in a food riot in Naples in 1946 and watched one of the biggest Communist demonstrations in the post-war period on May Day 1947, in Milan when the Italian Communist party was at the height of its power and enthusiasm. I first visited the Pentagon during the late forties when my father worked there as an Army colonel. I joined the military at age 17, attended the United States Military Academy, and graduated in 1956.

After 21 years with the United States Army, I spent the next 30 years as an Air Force officer. My wife of 30 years, Connor Dyess Smith, is the daughter of a Marine Corps officer who is the only person in history to have earned both the Carnegie Medal (for peacetime heroism) and the Congressional Medal of Honor. (He was killed in the Marshall Islands on February 2, 1944.) As you would expect, our family's relationship with the U.S. Marine Corps has been a close and warm one. The United States Navy named a destroyer (DD 880) in honor of her father, A. James Dyess, and the Navy demonstrated great hospitality toward Connor and our entire family for many years. My years at the National War College as a young faculty member and later as commandant increased my knowledge of and respect for each of our four services.

As I wrote this book, I was not constrained in any way except by my desire not to reveal any classified material. It has been great fun putting this together—probably more fun than any other book I have written. I have written it not using the language of a scholar but the language of the Pentagon. I have done this purposefully, since part of learning how the place operates is learning the unique phrases that are so commonly used within the halls of the Building.

I have asked lots of friends, most of whom I knew at the National War College when they were students there in the mid-1980s and are now working in the Building, to look over the manuscript closely and critically. As a result, I have received great feedback from individuals in all services and from all of the major offices in the Pentagon. I will not acknowledge most of them. Some of the things I say in this book are controversial, and I do not, in any way, want to hurt any of those who gave me such great assistance. Since they know who they are, I acknowledge, up front, their assistance and thank them deeply for it.

I would also like to acknowledge the assistance of the following individuals who no longer work in the Building. Each of these people reviewed my manuscript and gave me many useful ideas, insights, and criticism. They were particularly helpful in pointing out important areas that I had overlooked: Howard Barnard, Bob Plowden, Bob Hilton, Sam Packer, Bill Brehm, John Rose,

Bob Ward, Russ Dougherty, Dick Daleski, John Baker, Monte Montgomery, Emilio Tavernise, Dick Dowell, Giles Harlow, Jim Dalton, Tom Cardwell, Pat Wheeler, J. R. Allen, Jed Peters, Doug Olsen, Steve Pitotti, Tom Berry, Mark Cancian, David Lopez, and Larry Outlaw. Also, a word of thanks to four colonels who worked in the Building in the 1970s who taught me the value of high standards in staff work and the overwhelming priority of high integrity—Ray Dunn, Bud Rose, John Nolan, and Harry Lauterbach. Frank Margiotta, Don McKeon, and Vicki Chamlee of Brassey's deserve a special note of thanks for their great enthusiasm for this enterprise as well as for their thoughtful criticisms and useful ideas. And thanks also to Nancy Hoagland for carefully editing the manuscript.

Two experiences in the early 1990s have further enriched my understanding of the Pentagon. When I was a full-time military analyst for Cable News Network (CNN) during Desert Storm, I learned how willing most Pentagon officials were to share information with someone in the media whom they trusted. My commentary on CNN, both during the Gulf War of 1991 and since, has been enhanced by the information and insights I receive from more than 30 officials in the Pentagon.

Working closely with President Bill Clinton's national security transition team prior to January 20, 1993, helped me better understand the selection process for high-level officials in the Department of Defense. Secretary of Defense Les Aspin's team of Bill Perry, Frank Wisner, Walt Slocombe, Ted Warner, Graham Allison, and others is fully committed to restructuring the Office of the Secretary of Defense and the entire Defense Department so the U.S. military can effectively meet the diverse challenges of the post–cold war era.

2

THE PENTAGON:
REALITIES AND MYTHS

Common sense is the knack of seeing things as they are.
—E. C. STOWE

The Pentagon is a vibrant city, a unique subculture, a way of life. It has its own momentum, language, and life-style: almost a Starship Enterprise. Over 23,000 people, civilian and military, work in the 3,700,000 square feet of office space. Even 50 years after it was designed, it remains one of the largest office buildings in the entire world. It is twice as large as the Merchandise Mart in Chicago and has three times the office space of the Empire State Building in New York. The U.S. Capitol, the most impressive structure in the nation's capital (with the possible exception of the Washington Cathedral), could fit in one of the five wedges of the Pentagon. The Defense Post Office handles over a million pieces of mail monthly, not including the internal papers, memorandums, and circulars that comprise most of the written communication in the Building. Over 200,000 telephone calls are made each day from the over 80,000 telephones (almost double the 44,000 of a few years ago). There are many libraries, including the Army library—the largest and most widely used—which contains over 300,000 volumes and 1,700 periodicals.

Most insiders refer to the Pentagon simply as the "Building" or more affectionately as the Puzzle Palace (and, when they are in a

7

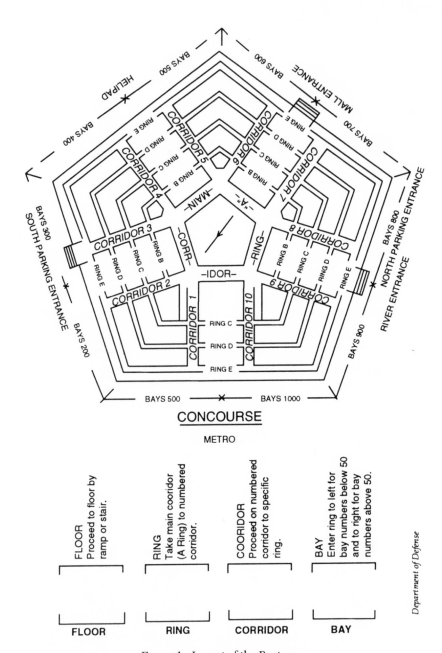

FIGURE 1. Layout of the Pentagon

more critical mood, as Fort Fumble, the Fudge Factory, the Squirrel Cage, or the five-sided wailing wall).

The Building has been, since it was first occupied early in World War II, one of the most efficient office buildings in the world. Even though it has over 17½ miles of corridors, it takes less than 10 minutes, at the normal, brisk Pentagon walk, to get from any one office to another. Working within this famous building is a very large number of employees with great talent, resilience, and dedication. If I were to pick one long-term employee who personifies the very best in the Pentagon, it would be Melba Boling. She combines efficiency, style, and personal warmth in such a way that she worked her way up to the position of the confidential assistant to the deputy secretary of defense. More about Melba later.

To understand the Pentagon, one must understand the U.S. military—its history, culture, numerous subcultures, life-style, language, dreams, mentality, family life, passions, calling, nomadic nature, and value system. Much has been written about the "military mind," and most, if not all, of it is misleading. To many, especially among the American intellectual elites, the military professional is considered to be authoritarian, reactionary, and bounded by a strong macho culture. The harsher critics see the military as an anti-intellectual group that is unreceptive to constructive criticism from the outside or the inside. These critics sometimes suggest that many military professionals, fearing that they could not find work in the outside world, tend to cling to the security of a regular monthly check and a guaranteed pension. There is a whole body of literature that is highly critical of the military and its parochial and wasteful proclivities.

In reality, the American military reflects the values, hopes, dreams, aspirations, weaknesses, and strengths of the American culture. Although at one time is was well isolated from American society, this has not been the case since the early 1940s. The military has become a force for social change (serious efforts in racial integration in this country began in the U.S. military under President Harry Truman), for the education and training of the less privileged in America, and for the broadening of the individual American experience in international affairs, and culture (the popular phrase after our big international adventure in World War I was "How ya gonna keep 'em down on the farm after they've seen Paree?").

Our military is a vast meritocracy and as such it reflects something that is fundamental to the American experience and the American dream—that is, equality of opportunity. Our military has never had a coup mentality; the "man on horseback" who might plan a military takeover of the government has been a rare (some would argue nonexistent) phenomenon throughout our history. This abiding commitment by our military leaders to civilian control must be understood if someone is going to grasp how the Pentagon works and how it may differ from defense ministries in some other locations around the globe.

What is it, then, that gives the Pentagon a special flavor? Let me list a few aspects, using the "bullet" format of the "point paper" that is so commonly used in the Building to give the busy officials information in a condensed and useful format:

- The urgency and level of importance of issues and actions
- The unexpectedness of some of the questions
- The camaraderie among those who are the producers (as opposed to the non-producers—the so-called lightweights)
- The close contact of the action officers (the standard name for Pentagon staff officers) with many senior individuals, who are busy and demanding but for the most part understanding and accessible
- The amazing number of issues being addressed on a daily basis
- The requirements for extensive coordination
- The frequent frustration in trying to get support for almost any position
- The occasional "crashes" when individuals of various ranks work through the night or a weekend to deal with a crisis
- The pressures, the deadlines, and the inability of most to get to the bottom of their in box
- The uncertainties of fiscal support

MYTHS ABOUT THE PENTAGON

Any listing of myths, realities, truisms, or rules of thumb about the complex, multidimensional environment that is the Pentagon must be preceded by some words of caution. Much that happens in that complex building is situational, and although there are many constants, there are also many variables. The same issue may be treated quite differently by the same people at a later time because of changed attitudes, changed outside forces, an altered budgetary climate, shifting congressional support, or a different international environment. Since the past is not always prologue and precedent often does not apply, there is a need to remain somewhat skeptical about any advice that I or anyone else might give about operating effectively within the Building. Keeping this caution in mind, please join me in exploring a number of myths about the Building with which you may have to deal in the weeks, months, or years ahead.

Everybody works 14-hour days. In reality most of the employees work between eight and ten hours a day. The mass of workers hustling to work between 7 and 8 A.M. and surging out of the building between 4 and 5 P.M. attests to this fact. When the time for commuting (and walking to and from the faraway parking places) is added to the work day, the time away from home averages around 11 hours. As in all large organizations, there is a certain percentage of "goof offs" (perhaps 5 to 10 percent), but, on balance, this is a more talented, dedicated, and effective group than you will find in almost any other government office building in the world. There *are* people who do work 11-hour days or longer on a regular basis. This group comprises from 10 to 20 percent of the Pentagon work force. However, some staffs are caught up in such a habitual pattern of longer hours that the percentage there is much higher (the part of the Army staff that works for the deputy chief of staff for operations would be one example).

Regular weekend work that was common throughout the Vietnam War and Desert Storm has dropped off. Sunday work call has become rare except in those offices and command posts that must stay open constantly. Saturday and Sunday "loyalty checks," where you are expected to be in the Building irrespective of whether there is important work to do, are less prevalent today than they were from the frenetic days of Robert McNamara through the workaholic days of Jimmy Carter. In fact, with the Total Quality

Management (TQM) Programs, weekend work often requires supervisory permission.

Everybody hates working there. This is probably the most widely held myth of all. First of all, there is a large number of people who have committed themselves to spending the majority of their professional lives working in the Pentagon. That commitment is often made on the basis of the fact that they love their work, find it interesting and enjoyable, and feel that they are able to make an important contribution to the development of important public policy. Second, military members usually complain that they would rather be out in the field, out with the fleet, or out flying airplanes, yet quite a few quietly extend their tours or volunteer to return after being away for a while. Of course, there are those people who hate the place and think that the best view of the Pentagon is from their rear view mirror on the way out of town *permanently.* But clearly that group is a minority.

All the office secretaries are incompetent. Some are, but lots are great. With a couple of notable exceptions, the best secretaries that I had during my thirty-year military career were my secretaries in the Pentagon (thanks Chili, Donna, Norma, Barbara, Melba). Without question, most need, want, and deserve your support, concern, and care. On the negative side, the worst secretary I ever had was in the Pentagon. I and others encouraged her to leave government and find employment in the private sector, and she did, thank goodness.

At the branch and division level, the turnover of secretaries is a horrendous problem. Of course, the very best secretaries rise rapidly and soon work for the big bosses. These higher-level secretaries can be of great assistance to individuals at the branch and division level for they tend to know the system and understand their bosses well. They can often help in improving staff papers, in suggesting where help can be found and, most important of all, in finding time on the boss's schedule. In a real crunch, they often will dive in and help "fix the package" for you, type up a quick memo or background paper, or otherwise make important things happen.

It is impossible to fire anyone. It is tough to fire people, particularly long-term civilian employees, but it can be and is done. It does require good documentation (counseling sessions, records of absences, performance records, etc.), lots of stick-to-it-iveness, and much patience. Having watched a number of people eased out of the Building and having removed three subordinates myself, I can say, with some empirical data to back me up, that firings occasionally do take place in this five-sided building.

Everyone is so busy that no one has time to think or plan. Those who manage their time well, have lots of energy, and "discipline" their in boxes and telephones do have time to conceptualize, think, and plan. It really helps if you have a quick mind and are well read, self-confident, and experienced in working within large organizations. It also helps if you have lots of talented people working with you—which, happily, is the case in most offices in the Building.

Bosses tend to ride a good horse until it drops. Superb action officers do tend to get loaded down with work, but most division and branch chiefs work hard to distribute the work load so that the best people don't get burned out with too many demanding actions piled on top of one another.

The Office of the Secretary of Defense is full of power-mad bureaucrats. The Office of the Secretary of Defense (OSD) got a very bad name during the time that Robert McNamara was secretary of defense in the 1960s. A number of so-called whiz kids whom McNamara had recruited treated the veteran Pentagon officials (both military and civilian) with contempt. Today the situation is better. There are lots of people who work in OSD who are not only competent but also easy to work with. Unfortunately, the transgressions of the past and the occasional stupid power play on the part of the odd official have sustained the bad reputation to some degree. Clearly, the power of the staff of the secretary of defense diminished considerably in the 1980s as Secretaries Weinberger and Carlucci worked hard to decentralize the department. They both returned power to the military departments, the commanders in chief in the field, and the chairman and vice chairman of the Joint Chiefs of Staff (JCS). In general terms, when the Republicans are in power there tends to be more decentralization within the Department of Defense than when the Democrats control the executive branch of government. However, even more fundamental, it is the management style of the secretary of defense and his deputy that determines the role and the power of the staff that works directly for them.

Joint papers are so watered down through compromise that they are best described as multihumped camels. When there is Joint Staff along with all four services' agreement on an issue, strong, punchy papers are written. However, when there is disagreement, there can be much compromising and waffling in the joint arena. The upgrading of the role of the chairman of the Joint Chiefs of Staff, the creation of a strong vice chairman, and the strengthening of the incentives for joint duty have all made a considerable difference in the quality of the work and the power of the Joint Staff since 1986 when the Goldwater–Nichols Act became law. Since the late 1980s, the Joint Staff officers no longer have to spend so much time accommodating the positions of all four services. Hence the papers tend to be more to the point rather than watered-down compromises.

No one really has a handle on how the place works. Although the numbers are rather small, there are some people who have worked in the Building for a long time in a number of jobs who really have a sense for the place both in general and in considerable detail. Let me name a few: Melba Boling, confidential assistant to the deputy secretary of defense for many years; David Chu, who ran the analysis shop in OSD throughout the 1980s (and well into the 1990s) and was closely involved in the evolution of the Defense Planning and Resources Board; Andy Marshall of Net Assessment fame, who for over 20 years helped the Department of Defense take a broad strategic view; and Doc Cooke, the director of Washington Headquarters Services—the "mayor of the Pentagon" for so many years. There are many others who no longer work in the Pentagon but retain a great deal of knowledge about how it works. Jim Dalton, Harry Train, and George Seignious worked effectively in the joint arena. The dedicated work in the policy arena by Bob Hilton and John Bellinger in many different jobs has been noteworthy. Jim Wade grappled for years with issues of arms control, nuclear policy, and the weapons acquisition process.

Within each service there are several individuals of this type. Often they are senior civilians who have served at high levels for many years. Executive secretaries who know how to get things done and know where the bodies are buried are a very special breed. There are also a few officers in the pay grades of 0–6 through 0–9 (colonel/captain through lieutenant general/vice admiral) with five or more years of Pentagon experience who have their fingers on the pulse of the Building. There is always a sizable number of experienced staff officers. By the three-year mark in their Pentagon tour, most of these action officers have a fine grasp of what is important and how to get things done. Finally, there are some very sharp enlisted personnel with an excellent grasp for "institutional memory." Many of these enlisted personnel have served in Washington for extended tours and have an uncanny feel for how to get things done. If you are fortunate enough to have the opportunity to sit at the feet of these kinds of people and you take the time to listen carefully, the learning benefits can be extraordinary.

3

Rules of Thumb: Helpful Hints on How to Get Ready to Work, Survive, and Thrive

If you wish success in life, make perseverance your bosom friend, experience your wise counselor, caution your elder brother, and hope your guardian genius.

—Joseph Addison

So, you have the word that a Pentagon assignment is in the works, and the possibility of ducking out of the job is about zero. You have heard lots of horror stories about the place, and you have so much conflicting information that you have no clue as to how best to prepare for the assignment. Let me share with you some rules of thumb and insights that I have gained from many of my students at the National War College who had Pentagon experience and from the seven different jobs that I had on the fifth, fourth, and third floors of that building.

A few months before I went to my very first job in the Pentagon, I visited for a day and a half and received the following advice from three friends.

16

1. "Whatever you do, don't come; this place is too damned political. You will hate it."
2. "Nobody knows anything about national defense unless he has worked here."
3. "You will not believe the hours; you will work for weeks in a row without one day off—not even Sunday."

Although there is some truth in all these comments, they are all generally misleading. The place *is* political, as is almost everything that takes place in Washington, but Washington is the seat of the federal government. The military is too large to be outside the political process, and political issues are intriguing and often very important. In addition, although many will never admit it, most people in the Pentagon like their work, find it very rewarding, and often extend their tours voluntarily.

As for knowing national defense, if you have been keeping up with your operational or technical specialty and reading magazines like *Army,* the *Marine Corps Gazette, Proceedings, Armed Forces Journal International, Aviation Week, International Security,* and *Foreign Affairs,* and an occasional book like *American Defense Annual* and the novels of Tom Clancy, you will have much to contribute in your new job.

And yes, the hours are sometimes long and it is not unusual to work right through a weekend or work past midnight on a crash project, but there are quiet times and there are free weekends for all but the most committed workaholic (and those who work for workaholic or insecure bosses). So take what you have heard about life in the Pentagon with a certain amount of skepticism, and let me walk you through a few basics.

THINGS TO DO BEFORE YOU CHECK IN

Read two or three books. My recommendations: *American Defense Annual* edited by Joseph Kruzel (get the latest edition); the *Annual Report to the Congress* by the secretary of defense, and, for those headed to the Joint Staff, *The Joint Staff Officer's Guide* (written by the Armed Forces Staff College and commonly known as the "Purple Book"). When you get tired of this rather heavy reading, pick up *Murder at the Pentagon* by Margaret Truman. Although the story line is farfetched, Truman captures the language of the Pentagon rather well, and there is plenty of good suspense, especially in the last half of the book.

For good escapism, rent the videotape *No Way Out*. It is wildly implausible but quite entertaining. (The great short scene [not counting the intense scene in the limo] is early in the movie when there is a Washington party and the lieutenant commander, played by Kevin Costner, meets the secretary of defense for the first time. The way people look over the shoulders of those they are talking to in order to spot someone more important is captured in that scene with skill.) This film also captures the hustle and bustle of the Building quite well.

There is one other book worth glancing over before you check in—the *Department of Defense Telephone Directory*. It is packed with good information about the Building.

Take a speed reading course. If you are a slow reader, you are in for some awfully long hours and some agonizing times with short deadlines. Speed reading and learning how to skim material with a practiced eye is really helpful. It can shorten your work day by an hour or so. I suggest the book *Speed Reading Naturally* by Lillian P. Wenick (Englewoods Cliffs, N.J.: Prentice Hall, 1983) or *Speed Reading*, an inexpensive software program by Davidson, that is available in most large computer and software stores.

Keep family responsibilities in mind. Try to get the family well settled before you dive into your work. In addition, try to establish a mindset of family support. If you become so consumed with your work that you neglect your family for three or four years, you will regret it. Your family can and will provide you marvelous support, especially when you have a major setback or a string of bad days or weeks. But please don't fail to give them some of your "quality time." Really listen when they try to communicate with you rather than always having your mind on the job. If you have a tendency to be a workaholic, the Pentagon environment will reinforce that tendency. So watch out. If nothing else, save Sundays for the family. Give the family that day completely and don't let your mind be elsewhere when the family members are looking for company, support, and advice. Remember, arms are also for hugging.

Get your personal affairs in order. Since you are about to dive into a highly intense environment and you may never get to the bottom of your in box, it is a good idea to get your personal life in order before you check in to the Building. If you are an officer in any of the military services, I strongly suggest that you join the Army and Air Force Mutual Aid or the Navy Mutual Aid. These societies, which were chartered many years ago when tax laws were more liberal, provide many wonderful services. The insurance they sell is very competitive, but the biggest factor in joining is the peace of mind you will have knowing that if anything happens to you, some wonderful, caring people will take care of many matters for your family at no cost. Both these associations are within five minutes of the Pentagon. The Army and Air Force Mutual Aid (522–3060) is at Fort Myer, and the Navy Mutual Aid (614–8683) is at Henderson Hall.

One of the services that both the Navy Mutual Aid and the Army and Air Force Mutual Aid provide is they will store all your important records, including wills, insurance policies, birth certificates, and marriage licenses. Whenever you need them, just call up and they will send you copies. Many members leave their records there permanently and therefore don't have to haul them all over the world from one safe deposit box to another.

GROUND RULES FOR THE FIRST FEW WEEKS

Get to work early. There is much to be said for getting on the road by 6:00 A.M. so you can get to the building by 7:00 A.M. This is a great way to beat most of the traffic (although if you live in some places, such as Woodbridge or Dale City, you may want to get going a bit earlier). Since life starts getting very hectic about 8:00

A.M., a 7:00 A.M. arrival will give you a reasonably quiet time when you can get a lot done. If early morning is not a time for you to do your best staff work, take an early morning jog out of the athletic center (it opens at 6:00 A.M.), meet someone for breakfast or read the "early bird" news summary. (The early bird, which is published in the middle of the night, has a fine collection of newspaper articles on national defense that appear in the early editions of a number of first-rate newspapers such as the *New York Times*, the *Wall Street Journal*, the *Washington Post*, etc.) Also, early morning is a fine time to get in your calls to Europe or the Middle East before the lines get overloaded and before the people in those areas go home. There is a final reason to get to work early that some of you may find compelling: you may impress your boss or bosses. You will probably prefer to impress bosses with the quality of your work but, let's face it: some bosses are also impressed if you are there early to help with some early morning activity (often called crashes).

Join a car pool. This is a good way to preserve your sanity, get to be friends with a few others, stay "tuned in" with what is happening in others parts of the Building, save on gas, get a free and better parking place, and force yourself to go home at a decent hour. Many new arrivals think car pools are wildly impractical, but the Pentagon has become well adjusted to the realities of car pools. It is quite easy to find one to fit your needs and hours. You should be able to find a few folks who keep about the same hours you do, who enjoy not having to drive every day, and who love the faster-moving car pool lanes.

Get a copy of **Tongue and Quill.** This is the best guide to practical writing and briefing that I have been able to find. It is an Air Force pamphlet (13–2), but it applies to all the services and the Joint Staff. There are lots of copies around the Pentagon. So far there have been over 1.6 million sold (and not a nickel of royalties to that marvelous guy from Air Command and Staff College, Hank Staley, who put *Tongue and Quill* together). Each service has an administrative publication, for instance, the Air Force one is HOI 10–1. The Army Style Manual is excellent.

Buy a watch with at least three built-in alarms. Missing key meetings can ruin your whole day and lead to dire consequences. One way to alleviate that problem is to set your alarms each morning to go off thirty minutes before the next key meeting. That way you can concentrate on your current project and be reminded in time to get ready for the next meeting. These watches also can be useful ways to excuse yourself from a meeting. When it goes off, you can leave and race off to the next meeting or appointment. One major caution, however, about watches with built-in alarms: don't let your watch beep in the presence of senior officials, some of whom find it distracting and impolite to have watches beeping all around the room during meetings and briefings.

Join the Pentagon Athletic Club. This recently remodeled facility is a fine place to grab a bite to eat; the exercise facilities range from good to excellent; and it is a great place to meet interesting people, to get rid of some of the frustrations on the job, and to stay in reasonably good shape. If you are a jogger or a runner and are fortunate to live fairly close in, you might consider running to work. Or you might want to drive to work and take an early run through the parks around the Pentagon. Lots of folks do just that or take a run at noon, at a quiet time in the middle of the afternoon, or just before going home to give the evening traffic an opportunity to thin out.

For the serious athlete, there are opportunities for athletic competition at night and on weekends: running, squash, racquetball, handball, etc. The POAC (the official name is Pentagon Officers Athletic Club) is a great place to conduct business, to catch up on important happenings, and to exercise your network of contacts. The POAC serves the same purpose as the corporate golf match. In fact, people will often tell you more on a thirty-minute jog than in the office. Don't wait to join; do it now.

Get a pad, keep it with you, and take good notes. A steno pad or notebook is easy to carry with you at all times. If a senior official grabs you and wants to give some tasking or guidance, it is a little awkward to ask for a pen and paper. If you don't have a means to take some quick notes, you may forget something important by the time you get back to the office. If you use a steno pad, you may want to put the tasking on the left of the line down the middle and the actions taken on the right. When you use up the entire pad, don't toss it into the classified waste; keep it in your safe—it may come in handy at some later point.

Learn how to use the computer or word processor in your office. Since secretaries have become so scarce, action officers must be competent with personal computers if they are going to be effective and successful. In fact, most action officers (and many senior officers) today use computers on a regular basis, know how to make their own slides, and are wizards at word processing and using various software packages such as WordPerfect, Harvard Graphics, Lotus 1-2-3, and dBASE.

Buy a computer for your home. If you are truly computer literate, you will be much more effective in an environment that relies more and more on computers, speaks computer lingo, and depends on analysis that is largely driven by computer input and output. I must highlight a major caution, however. To prevent computer viruses from being introduced into Pentagon computers, you may not be permitted to do work at home and then bring in your diskette for use in your Pentagon office. Be sure to check the rules in your office carefully in this regard.

Find out where the photocopying machines are. When things are moving fast and you need to reproduce some papers, that's when your favorite photocopier breaks down and the one just around the corner is all tied up. You should know where a number of machines are, which ones tend to be less used, and which ones are available to you at night and on weekends. Although many offices now have printers and photocopiers, it is still useful to know where to go when yours break or the electricity goes out in your part of the Building.

Find out where the secure phones are and how to use them. Since much business just can't be done over the regular telephone because of the sensitive nature of the work being done, using the secure phone is necessary. Knowing where to locate a secure phone when the one in your office is tied up is vital in many fast-moving situations.

Develop and maintain a handy list of addresses and phone numbers. To a very considerable degree, communication is what makes the Building function. If you maintain a Rolodex, a well-organized notebook, or, if you like the high-tech approach, a Casio databank, you can save lots of time.

Develop a good list of points of contact and keep it current. Visit and revisit your points of contact and keep them informed of important actions you are working on and tidbits of new information you have picked up. When they ask for help, try to assist them so that when you need assistance they will be there to help you.

Learn how to give short, crisp, issue-oriented briefings. Briefings make or break a lot of people. Those who know how to construct interesting and easily understandable slides, to brief without notes, to take a thirty-minute briefing and boil it down to three minutes on short notice, and to field the tough and sometimes nasty questions of the senior officers and civilian officials can be very effective and successful. Some call the short three-minute briefings "elevator speeches" since they last about as long as an average trip in an elevator. Remember a very basic rule of thumb: "Tell your bosses what they need to know, not what you know."

Have a position on issues for which you are responsible. When I was the director of plans for the Air Staff, every few weeks I would sit down with my new officers and explain to them that, when they were "running an action," I wanted them to think through the issue carefully and take a position. I explained the situation along the following lines.

"Often I only have five minutes or so to get ready for the next meeting. It is not helpful to me to have you explain that this is a complex issue, that various agencies have different views, and that you are not sure what the Department of Defense and the nation ought to do. If I don't like your advice I will question it. However, you have a lot more time than I do to think through the problem, and I need your mature and objective advice."

Action officers and others who are too insecure, too shy, or too careerist in their motivations to take a position normally fail. As I used to tell division chiefs after an action officer had let me down by not having a position for me to defend, "I am not smart enough to know precisely what to do on all of the many hundreds of issues I must deal with. I needed help and I didn't get it."

Action officers should have information papers on hand (or in their computers) on each of their major actions. They need to keep these information papers up to date as they find time.

THOUGHTFULNESS AND KINDNESS CONSIDERATIONS

Treat your secretaries with great kindness. They can make or break you; if you treat them like dirt, they can destroy you. If you are not kind to secretaries, just when you are desperate to get your secretary, or *any* secretary, to work overtime some evening, you will find that they will have other commitments. If you mistreat secretaries, the word spreads quickly. When you do keep secretaries working late at night, after your work is finished, walk them to their cars or give them a ride home. This is a kindness that will be greatly appreciated.

Share your ideas and your writing gifts with others. Everything you write and every idea that you come up with is in the public domain. If people plagiarize your work and steal your ideas, consider yourself well complimented. Try to be magnanimous and take quiet satisfaction even when someone else takes credit for something that came from your fertile mind. After a while, your bosses will begin to recognize your talents and appreciate the fact that you have the maturity to allow others to use your ideas without resentment.

If you obtain good ideas from others, give them credit. This is the flip side of the point made above. If you give full credit to those who help you, the next time you are looking for assistance, you'll probably receive it.

When you win a victory over an opponent, be very kind to him or her immediately afterward. If you gloat or remind opponents constantly of their losses, they will remember and look for ways to shoot you down at some later point. If, however, you treat your opponents of the day with thoughtfulness, if you give them good arguments that they can take back to their people to help explain why they did not win all their points, if you invite them to lunch or send their boss a nice note, you will be less likely to be treated as an arch enemy in future bureaucratic battles.

Be thoughtful toward the folks in your graphics shop and your information-management shop. These people can be absolutely invaluable to you especially when you need some fast graphics, or fancy slides that you cannot make yourself, or advice on how best to display some complex data. If your computer goes down, the information-management shop can often help you. If you get to know these graphics and computer folks well and they learn to like you and respect you, they can help you design graphic presentations that are effective and dazzling or find lost files in a hard disk that has "dumped."

Be magnanimous. Give credit where credit is due. Go out of your way to thank others who have helped you. Handwritten notes of thanks, official letters of praise from your boss to the boss of the person who helped you, a telephone call to a spouse to explain why you have worked someone so hard on an issue—all these are useful ways to thank people. In addition, try very hard to avoid criticizing others, particularly those from other services and agencies. If you are a constant critic, if you have a compulsive desire to compete aggressively with people and organizations, you will slowly diminish your effectiveness when the word gets out that you love to challenge or "badmouth" others.

ADMINISTRATIVE RULES OF THUMB

If you keep any files on a computer, be sure to back them up. As we all become more dependent on computers and sophisticated word processors, it is easy to become complacent and forget to make back-up copies. When you can't "boot up" the hard disk or it dumps everything, you can really be at a loss. If, however, at the end of every day, you copy the day's work on a diskette and file the diskette in your safe, you should be in good shape.

When you are carrying classified material, be sure to have it in a folder and be sure that the folder is properly labeled as such. The beauty of using a folder is that it is much less likely that any classified material will fall out than if you just grab some papers, stick them under your arm, and race off down the hall. Having the folder properly labeled is a normal security requirement. If you do leave the folder somewhere by mistake, someone will quickly see the classified label, realize that something is wrong, protect it, and in most cases, return it to you promptly.

After copying, always check and double check for classified materials. One of the most common security violations over the course of the last thirty years or so has been classified material left in or near photocopiers. Of course, within that context the most common mistake is to leave the very last page in the machine itself. If someone is copying right behind you, your mistake will be caught, but, if not, the next voice you hear will be a security officer's.

Fully coordinate your papers. Any action paper in the Pentagon requires lots of staff coordination. When the top leaders finally make their decisions, they want to do so with the confidence that all the key staff and line organizations either concur with the thrust of the paper or have had the opportunity to express their disagreements before the decision is made. Action officers who skip some key offices when they run the coordination do their bosses and themselves a great disservice. Often, however, time is short and there is no opportunity to coordinate a paper completely. In this case, it is the wise action officer who always checks with those offices that are likely *not* to concur while skipping those that are likely to agree. It is also very prudent to inform the skipped offices after the fact, to apologize for skipping them, to explain the issue to them, and to leave them a copy of the package, if at all feasible.

PHILOSOPHICAL ADVICE

Compete against a high standard, not against your peers. Most of you are highly energetic individuals who love the opportunity to engage in competition. May I suggest that you treat your Pentagon assignment like you would a marathon run: Prepare by studying and getting yourself in mental shape, set some personal goals, and pace yourself for the long haul. Your goal should not be to beat others, but to meet or exceed those goals you have set for yourself.

Retain your sense of humor. The very intense and superserious person usually fails in the end. If you can't laugh at yourself, your service, the system, and the procedures, you may be in for a nervous breakdown or a heart attack. More likely, you will become so cynical that people will start avoiding you, and you will slowly lose your effectiveness.

Be sure of your facts. You will be dealing at levels where it will be assumed that your facts are right. Do all that you can to ensure that this assumption is correct. There are few things as devastating as having someone point out that one or more of your key facts is not a fact at all but something you picked up somewhere and didn't check out.

Give everything a commonsense check. Some people tend to drift off into an "Alice in Wonderland" (or Orwellian) world as they try to handle the many pressures of the job. When someone is pushing an idea that just doesn't make sense, be sure to ask the tough questions. If you don't and you accept the strange idea, paper, or briefing, one day you will have to face these tough questions yourself when your boss asks, "Did you coordinate on this piece of garbage?"

Don't waste time reinventing the wheel. Before diving into an issue, it is useful to research what staff work has been done already. If previous staff work has been accomplished (this almost always is the case) and it has been done well, you may be able to save yourself a great deal of time and effort. There are few things more frustrating than working hard and long for weeks, coming up with solutions to thorny problems, and then finding better answers already in the file or in another office.

Don't be cavalier in your treatment of commands in the field. Just because you operate out of the Pentagon, work for top bosses, and help formulate important plans and policy doesn't mean that you are wiser than those people out in the field. Keep those key staff officers informed, listen to them as they pass on their ideas and frustrations, and help them solve their bureaucratic and substantive problems. It is especially important to stay in close (and in warm) contact with the major commands in the field. Try to avoid slipping into a "higher headquarters" mentality. The Pentagon does *not* always know best.

Answer your mail and return your phone calls. If you want to stay tuned in, you must not cut off communication with those who want to deal with you. Don't wait until tomorrow to return that call—it may be someone else's crash project; by helping someone in dire need you may have just made a friend for life.

Keep your antennas out. Walk the halls, get to know people who are knowledgeable and helpful, expand your circle of acquaintances to the other services and agencies. Don't bury yourself in an office and only surface when it is time to go home. A tuned-in person in the Pentagon can be enormously influential. Be one, and people will notice, seek your help and advice, and give you the more interesting actions.

When you promise, deliver. The coin of the realm in the Pentagon is trust, even among adversaries. It is one of the things about the Building that makes work there bearable. If someone promises something, it is almost always delivered. It may be late and it may not meet the needs, but it *is* delivered. One of the biggest mistakes I made when I was director of plans for the Air Force was to promise to provide a study for a congressional staffer; then I got so busy and distracted that I totally forgot about it and failed to get it done. (I found out years later that the staffer had spread the word around Capitol Hill about how unreliable I was.) A corollary to this rule is: "Don't promise unless you can deliver."

Know when to say "no." When someone asks for help, you should almost always try to assist. But there will be times when you are crashing on a hot project and just have to say "no" and send folks elsewhere for help. Also, you should establish some priorities and not jump into every project that turns up. Time management and good self-discipline are important qualities to develop, no matter where you work in the Building.

Avoid being a sycophant. Too many people come to the Pentagon with the supreme motivation of getting ahead by pleasing their bosses. They are the ones who sit around and try to figure out what the boss really wants and then feed that back to him or her. Although this technique sometimes works, it certainly has a number of disadvantages. With the thousands of issues that are floating around the Building at any one moment, most bosses don't know what they want on many of them. This is not because they don't care or aren't smart or experienced, but because they don't have time to research and think through the issue completely, or the issue is far outside their areas of expertise. A second problem with sycophancy is that it leads to "group think" and dumb answers to important questions. A leader will not be well served if he or she doesn't encourage subordinates to be innovative, to question conventional wisdom and current policy, and to take on the boss occasionally.

A FEW RULES TO BROADEN YOUR HORIZONS

Get to know the Joint arena. The name of the game in the 1990s is "joint." Get to know your counterparts on the Joint Staff and help them. If you don't establish warm relationships, these Joint Staff officers may feeze you out on key actions. If you are not going to a joint job, try to work on some joint actions, car pool with a person on the Joint Staff, or volunteer, after a year or two on a service staff, for a move to the Office of the Secretary of Defense or the Joint Staff. One clear message from our experience in Desert Storm is that warfare is a joint undertaking. Where services and organizations do not willingly act jointly, they suffer.

Volunteer to work with Congress. The learning experience is invaluable and you will be much more effective in the field or in the fleet if you know how Congress works; are familiar with key committees, congressmen, and staffers; and understand the interaction between the Department of Defense and Congress. If you don't get a chance to work with Congress (being a witness can be an especially useful experience), at least go over to the Hill a few times to sit in on hearings and watch the process. On your next Pentagon assignment, you are likely to be called upon to be a witness.

Get out for short visits to the field when the opportunity permits. All Pentagon warriors begin to lose touch with the changing realities of the operational world unless they "burst out" of the Building on occasion. Taking a trip with a boss is a quick and easy way to get batteries recharged. On the flight back, you and your boss can sort out what you learned. An occasional trip is also a good way to identify talented people who may one day come to the Pentagon to work for you (or perhaps replace you so you can get back to the field or fleet).

Visits to key headquarters that you work with on a regular basis are also useful. Good chemistry can be established by sitting down with people at their work places so that they know you better.

Telephone friendships need to be reinforced periodically by personal contact.

Don't eat your lunch at your desk. Use the lunch hour as a time to get together with people and find out what is happening outside your area. Most people can't afford to spend an hour at lunch but half an hour with a different colleague each day can be time well spent for someone who wants to stay abreast of issues. Office lunches once a week are also helpful.

Visit the Pentagon bookstore once a week. If you are going to be truly effective in the Building, you will need to be smarter than your personal experiences, your in box, your television, and the insights of your office mates. The Pentagon Bookstore has a fine collection of classic books on the military and on defense policy as well as excellent new books. If you read one or two good books a month, you will build on your strengths and fill in some of the gaps in your knowledge and experiences. This bookstore maintains a listing of the best of the new books, will order books for you, and will accept your personal check if you are short on cash.

The Pentagon Bookstore is a great place to send visitors who have some dead time between meetings and appointments. Foreign visitors often buy large numbers of professional books to take back home with them.

Watch the first 10 minutes of the "MacNeil/Lehrer News Hour" (if you get home by 7:00 P.M.). This is now the best news broadcast on television. Since there are no commercials, you get your news faster and better than anywhere else. Tom Brokaw, Dan Rather, and Peter Jennings just can't compete with MacNeil/Lehrer as far as substantive news is concerned. If you throw out the commercials and the "junk news," the commercial nightly news shows give you barely 10 minutes of substance. If it appears that the "MacNeil/Lehrer News Hour" will discuss an issue relating to national defense or foreign policy later in the program, stay tuned in. This program will introduce you to many important officials in the national security business, and you can benefit from knowing what's on their minds and what positions they are taking publicly. CNN has established itself as a source of useful information and intelligence. It is monitored in all command centers and is watched closely by key decision makers during crises and war. Listening to CNN radio (AM 730) to and from work is another way to keep up with the news. If you don't like CNN, WTOP (AM 1500) or National Public Radio are excellent alternatives.

RULES OF CAUTION

Learn from the bad folks. The good people are plentiful and priceless. However, you can learn more of what not to do from the bad people: the slick operators, the sycophants, the manipulators, those who play fast and loose with the facts. The sleazy ones who would sell their souls for a promotion, a lucrative job offer from industry, or for a bribe badly damaged the Building's reputation for high integrity when the Pentagon scandal of 1988 broke (in June of that year). It will be some time before the reputation of integrity can be reestablished. Even when it is, there will always be a few of these people roaming the halls, so be on the alert.

Learn whom to trust and whom not to trust. Get to know the "street smart" folks early and ask for their advice on identifying the good people from those who are not. Some people are lazy but glib, some are dishonest, others are hyperambitious, a few are chronic procrastinators, others love to toss "hot potatoes" at you, and some are only interested in working on the high-visibility issues. It is vital that you become wise about people, about issues, and about how to get things done quickly. Of all the "street smarts," knowing whom to trust is, by far, the most important one. The sooner you learn whom you can or cannot count on, the quicker you will become truly effective.

Maintain your integrity. In the jungle of the Washington scene, it is quite easy to sell your soul incrementally without even realizing what you are doing. There are certainly lots of temptations to "cook" the numbers, to tell only a part of the story, to fail to bring up some bad news at a crucial time, to use half (or three-quarters) truths, to mislead a congressional staffer, or to hide important information behind security barriers. Lying to further personal ambitions, serve parochial interests, stay out of trouble, avoid over-time work, help a contractor win a competition, or for any other reason is just plain wrong. If something that you have done during the day causes you to lose sleep at night, correct your mistake the very next day.

When I was director of plans in the Air Staff, I arrived late to a meeting one day and the decision was being made to "bury" some extra money that we had into a special program that was not being closely scrutinized by the Office of the Secretary of Defense (OSD). The fear was that the budget cutters in the OSD would grab the funds. I went along with the recommendation. As I thought about it that night, the decision bothered me more and more. The nice part of this story is that others also had second thoughts, and the decision was quickly reversed. Too many officials say what they want to believe rather than being truthful. Don't let your optimism about your program cause you to mislead others.

Curb your personal desire for self-aggrandizement and power. Those who love power trips tend to be identified as overly ambitious by subordinates, peers and, eventually, by bosses. To be successful, you must understand and use the reins of power, but you should try to use power for important institutional purposes rather than to serve your own ambitions.

Beware of those who operate outside the system. Those who refuse to play by well-established Pentagon rules, who enjoy the clever games of "end runs" and "back channels," who tend to lie, cheat, and/or steal to win some bureaucratic battle will eventually embarrass themselves and their organizations. If you join them in their manipulative machinations, your reputation and your effectiveness can also be badly tarnished.

Watch out for "loose cannons on the deck." In the earlier days of gunpowder, cannon, and sailing ships, a cannon that broke loose on deck could cost limbs and lives. (A cannon that broke loose from the systems of lines and blocks used to absorb recoil and then haul the gun back into the battery prior to firing again was a real threat. This loose cannon would go careening back and forth across the always inclined, and often rolling and plunging, deck of the sailing ship. Sailors in their haste to avoid these cannons would slip and slide on the decks washed by the roiling seas and the blood of their wounded and dead comrades.) Those individuals who are loose cannons in the Pentagon shoot before they aim and cause great damage. Too many new political appointees take the basic approach to decision making of "ready, shoot, aim" (even worse is the "shoot, ready, aim" technique). In addition, there are a few loose cannons at every level who violate good judgment (and in some cases, the law) to serve their ambitions or personal agendas. Zealots, hip shooters, and people who are "all velocity and no vector" are not only a menace to orderly decision making, but also give the Pentagon a bad name. The best approach is to identify these people as early as you can and devise ways to head them off or figuratively dump them overboard before they cause you, your organization, and the nation too much harm.

Be pepared to be fired. It is a fact of life that some people get fired for reasons that include incompetence, lack of integrity, bad chemistry with the boss, or an inability to write or brief well (among many other reasons). Although being fired can certainly be damaging to your career, it is important to understand that numerous people are "soft" fired (removed from a job gently with a favorable effectiveness report written by the boss) and the damage is minimal.

When the deputy secretary of defense fired me as his military assistant, I was not prepared even though I knew that the chemistry was bad. I knew that he did not respect my advice and seemed to think that I was a spy for my service, yet I thought things would improve. They didn't. It was probably the best thing that could have happened to me. I got back to an operational unit and was soon checked out in that single-seat marvel, the F-15. Within two years of leaving the Pentagon, I was granted the great privilege of commanding the 4,000 professionals who were members of the 36th Tactical Fighter Wing at Bitburg, Germany. The bottom line here is that although being fired from the Building is a big setback, there is life after the Pentagon even if your departure is less than auspicious.

Treat your retired friends with discretion. Many of your friends in the Building will retire and accept positions with research firms and with defense contractors. On occasion, they will call on you, as an old friend, to help them out. Sometimes, often out of ignorance of the rules, they will ask you to do something for them that is illegal, unethical, or against DoD directives. You must know the rules well and turn your friends down when they ask you to violate the rules.

Use the research companies around the beltway with caution. There are many high-quality firms doing excellent research on defense matters in the Washington area. Within these firms there are smart, hard-working, and experienced people, many of whom have recently retired from some key jobs in the Pentagon. However, some of these companies deserve the title "Beltway bandit" (bandits for short). People who work for these bandits come in and interview people, collect some data from you, review old studies, and issue a report that tells you what you already know. They then walk away with big bucks. Many precious tax dollars are squandered in this way. If you have some influence in picking research firms to assist your office, try to pick those that are likely to give you fresh ideas and new approaches to thorny problems. Pick those with excellent reputations and a good sense for bureaucratic realities so that their better proposals have some chance of being accepted and implemented.

Learn to survive bad bosses. Let's be totally candid: there are a number of bad bosses in the Pentagon. In the latest version of my book on leadership of large and complex organizations, *Taking*

Charge: Making the Right Choices (Garden City, N.Y.: Avery Publishing Group, 1988), I identified a number of categories of problem bosses (Wimp, Power Seeker, Type A, Country Club, Mother Hen, Inflated Ego, Captured by the Staff, Retired in Place, Laissez-Faire) and described briefly how to deal with each type.

The demands and pressures of the Pentagon sometimes bring out the worst in people when they are in leadership jobs. Many become authoritarian, demanding, impatient, and distrusting. It is tough enough to deal with an overflowing in box and a demanding meeting and deadline schedule. Having a bad boss can make life almost unbearable. Fortunately, bosses come and go quite rapidly, and the really bad boss is usually eased out or fired in a year or less. In the meantime, learning to work with and around a bad boss is a necessity. Patience, tolerance, and innovation are essential (see chapter 9).

Be cautious about advice from the cynics. The crusty old heads will often give out advice containing much wisdom and insight, but some of these people have become so jaded that their cynicism can rub off on you. Let me give a specific example. I have a few acquaintances with over twenty years of service in the Building who have evolved into cynics. Here is some wisdom I received from a couple of them when I told them I was writing this book.

1. Always be cheery around your bosses.
2. Always have a folder in your hand with a top secret label attached.
3. Try to be seen in the hall talking to important people.
4. Always look busy and somewhat harried.
5. When you go home early and grab your coat, don't leave by way of your boss's office or the E ring.
6. When you come in early, be sure to walk down the E ring and pass the offices of your various bosses.
7. When your boss gives you some dumb task, say "Yes, sir" right away (if you argue the task will just get dumber, and the guidance will get more specific).

My point is when you start believing that these are the real secrets to success in the Building, you may have "lost the bubble." Substance still counts more than form, although I would be less than candid if I didn't admit that I have seen a few cases where some of the above maneuvers did carry weight with the less discerning bosses.

DEPARTURE RULE

When you get reassigned, take a recent DoD telephone directory with you. You will find many opportunities to call back to the Building for advice and help. The DoD phone book is invaluable for that purpose.

One of the great advantages of a Pentagon tour is that you can really help the folks who will be working for you when you return to the field or the fleet. You will not be intimidated by someone who says that what you are trying to do is against DoD, Navy, Marine, Army, or Air Force policy. With your vast knowledge of the Pentagon and with your DoD telephone book in hand, you will know how to change policy (or get a waiver) and whom to contact to do so. If there are no extra copies in the office, buy one from the Government Printing Office or the Pentagon Bookstore.

4
PENTAGON TRUISMS

Knowledge and intelligence are two separate and distinct attributes. You must possess both to succeed in a big way.

—E. B. GALLAHER

With so many ambitious, hard-working, and intelligent people working in the complex environment of the Pentagon, there is much wisdom and insight available to help ease the burden of those who may be new to the scene. Let me share with you some of my wisdom, offered with a note of caution that these rules could be wrong or misleading in certain situations. Hence all of the truisms outlined below should be accepted with a bit of skepticism. However, *most* of this stuff is valid *most* of the time.

PEOPLE TRUISMS

If you are going to get moved to the "second team," it will probably happen in the first few months. Life in the Pentagon is not unlike flying fighters in combat—the risks are the highest when you have not yet learned how to operate well enough to dodge the missiles and bullets aimed your way. Early in the game, you may do major damage to your future effectiveness in the Pentagon when you "bomb out" giving a briefing, preparing a paper, or engaging in a discussion at an important meeting. For instance, if you brief a

general or admiral prior to an important meeting and fail to tell
him some key point or fail to warn him that some deputy assistant
secretary is about ready to attack him, that general or admiral may
not want to be briefed by you again. If that official is one of your
immediate bosses, that may considerably limit your ability to make
a contribution from that point forward. Since the boss no longer
trusts you or values your advice, you may spend most of your time
dealing with backwater issues.

There is a subtle point here that needs emphasizing. Many people roam the building wondering why they never get any "hot actions." The reason is usually because they failed a couple of times
when they "ran some hot papers," and the bosses are afraid to give
them other important actions for fear they will fail again. Their advice and input are often ignored or heavily discounted. To return
to the combat fighter pilot analogy, you may remain a wing man for
your entire tour and never get checked out as a flight leader.

So what's the answer? "Overstaff" your first few actions to be
absolutely sure that you identify *all* the issues, completely coordinate the papers, have background papers and point papers in the
package that cover each issue, practice your briefing before the
very best colleagues in your office. Don't assume that since you
were a good briefer at Benning, Pendleton, Mayport, or Nellis, you
will be automatically a great briefer in the Pentagon. Also, listen
carefully to the criticism you get from colleagues and branch and
division chiefs. If you don't understand why they suggest that you
change a slide or raise an issue that you think is unimportant, ask
them! There may well be a hidden but important point that they
understand and you don't. Also, before giving a briefing, brain-
storm with your colleagues, and ask questions that the boss might
ask (these sessions are often called murder boards, skunk missions,
or skull missions). Probe deeply for mine fields that you need to
warn your boss about.

Whatever you do, don't leave important issues out of the package under the assumption that you will have time to brief adequately before the meeting. Often the briefing will be canceled or
you will only have four minutes to give your thirty-minute briefing. If the information is not in the package that the boss carries

into the meeting and can't be found when needed, you may soon be in big trouble.

You can't pull the trigger for your boss. You can give your boss lots of ammo. You can arm him or her with the best weapons. You can help your boss aim. But if the boss is too insecure, too weak, too ambitious, too lazy, or too tired, he or she will not win the argument in the key meeting. Understanding this truism can help you understand and rationalize the great disappointment you may feel when your boss lets you and your organization down despite your very best efforts to help. Also, if you send your bosses into fights with insufficient ammunition, they will return with wounds and scars. It is wise to "save" your boss for the important battles. Finally, if you mount your bosses on white chargers and send them into the valley of death too often, they may not be willing to mount up when you really need them to do so.

Planners tend to mortgage the present for the future, and operators tend to mortgage the future for the present. The military services and the secretary of defense could do a lot better job planning and programming for the department if they knew when and where the next war was coming. Since they don't, they must make lots of decisions about how much to spend for immediate military capability and how much to spend for the research and development (R&D) that will make us ready for future challenges. In other words, is this year like 1922 or like 1939? The operators tend to think it is 1939 while the planners tend to think it is 1922; these differing mindsets help to explain some of the tension that exists between planners and operators.

Forecasting future events is just plain tough. There is an old story of the planner who hears that there is a new computer in the basement of the Pentagon and goes down to try it out. He types into the computer, "Will there be war or peace in the next ten years?" The computer, after grinding away for a while, types out, "Yes." The general, not finding the answer too helpful, types back, "Yes, what?" And the computer very quickly replies, "Yes, Sir!"

Jazzy new phrases and concepts are almost always overused.
Every once in a while some clever action officer, scholar, or defense contractor comes up with a new phrase, concept, or idea
(proactive, stealth, Strategic Defense Initiative, paradigm shift).
Soon the phrase becomes so commonly used that it becomes overused and misused. These phrases also seem to generate similar
phrases. For example, Strategic Defense Initiative leads to Conventional Defense Initiative. Window of vulnerability leads to
window of opportunity.

*The language of the Pentagon is the shortcut language of newspa-
pers, big business, sports, and warfare.* When time is very short,
senior officials get very impatient with anyone who takes three or
four sentences to say something that can be articulated in a short
phrase. Hence, tough, punchy one-liners have become the *lingua
franca* of the Pentagon.

- "Let's get this paper on the street."
- "The train just left the station."
- "I just got slam dunked by the boss."
- "Are you willing to fall on your sword on this issue?"
- "We are walking through a mine field here."
- "My in box is full of sticks of dynamite."
- "Just give me the bottom line."
- "Who is going to grab this hot potato?"
- "But that's the old man's gold watch—we can't cut that pro-
  gram."
- "Those R&D guys are always chasing the next hot biscuit."
- "We are going to spend so much on intelligence and communi-
  cations that we sure will be smart when we surrender."

These phrases should be used, when appropriate, in oral discussions (see, also, chapter 5). In more formal communications, such
as briefings and staff papers, they should normally not be used
since some senior officials object to the use of slang in any correspondence or communication that may reach the White House,
Congress, or the Office of the Secretary of Defense.

A good way to influence policy is to walk down the hall with the big boss on the way to the key meeting. Since in many cases the boss has not had the opportunity to study the issue closely, your candid input can often shape last-minute opinions. On the other hand, if the person walking with the boss to the meeting is not familiar with the issues, he or she can really confuse the boss. It is the wise big boss who grabs the action officer rather than someone in middle management if he needs a bit of last-minute wisdom just before he enters the meeting. In any case, it is absolutely amazing how much work gets done "on the move" in the Building.

Weekend loyalty checks are a sign of bad leadership. If you find yourself coming in on Saturdays and Sundays regularly because your boss expects you to be there, there is a leadership problem in your staff agency. Too many bosses come to work on the weekends when they don't really need to. They invariably drag in large numbers of staff officers who feel that they are expected to be there in case the boss calls. The worst example in recent times was a vice chief of staff of a service who loved to work on weekends. Lots of generals, colonels, action officers, and others came in to answer his queries. What he never seemed to understand was that he was doing major damage to the morale and the efficiency of the staff. Weekend work is sometimes a necessity, but routine work that spills over into the weekend because some senior official is happier on the job than at home is nonsense.

If you are a boss and have work that must be done on the weekends, get a safe for your classified material placed in your home and take the work home with you! If you must come to work, don't bring in anyone with you and occasionally walk the corridors to be sure that a lot of insecure mid-level supervisors have not dragged in a bunch of unneeded folks (just in case the bigger boss might call). If you find that many have drifted in, make the point in your staff meeting on Monday that you don't want this to continue and that if you need help you will call them at home.

The higher up you get, the more important chemistry becomes. A top leader in the Pentagon can look to lots of people and places for advice and assistance: deputies, executive officers, military assistants, key subordinates, outside consultants, colleagues in other agencies, old friends, and retired officials. Hence, if you work for a top boss and he or she does not value your advice or trust your judgment, or feels that you may be a spy for another organization, your boss can easily cut you out of the process and ignore any advice or assistance that you may offer. Here are some signs to look for:

- not being invited to key meetings,
- never being invited to travel with the big boss, or
- being ignored when you raise an issue in a staff meeting or send in notes.

If the chemistry is really bad, it is usually best to sever the relationship by quietly suggesting to the big boss that you should move on to some other position where you could make a greater contribution to the mission.

The military tends to moderate ideological swings in the political system. When President Carter came up with such ideas as bringing the troops home from Korea, the military helped get him back on course. When Ronald Reagan's right-wing rhetoric got a little heavy, the military was able to help him understand the disadvantages of his hyperbole. Although it is clear that the Pentagon is more comfortable with conservative presidents, the military and the professional civil servants in the Pentagon actually provide useful constraints to the more radical and ideological proclivities of both liberal and conservative administrations.

Friends come and go but enemies accumulate. People in the Building who, because of their abrasive nature, their hyperambition, or their disloyalty, tend to make enemies and lose their effectiveness over time. As more enemies accumulate, these people find it harder and harder to get things done. On the other hand, the caring and helpful individual collects more and more friends and admirers. Over time, they gain the kind of stature and support that lead to continuing success. I have two models in this regard: General Russ Dougherty, USAF (ret.) and Colonel Bob Ward, U.S. Army (ret.), both of whom gained more and more friends and admirers during their many Pentagon tours.

Most high-level officials in the Pentagon favor arms control. This fact has been true for many years and became quite evident in the late 1970s when the Joint Chiefs joined the secretary of defense and the president in supporting the SALT II Treaty. Support for the INF Treaty of the late 1980s is another manifestation of this phenomenon. All of the services use arms control as part of national military strategy to produce stability at lower force levels. None of the military services enjoy spending money on nuclear weapons. Let's face it: it is easier to love airplanes and ships than nuclear missiles. In general, the services work hard to build a balanced force structure to provide deterrence and war-fighting capability across the entire spectrum of conflict. Collectively, they want a force structure that can deal effectively with all known threats. Verifiable arms control tends to serve the goal of a balanced force posture.

One caution is in order here. Arms control is per se neutral. The military should support it only when it enhances national security (or at least does not diminish it). Top military leaders who are pressured to support a flawed treaty should resist.

The Pentagon is a vast meritocracy. Although there is certainly some cronyism in the Building, most people are in the positions they are in because they have demonstrated their excellence. If you are quick-minded, tuned in, and on time, you will be recognized and rewarded with more important work. This new work will keep you very busy but will allow you to make a significant contribution to national defense. For those who are not very talented, the Building may seem a ruthless place. A comparison to Wall Street may be in order. The "what has he or she done lately?" question comes up a lot. To put it in the vernacular, "You may have been a great commander in the field but if you can't hack it in the Building than you're *out of here.*"

Both the Peter and Paul principles are at work. People do, in fact, reach their level of incompetence in the Building and get stuck there (the Peter Principle). The Pentagon caveat to the Peter Principle is that these incompetents usually get reassigned after a year or two rather than get stuck in their positions of incompetence for many years (as is often the case in the business world). The Paul Principle is also at work: some bosses are competent when they first take over but become more incompetent every day—they either fail to keep up with the issues, people, or technology, or just get burned out.

Commuting times are usually calculated on Sunday mornings. Whenever you are talking about commuting times to a real estate agent, a colleague in your office, your secretary, or a neighbor, be careful. The time that they will quote from home to the Pentagon is almost always understated. So, take any estimates in this area with more than a few grains of salt. With economic factors forcing more and more people to live farther and farther away, the average commuting time is probably 45 minutes each way, with lots of people enduring an hour or more each way, every day. Don't be deceived by the summer traffic: it is always less than the winter traffic. Traffic gets quite worse when schools are in session (about half the high school students in this area get to and from school by automobile), Congress is in session, and it is raining, sleeting, or snowing. The enormous influx of tourists in the spring has made that time of the year the worst as far as traffic is concerned. From cherry blossom time in late March until school lets out in mid-June is the very worst time as far as traffic is concerned.

If you do quite well and are reassigned out of Washington, you will most likely come back. All of the military services need people at high levels in the Building who have a proven, successful track record in the Washington environment. So when you get your assignment and are headed out of town, don't forget that there may be a Pentagon in your future. Hence, burning bridges, telling off problem people, or selling your house may not be wise. When should you expect to be back? In three to five years.

PROCEDURAL TRUISMS

Debriefings and back briefings are crucial. With so many people running off to so many meetings, it is awfully easy for individuals to get confused about what is going on. Two very useful systems have evolved over the years to help alleviate this real problem. At all important meetings, those in attendance are responsible for taking careful notes and debriefing others on what happened and what was decided. Senior officials are responsible for debriefing appropriate staff officers and answering their questions. Senior officials who fail to do this or who debrief only their deputy, executive officer, or secretary are making a big mistake. An action officer who has spent months on an issue has a right to know what happened in the key meeting and to learn it directly from the boss. This is particularly important when there is some additional tasking (which is often the case) for those staff officers. If these staff officers can get this tasking directly from the big boss, they are much more likely to be responsive than when they receive it secondhand or thirdhand from an executive officer or secretary.

The back briefing system is quite similar. Action officers often get to sit in on meetings and discussions with big bosses that their intermediate bosses miss. It is the responsibility of these action officers to take good notes and brief their bosses on what happened, what tasking was handed out, what suspenses were established, and what decisions were made.

If you want it bad, you will get it bad. This is well worth considering if you are a new branch or division chief and you are inclined to press your folks for quick responses to complex questions or actions. The people who work on the various staffs will do their best within the allotted time. But if that time is too short for them to do a decent job, you are likely to get a paper or a briefing that is full of holes, not fully coordinated, and ready to blow up in your face when your boss or some other high official with lots of experience takes a close look at it. If your people tell you that they need a little more time to do a good job, give it to them if you possibly can. The results and your credibility, both up and down the chain of command, will be enhanced.

"It's déjà vu all over again." Yogi Berra, who coined this phrase, must have worked in the Pentagon before he became a famous baseball player, manager, movie critic, and sage. In the big bureaucracies, the same issues keep reappearing. Just when you think you have put something to bed and can move your attention to a new and more interesting issue, someone in one of the many offices above you takes an interest, gets mad, faces a hearing, or gets a call from a war lord in the field and *bang!* — that same item is hot again. The answer to this is lots of patience, a good filing system, and a willingness to take a fresh look at an issue that you have already examined in what seems a thousand different ways.

The iron law of unexpected consequences. No matter what you do, or how well you think it through, coordinate it, and implement the decisions, you will find that months or years later the final result will be different in some ways from what you or your bosses intended. Sometimes the results are better than you had hoped, but in other cases the results are worse. The discovery of this iron law is a sobering realization, yet it helps you in your future work because it forces you to ask more questions and make better decisions. Let me give a non-Pentagon example of this phenomenon. Morris Silver demonstrated that government policies in Egypt to keep grain prices low in time of scarcity led not only to famine but to outbreaks of bubonic plague. Fearing prices would go up, people hoarded grain in their households, a practice that brought in rats, fleas, and eventually, the plague. Hence, what may have seemed to decision makers to be enlightened public policy led to a double disaster. The famine might have been predictable but the bubonic plague was not.

Another example is from my personal experience in the Office of the Secretary of Defense. When I was a military assistant to the deputy secretary of defense in the mid 1970s, I had a good opportunity to watch the activities of the Clements Committee. This committee was in the process of examining officer education in the military services, and Clements had some very strong views on the subject. He had been on the board of Southern Methodist University and felt he knew a lot about higher education. A major initiative of this committee was to create a university (the National Defense University) to consolidate the administrative functions (library, personnel, comptroller, logistics) of the two war colleges in the Washington area (the National War College and the Industrial College of the Armed Forces), save some money and manpower spaces, and reduce the infighting between the two colleges. The results, of course, are considerably different from what Secretary Clements and his committee anticipated. The National Defense University has grown into an organization larger than anticipated with a budget much larger than the combined budgets of the two war colleges prior to the consolidation. The size, structure, and philosophy of the National Defense University is quite different from what the Clements Committee planned in the mid-1970s.

The perfect is the enemy of the good. Too many people arrive at the Pentagon with a perfectionist mentality and are therefore ineffective. A very good, workable decision that has a strong chance of being faithfully implemented is much better, in almost all cases, than a perfect solution that can never be coordinated or implemented. The decision-making process in the Pentagon is a complex one that works only if large numbers of people are willing to collaborate in order to arrive at workable solutions. The best solutions are those that will be supported by the various services, the commanders in the field, the Joint Staff, the Office of the Secretary of Defense, the Office of Management and Budget, the White House staff, and Congress. Perfect solutions almost never work because perfect solutions for one department or agency are often anathema for another.

Any issue can be summarized in a short briefing or on a one- or two-page staff summary sheet. Too many new people in the Pentagon prepare overly long briefings and staff summary sheets. They fear that they may leave something out and therefore go overboard with detail and minutiae. The secret is boiling down the really important information into a few words and putting the less important stuff into background papers. If you can't figure out how to do this, someone else will have to do it for you. Get your service staff officer's guide and follow it.

A *victory is seldom permanent.* A victory in the bureaucratic wars of the Pentagon is just the beginning of the next fight on the same issue. One of the great mistakes that many new people make is to assume that a decision will stick—that a decision is, in fact, permanent. Even the major decisions by top leaders often fail to stick for long.

Parkinson was right. The small classic book *Parkinson's Law* rings true as far as the Pentagon is concerned. You may remember that C. Northcote Parkinson wrote *Parkinson's Law and Other Studies in Administration* long before such works as *The Peter Principle, Up the Organization,* and *Augustine's Laws* appeared. Yet Parkinson's insights ring true more than 30 years later: "Work expands so as to fill the time available." In the Pentagon, the only exceptions are a few magic times like over the Christmas holidays, the middle of the summer, and perhaps somewhat more curiously, when there is a major international crisis going on. TQM may help prove Parkinson wrong by the late 1990s. We shall see.

Christmas has remained a time of relative leisure most years. However, Christmas "massacres," such as what took place under President Carter and, more recently, when Defense Secretary Frank Carlucci mandated major budgetary cutbacks, do occur on occasion. When these budgetary drills take place, the Christmas holiday season is spoiled for many. These Christmas massacres usually are the result of revised fiscal guidance being provided to the military departments in early December. The entire budget has to be redone over the holidays so that the president can submit his budget to Congress early in the new year.

Midsummer is usually slow because of the big turnover of people. In addition, many of the bosses have been reassigned, and the new bosses are not settled in enough to put heavy new burdens on the staff. A big international crisis ties up the big bosses so much that they don't have the time or the energy to give too much attention or new work to the staff members who are not directly involved in the crisis.

The most common approach to most new actions is delay. Unfortunately, there is a strong bias toward delay in the Pentagon as a result of a number of interacting factors. Any new action or initiative normally leads to lots of work. Since in boxes are already full, the natural reaction is to pursue one or more of a number of delaying actions. "Let's conduct a study" is a common theme. This is almost sure to delay the action for at least three months and often a year or more. This approach is taken for a number of reasons. Some feel that the issue really ought to be studied more fully allowing the key decision makers to better understand all the nuances and implications and to consider the full range of options. Getting a study underway usually requires the establishment of "terms of reference." Just the process of getting these set up can take a number of weeks or more, depending on how controversial the issue is. In addition, finding manpower and money to do the study usually takes a minimum of a few weeks. Often, when the study is finished, the interest in it has so diminished that no action is taken on the recommendations. An enormous amount of time, money, and effort is spent on studies. Some of this is worthwhile but, sadly, a good proportion, perhaps as much as 30 percent, is totally wasted. If you are assigned to a study that is not going to result in anything other than wasting time and money, it can be a very frustrating experience.

"Let's query the field" is another approach that is taken with new actions. This is an appropriate action in most cases, but those who manipulate the system use this approach to delay addressing an issue. Sometimes these people hope the field agencies will come back and disagree with the idea. Sometimes manipulators will quietly go out to the field by message or phone call and get a return message written that says what they want it to say. Some Pentagon officials go as far as writing the message for a field agency and having someone at a high level in the field send it back to them verbatim.

Hardly anybody is cleared for all the "black" programs. There are at least four areas where programs are of such a sensitive nature or so highly classified that they are compartmentalized: that is, only a very few people are given the very specific clearances that give them access to all of the compartmented aspects of a program. These are commonly called black programs. There are black programs in space, in the operational world, in the general area of R&D, and in the various intelligence worlds. Examples are certain satellite capabilities (space), certain spooky ongoing activities such as the Iran–contra arms deal (operational), stealth airplanes and other low-observable developments (R&D), and agents in certain unfriendly countries (human intelligence).

The great majority of people in the Pentagon are not dealt a full deck of cards and may not even know it. A few years ago a man who had just been selected to be a chief of staff of one of the services announced to his staff that he had just been cleared for all the black programs in his service. A wag in the audience said, "How do you know?" During Desert Storm, a number of black programs "turned white." For instance, the public knows much more about the F-117 (stealth fighter) than it did before 1991.

Institutional momentum is very important. The key to decision making is not only getting the right decision made but also ensuring that the decision is fully implemented. As the sportscasters and the politicians say, "You've gotta have the big mo." You have to check on the implementation process periodically to ensure that the decision and plan you worked on so hard is carried out fully and faithfully. If momentum is lost you may have to go back to the big boss and have a message sent out to the staff or to the field that reminds everyone that the boss was serious about the full implementation of the decision.

Some defense contractors are more effective than others on Capitol Hill. If your service has picked a contractor to build a weapons system and that contractor is not effective in gaining congressional support for its programs, that system may never be built. This can be a source of great frustration if the system is badly needed and the contractor clearly has designed the best system to accomplish the needed tasks. It can be even more frustrating if the best contractor is not even chosen for fear that the system will not survive the scrutiny of the legislative process. This is one of the reasons why in 1982 the U.S. Air Force chose the C-5 over the more advanced C-17. The Air Force chief of staff and secretary realized that if they wanted a large airlift aircraft built in the early 1980s it would have to be the C-5 because of the strong lobbying team of Lockheed and the effectiveness of Georgia's congressional delegation (the major Lockheed aircraft production lines are in Marietta, Georgia). Unfortunately, this is but one example of a common practice in Congress of forcing the Department of Defense to buy something less than the best or, in the more absurd cases, to buy something that the military services do not want or need.

Personnel accounts spend money much faster than do procurement accounts. This truism has enormous implications especially when it is time to make big budgetary cuts. Over 90 percent of personnel money is spent during the present year, whereas procurement money, for, say, a large ship, may be spread over ten years or more. Hence, if you cancel ships early in their construction cycle, you may be able to save 10 percent of the cost of that ship in the first year, but if you cut manpower you may be able to save 90 percent from certain accounts. Consequently, there is pressure in each budget-cutting drill to reduce manpower.

The last weapons systems to be cut tend to be those that are best at signaling intentions to a potential enemy. It is easier to cut submarines and strategic nuclear missiles (which are poor signaling devices) than it is to cut large surface ships and AWACS aircraft that can so easily be used to signal intentions, commitment, and resolve. Gunboat diplomacy has, for many years, been an important instrument in our national security policy; AWACS diplomacy has begun to play a somewhat similar role. A related point should be made here: It is also easier to cut down on the procurement of spare parts or munitions than on the "big ticket" weapons systems such as combat aircraft and major ship programs that have strong congressional support.

Future inflation rates are usually set for political reasons. In most cases, what you plan to buy will turn out to be more than you will actually get. Any forecast is problematical in the Pentagon, but those that are heavily influenced by political factors are even less reliable. Expected inflation rates for future years in the defense arena are set by the Office of Management and Budget (OMB) in the White House in coordination with the Office of the Secretary of Defense. There is a natural tendency on the part of OMB to assume that these rates will be low so that the Department of Defense can be allocated a smaller amount of money to buy the things it needs to have an adequate military capability. In this way, projections of overall deficits can be lower, which is always politically attractive. This factor, in combination with the fact that defense industries tend to have a higher inflation rate than the rest of the economy, means that forecasts of force structure growth, readiness levels, and sustainability factors almost always fail to be met.

Innovation takes place best in times of great budgetary change and in black programs. Innovation is characteristically very tough to attain in the Pentagon since there are so many forces for stability, and since many agencies and people feel threatened by innovation. On the other hand, in the compartmentalized programs—which exclude many bureaucratic reactionaries—and in times of great budgetary change, the forces for innovation have a much better chance. For instance, during the early 1980s some of us were able to push the Air Force into accepting the phase-out of a number of systems, such as the B-52D, the mid-Canada radar line, and the Titan missile, largely because we could show the commanders in the field that major new systems were being funded. If those new incentives had not been available, it would have been much harder to force through the phase-out of obsolescent but still somewhat capable systems. Of course, all the services have been able to phase out or cancel some systems that were becoming obsolescent (or not living up to expectations) during a period of major budgetary decline. A bigger challenge in time of major budgetary decline is how to begin new systems that should be started to preserve the long-term capability of the military services. The most difficult time to push innovation is when budgets are growing modestly and the bosses who helped make the present policies, programs, and weapons systems see little need to change. Bureaucratic stagnation is so pervasive that the innovators are often frustrated.

In every service and agency there are people and offices that serve as informal clearinghouses for new ideas. New people soon learn that some of their best ideas get shot down within their own office or by a boss who is one or two levels above them. This can be a matter of considerable frustration, but there is an option that can be pursued if done with care. Long-range planning divisions, small staff groups that work for the chief of staff or secretary, and special assistants to top officials are always looking for new ideas. These groups are universally careful not to undercut the chain of command, but they also have a responsibility to ensure that brilliant ideas are not lost behind the unimaginative middle-level bureaucrats. Finding out where these places and individuals are and feeding them with ideas is one of the most fascinating aspects of life in the Building.

The Pentagon spends much time on budget formulation and little time on budget execution. While the corporate headquarters of a large business might spend a major part of its effort on the execution of its budget, the Pentagon does not. Budget formulation is certainly important. Top leaders should work hard to formulate the budget and help it through the approval process. However, neglect of the execution phase by these same leaders explains, at least in part, why the Department of Defense is constantly being criticized for cost overruns and wasteful practices.

When it's time to cut the budget, the "salami slice" approach normally prevails. Rather than cancel a big program, the military departments usually cut small amounts of money out of hundreds of programs. This incremental approach often leads to inefficiency in production rates, reduced amounts of spare parts for weapons systems and other equipment, reduced training time and flying hours, and poor morale in the field and in the fleet.

It is much harder to discard yesterday's success than yesterday's failure. If your organization, agency, department, or division is "on a roll," if you have had a number of significant victories in recent months, be careful. Complacency and rigidity may set in, and when it is time to unload something, perhaps something that was a success in the past but is no longer useful, your organization may be unable to dump the program. One of the hallmarks of the best Pentagon leaders is their willingness to face an issue and "kill" unproductive or excessively expensive programs. In many cases, canceling a program is much harder than keeping it alive, since the cancellation will cause the loss of jobs in many congressional districts—an unpopular move on Capitol Hill.

Actions once assigned to a branch or division tend to stay there. Certain branches and divisions try to hand off new actions to other divisions. Why? They know that once they accept the action they will live with it for a very long time. The administrative system and the computerized tracking system both point to that branch or division when future actions relating to the issue arrive in the Building. Branch and division chiefs should avoid being too aggressive in pursuing actions, or they will find out that they are overburdened and unable to accomplish any of the actions well. This is one of the delicate areas for branch and division chiefs to deal with. It is a mistake either to fight off too many good actions or to try to grab too many.

Crisis management is inherently chaotic. In many ways the term crisis *management* is misleading. Most crises with which the Pentagon must deal are created by forces over which the military has very little control. Those who are assigned to work in the crisis action or crisis management areas should follow a few basic guidelines.

- Gather as much information from as many sources as possible (including such valuable sources as Cable News Network).
- Be sure to touch base with all the important players.
- Be prepared for many long hours and weekend work.
- Watch out for hidden agendas.
- Don't expect systematic decision making and policy coherency during a crisis.

5
THE STRANGE LANGUAGE OF THE PUZZLE PALACE

Words should be employed as the means, not as the end;
language is the instrument, conviction is the work.

 —SIR JOSHUA REYNOLDS

You have been on the job for three days. You have figured out where to park, how to get to your office, where the nearest restroom is, and the names of some of your office colleagues. You know how to find the shopping area called the Concourse on the second floor, as well as a couple of places to grab a bite to eat. You are beginning to feel that you might figure out how this place works, if you have another week or two to watch how the office operates.

All of a sudden, your assistant division chief races in the door, turns to you, and says, "It just hit the fan, I need help now. I want you to put together a package on the NMSD. I'll need a full JCS package with talkers, background papers, point papers, all the right tabs—you know, the whole nine yards—and I need it by COB. We will need to shotgun the coordination. Also don't forget to stick the Jayscap (or something that sounds like that) and the UCP in the package." He then runs out the door without giving you time to ask any questions.

OK, so what is this NMSD (the NMSD is the National Military Strategy Document), the UCP (the Unified Command Plan), and the *Jayscap* (the JSCP is the Joint Strategic Capabilities Plan), and how do you put together a JCS package? At least you know that COB is close of business and have watched others in the office put together talking papers and background papers.

The shorthand language of the Pentagon helps to make the place operate more efficiently but if you are unfamiliar with it, the confusion can be considerable during those first few weeks on the job. Let me try to give you some of the more important phrases of the literally thousands of words, phrases, and acronyms that rattle around the Building day and night. It is a complex and quickly changing language, so there is no way that I can cover all the words and phrases, but these are some terms that seem to have both importance and some longevity. I have placed the terms within a phrase to give you an idea of the normal way they are used. They are listed by general frequency of use. Please notice how many are directly related to the most common business of the Pentagon— taking action on important issues.

Finally, at the end of this chapter I have listed, in alphabetical order, many other common phrases of the Building. May I suggest that you skim through this chapter, since you may be familiar with some of these phrases while others are fairly self-explanatory. This chapter comes early in the book since many of these phrases will be used in later chapters. The earlier you can become familiar with the language of the Pentagon, the quicker you will be able to operate with competence and speed.

RUNNING ACTIONS

Where is the *package*? The combination of the cover sheet, the coordination sheet, the staff summary sheet, the action paper or message and the background papers, point papers, and talking papers is known as the package. A Joint Chiefs of Staff (JCS) package is one that is used for JCS actions and usually requires a very specific format, with standardized tabs so that the chief of staff and his operations deputy can find the right paper at the right time in the negotiations in the JCS conference room (known as the Tank).

At which tab will I find the *implementer*? All packages are arranged in such a way that the key paper that will be signed out by the big boss is readily available to the people reading and coordinating on the package. The more complex packages often have a table of contents and a series of tabs along the righthand side of the package. The implementer is the message, the letter, or the memo with the signature block of the big boss that you hope to have sign it. This implementer is by far the most important paper in the package; it should be easy to find in the package and especially well written.

What is the *suspense?* Knowing when the work is due back to the big boss is almost as important as knowing what the issues are. A suspense is a deadline that is not to be violated unless a delay in that deadline is agreed to by the big boss *prior* to the original suspense date.

I need a three-day *slip.* If you can't get the package finished and fully coordinated by the Tuesday suspense date but can have it done by Friday, then you need a three-day slip or delay in your suspense.

Put it *on the street.* This phrase, which comes from the newspaper business, means that officials want you to publish the paper or release it for distribution now. Other terms that have the same meaning include *put it to bed* (another newspaper term), you are *cleared in hot,* and *go for it.*

Don't *miss the train.* This means that you are running out of time and if you don't move fast, you won't get the paper or the briefing to the right place or right person in time. If someone says you have missed the train, then all the work you have done is for naught, for the boss has already gone into the meeting, left for Europe, or headed across the river to Capitol Hill to testify. One way to get in trouble fast is to miss a couple of trains. Years ago, I watched an action officer miss a train when he overslept one day and missed his chance to brief his chief of staff who was on the way to see the president. We tried to find him, starting at about 6:00 A.M., but to no avail. He had worked throughout the night, had decided to grab a nap in an empty office at about 4:00 A.M., and could not be found.

I want *shotgun coordination* on this package. A package is usually coordinated by the staff officer who put it together. This action officer takes it from office to office so that if there are any questions on the package the original action officer will be there to answer them. If time is short, many copies of the package are made and the packages are sent out to many offices simultaneously. This is called shotgun coordination. Most joint actions are handled this way. The newest trend in quick coordination is "shotgun coordination" by means of electronic mail.

This is a *front-burner* issue. If you are working on a front-burner issue, this means it is one of high importance and usually one of great urgency. You might well work all night or all weekend on a front-burner issue. *Back-burner* issues are much less important but still must be dealt with when time permits. Since a back-burner issue can become a front-burner issue in a heartbeat, you should not neglect back-burner issues.

All of this is not to be confused with the term *burner,* which is short for fast burner or someone who is moving very rapidly up the ranks. Burners like to work on front-burner issues since they often feel that these issues will give them a better chance to excel and be recognized for their work. One problem with burners is that they sometimes try to turn back-burner issues or non-issues into front-burner issues in order to enhance their personal sense of importance. Big bosses should stop this from happening as soon as they realize what is going on. There are enough truly important issues in the Building for people to spend time on. As a boss I used to say, "Tell me, is there really an issue here?" If there wasn't, I would close down the action.

Who is *OPR* on this issue? This means who is the person responsible for this issue. OPR means *office of primary responsibility* but if often implies the *person* of primary responsibility. If it's you, everyone expects you to lead the way to success with this issue. "Who has the *lead*" has the same meaning as "Who is OPR?"

DEALING WITH BOSSES

Who *rolled the boss?* Getting rolled means getting bested by someone else. If your boss is so weak that he gets rolled often, you will find this to be quite frustrating. One of the reasons there is a lot of parochialism in the Pentagon is because bosses at all levels don't want to get the reputation of being rolled easily, since this causes morale problems among the troops. In other words, because they don't want to look weak, bosses sometimes support parochial positions that their staffs have put together for them.

He *shot the messenger* again. The boss who often overreacts to criticism or bad news and takes out his or her wrath on the person who brings in the bad news is guilty of shooting the messenger. Bosses who shoot too many messengers start losing touch with what is going on, since people become afraid to bring them anything but the good news.

Let's *wait him out.* If there are senior officials who are opposed to your initiative and about ready to retire or be reassigned, it is often prudent to wait until they leave before bringing up the issue. One of the great advantages of life in the Pentagon is that there is plenty of movement of key people. These personnel changes often give you an opportunity to dig something out of your idea file and try to get it moving again.

Let's solve this quick, before the *elephants* get involved. The elephants (sometimes called dinosaurs) are the top officials in the Pentagon. Many issues are handled best at the lower levels. The better elephants understand this and give their subordinates lots of opportunity to work out issues at the lowest possible level. Another common term for a top official is *bear. Feeding the bears* means giving information to top leaders.

The big boss has *gone soft* on our program. The strong support that we had in the front office has disappeared. This means big problems for you. Also, if you are a boss and you go soft, you should realize that you may be letting down your subordinates.

That issue is *above my pay grade.* One of the most often-used excuses in the Pentagon, this phrase means that the issue is so important that it must be decided by someone above them. Since Pentagon officials at all levels can have impact or influence on even the most important issues, to say it is "above their pay grade" is often a "Pontius Pilate" exercise—they could help, but they choose not to get involved. Having made this point so strongly, let

me soften it a little by pointing out that in certain compartmentalized or other very sensitive programs, you are not and should not
be involved in the decision process. In these cases, the "above my
pay grade" phrase may be quite appropriate.

But that's the old man's *gold watch*. When a senior official falls
in love with a weapons system, that system then becomes his or
her gold watch, that is, something so cherished that it can't be cut
no matter how much sense it makes to do so. There are lots of gold
watches in the Pentagon. It is the role of the top decision makers to
identify the gold watches and take action to throw them out when
the time has come to do so.

Another meaning of gold watch dates back to the early 1960s
when services would often recommend cuts in retired pay, knowing that the secretary of defense would not deprive the retired officers and enlisted personnel of their gold watch (their retirement
benefits). In more recent times, the military departments sometimes offer to cut the gold watch of the secretary of defense or a
key member of Congress in order to save other vital programs. The
services know that the gold watch offered will not be cut and they
hope the secretary or Congress will look to another department's
budget to find the necessary money.

Let's try *to get to the boss through the speech writers*. One of the
quickest ways to get policy made is to get a big boss to commit to
something in a speech or in congressional testimony. Speech writers can therefore be very powerful people and should be cultivated
in two ways. First, if you have helped them in the past and they
trust you, they will often check with you before they put major or
sensitive points in a speech. You can help them and the big boss
from making mistakes. On the other hand, if you desperately need
a big boss to commit to something and you are frustrated by incompetent people or bureaucratic barriers, you may be able to get the
speech writers to help you. One caution: don't get the speech writers in trouble. Be completely honest with them about what you are
trying to do and why you have chosen to pick this route of attack.
This is a very delicate area but clearly a fact of life. If you choose to
take this approach, be sure that your action will serve the nation
and not just some parochial or personal interest.

PHRASES FOR ALL SEASONS

Have you found the *heart of the envelope?* If you are a warrior and you have a target in your sights at the optimum range and firing parameters, that target is in the heart of the firing envelope. When you are running an action and your boss tells you that you are in the heart of the envelope on an issue, that is a real compliment.

Is there a *knee in the curve?* Sometimes in the procurement of weapons systems, it is more efficient to produce systems at a certain rate and less efficient to produce them at faster or slower rates. That optimum point is called the knee of the curve. Another meaning of knee of the curve is when a weapons system reaches a point of diminishing returns (as far as targets destroyed, for instance). At that point in the procurement cycle, it may be wise to cease production or modify the system to enhance accuracy and performance.

Let's try to *unload some dogs.* One of the toughest problems that the Pentagon faces is divestiture. Whereas in the business world something that is not working out is closed down or sold because it is losing money, the military tends to hold on to things long past their effective lives. Trying to unload dogs may get you in big trouble with war lords in the field or in the fleet (major commanders— usually of four-star rank) who want to keep the dog for a number of reasons (often quite legitimate reasons).

Let me give a specific example to illustrate the point. The 1980s was an exciting time for the former Strategic Air Command. Instead of developing no new bombers as had been the case in the previous 15 years, both the B-1 and the Stealth (B-2) bomber were in development. A number of us in the Building wanted to divest the older model B-52s (the 70 B-52Ds) since they had limited capability, were expensive to operate, and required lots of costly upgrades and modifications almost every year. We made the point that if SAC were to get two new bombers it had to give something up. Yet it was very hard to get support from the commander of SAC and his staff. His position was a perfectly legitimate one for an operational commander: "We will start giving up B-52s when the first B-1s start showing up on our bases." The Air Staff won the argument, but the debate became intense at times and those of us who were pushing hard for divestiture did not endear ourselves with the commander in chief of the Strategic Air Command.

That guy is *all smoke and mirrors.* Action officers who are good at tap dancing (slick briefings) can bedazzle audiences with their ability to defend programs with clever arguments. Like magicians trying to feel an audience, the idea is to cloud up the real issue with so much smoke until all you see is a mirror reflection of what they want you to see. One of the reasons that many weapons systems do not live up to expectations is because they have been sold using smoke and mirrors rather than substance and objectivity. Action officers who use a lot of smoke and mirrors are also known as *snake oil salesmen.*

We need to put some *silver tongues and golden pens* on this action. Those who are extraordinarily talented briefers and writers are labeled silver tongues and golden pens. If the big boss says, "I want to put a golden pen on this one," and you are asked to take the action, you have received a nice compliment. Since extremely talented writers are quite rare, they are usually identified fairly early in their tours in the Pentagon and put to work on the most important and sensitive issues.

That guy has a *fast pencil.* Those who can think and write fast, particularly in negotiating sessions such as in the Tank (the conference room of the Joint Chiefs of Staff), can be very influential. Although it may seem unfair that you are doing most of the writing in certain settings, it can be a powerful position to have. The power exists when the words that are the basis of the negotiation are your words rather than someone else's, who may be less smart or more parochial. The way to be helpful in a tough negotiation is to say, "I have come up with some words that may help everyone," or "May I try these new words out?" or "Can we find agreement on these new words?"

We can't even agree on the *terms of reference.* One of the sad facts of life in the Building is that getting a study underway can be a big problem. In order to ensure that a study is framed properly, terms of reference, which describe the scope, goals, and schedule for the study, are normally required. If the agencies and offices involved in the study have major problems agreeing on the terms of reference, the chances that the study will end up with productive conclusions are quite slim.

Did they *buy in*? Defense contractors often underbid on a contract in hopes of beating out the competition. After a contractor wins the competition (and often after a period of time), the company looks around to find ways to charge more than what it bid in order to make some additional money. The underbidding game has been common for many years. If you are involved in research and development, procurement, logistics, or contracts, you will want to watch closely for this. Another important but different meaning of buying in is when someone fully coordinates with or accepts your position and, hence, buys in.

The *iron majors* are in control. Big bosses are heavily dependent on the thinking, writing, and coordination of the majors, lieutenant commanders, lieutenant colonels, and commanders (the so-called iron majors). If these big bosses overrule them often, both the morale and the quality of the work at the action officer level suffers. After working on an issue for some time, these action officers often take a very rigid position, saying something like, "We can't afford to lose on this one."

They think they have found the *silver bullet.* Exciting new technologies have great promise for the future. However, one of the problems with revolutionary new technologies is that officials sometimes think they have discovered the ultimate weapons system, which will solve most of the problems for a service. These silver bullets (in some horror movies, the monster cannot be killed by a standard bullet; it takes a silver one) seldom live up fully to expectations.

That office has a big *not invented here* (NIH) problem. This means that an office is not open to new ideas from outside. If the people in the office didn't devise it, they aren't interested. This is one of the great impediments to innovation in the Pentagon.

Let's push that program to the *out years.* There are two separate meanings for this term. The out years are those years in the future that are beyond the upcoming Future Years Defense Program (FYDP). If a program gets pushed to the out years then it will be at least seven years before it will get strong support. Pushing programs to the out years often kills them since, in six or seven years, the program may look so old and out of date that it won't get much support when it comes up again for consideration. Another common usage of the out years is the last four years of the six-year program period. Hence when you hear this term used, listen carefully for the context: three to six years or beyond six years.

This is a *non-conversation*. Often there are phone conversations that concern delicate matters such as personalities, hidden agendas, rumors, or issues outside the chain of command. These discussions are important in order to accomplish things, but they should be held in confidence. Here's a specific personal example. When I was on the Air Staff during my first assignment to the Pentagon, I used to get regular calls from a close friend on the National Security Council staff (long before the days of Ollie North's years on the NSC staff). He would always remind me that we were not authorized to speak (all interaction between the White House and DoD was supposed to go through the Office of the Secretary of Defense). Then he would explain that he needed accurate information fast and he couldn't wait the few days it would take to get the answer through normal channels. I would get him an answer usually within a few minutes. Normal bureaucratic procedures are often much too slow, so there are lots of people making unauthorized phone calls in order to serve the tyranny of short suspenses.

Let me suggest a number of cautions about non-conversations. If you engage in them, you should be wary of someone trying to get you to do something that is unethical or illegal. Always remember to think before you speak when the conversation is a non-conversation. Also, use this technique sparingly. If you initiate lots of non-conversations, people will begin to suspect that you do not know how to accomplish things within the normal rules, and they may begin to distrust you.

PENTAGONESE—HANDY PHRASES
TO UNDERSTAND AND USE

The following is a short list of some of the more commonly used phrases that have not been described above. Although not all are unique to the Pentagon, the reader may not have encountered them before. They are listed in alphabetical order for everyone's convenience.

Across the river	Congress, the White House, or State Department; across the Potomac from the Pentagon
Analysis paralysis	Studying issues excessively
Back briefing	Passing on to others the highlights of a key meeting
Back channel	Communicating via informal or nonofficial ways
Beak	Upset, mad
Bedbug letter	An effusive, non-responsive answer to complainer (like the president of a hotel chain who never mentions the complaint of the bedbugs in his letter of apology)
Bells and whistles	Hyperbole to sell a system
Black programs	Compartmentalized, highly sensitive programs
Blue suiter	An officer or noncommissioned officer in the Air Force
Bogie	Proposed budget goal
Bow wave	Large budget requirements that can't be funded and appear just beyond the five-year program as a huge "bow wave" on program and budget charts
Bridging document	A short, easy-to-read paper that bridges the gap between an esoteric study and the real world
Brilliant flash	Having the light come on in your head (often known as *BFO*— blazing flash of the obvious)

Check's in the mail	Watch out—this thing may not be paid for
Circle the wagons	Tension is building
Crank it out	Get to work and start producing
Crash	A fast-moving action requiring top priority and lots of overtime work (used to be called *flap*)
Cut drill	Budget exercise to reduce program
Cut legs off	Undermine someone's position
Cut water off	Stop giving support
Dodging a bullet	Avoiding a major crisis or confrontation through skill or luck
Do later file	The place where actions get placed and all work stops
Don't break my rice bowl	Stay out of my business
Elevator speech	A short, two- or three-minute briefing
Face time	Time spent near big bosses in attempts to impress them with your diligence and loyalty
Fallen through the cracks	An important action is lost somewhere
Feet in concrete	Inflexible
Fenced	Money for a program that is reserved and cannot be used for other purposes
Flesh it out	Add more words to paper
Fort Fumble	Affectionate name for the Pentagon (also, *Fudge Factory, Five-sided Squirrel Cage*)
Gin up	Compose, get started
Go ballistic	Get overly excited

Going soft	Giving less support
Gold plate	Add lots of systems to a weapons platform
Golden moment	Something extraordinary has just been thought up or accomplished
Green door	A door behind which some highly sensitive activities take place
Green eye shade	Someone who loves numbers
Happy to glad	Nonsubstantive changes to a paper
Heavy hitter (or just *hitter*)	Someone with lots of power
The Hill	Capitol Hill, home of 535 members of the U.S. Congress and 20,000 staffers
Horizontal escalation	Attacking an enemy in a different location from where he is attacking you
Horseholder	Executive assistant (*go-fer, spear carrier*)
Implementer	The key part of an action (the message or letter to be sent out)
Kicking the can	Postponing decision
Line up your ducks	Do some advanced planning and coordination
Magic bullet	New system or idea that is supposed to solve many problems (and usually doesn't)
Mudfighter	A small, cheap attack aircraft
Mushroom treatment	Keep them in the dark and feed them "crap"
Night face	Face time with bosses at night (counts twice as much as daytime face time)

No brainer	An easy or a "no-issue" action
Non-starter	An idea that has no chance of being accepted
Package	All parts of an action, including the staff summary sheet, implementer, and back-up papers
Pearl Harbor file	A complete record of the package so that when disaster strikes you can trace the actions that led to disaster and protect yourself
Potomac fever	Falling in love with the Washington scene
Power trip	Pursuing power rather than the best solution to a problem
Prebrief	Briefing your boss about key issues before an important briefing (a briefing on a briefing)
Proactive	Go out and make it happen
Purple suiter	An officer working in joint headquarters, on the Joint Staff, in the Office of the Secretary of Defense, or in a defense agency
Put some meat on the bones	Add some more words and analysis
Rattle their chains	Challenge them with tough questions
Read ahead materials	Information provided to officials prior to a meeting (usually copies of briefing slides)
Reprogram	Move money from one program to another
Risk avoidance	Common conservative approach to most problems (minimize or avoid risks)
Rubber threat	When you design a weapons

	system to meet an expected threat and someone (often your bureaucratic enemies) changes the threat parameters
Rudder orders	Specific orders (micro-management)
Run an action	Grab an issue, write the necessary staff papers, and go from office to office to gain staff concurrence on your work
Same sheet of music	In accord completely
Scrub	Cancel ("scrub the mission"); another meaning—to revise
Scrub down	Eliminate unneeded funds in a program (or reduce length of a paper)
Spadework	Basic research
Spook	Someone involved in sensitive programs
Sprinkle holy water	Give approval
Stem winder	Long emotional speech
Strawman	A rough draft for discussion purposes
Street fighter	Someone who would sell his or her mother to win
Supplemental	Extra funds provided to DoD by Congress during the current fiscal year
Tap dance	A slick briefing (or answer to a question), usually lacking substance
Tasker	The requirement, usually in writing, that initiates a staff action
Test for gas	Check out idea for resistance (for gas pains)

To the right of Ghenghis Khan	Ultraconservative
Trigger	Start or activate an action or activity
Up the tape	Going up the chain of command
Up to speed	Finding out what's happening on an issue
Waffling	Watering down a paper
Walk in the woods	Negotiating off line (as Paul Nitze did with the Soviets in Geneva in the mid-1980s)
War lords	Major commanders in the field or in the fleet
Weekend face	Face time on weekends (counts four times as much as face time during daytime)
Weenie	Wimp, weak person
Whip it on me	Tell it to me straight
Who has the action?	Where is the office of primary responsibility? Who has the lead?
Win-win solution	Where all parties in a negotiation win
Wiring diagram	Organizational chart
Zebra study	Analysis of black and white programs in a coherent and complete way
Zero out	Cancel or close down
Zero-sum game	Where there is a winner and a loser rather than two winners

6

WHERE WERE YOU WHEN THE PAGE WAS BLANK? THE AGONY AND THE ECSTASY OF THE ACTION OFFICER

No one can really understand the complex nature of the Pentagon bureaucracy unless he or she has served there as an action officer.

—GENERAL DAVID JONES, U.S.A.F. (RET.)

Beyond a shadow of a doubt, it is the action officer who is the most important actor on the Pentagon scene. Normally serving in the rank of major/lieutenant commander or commander/lieutenant colonel (or in the professional civil service grades of GS–12 to GS–14), these individuals are the worker bees who make the Building hum. They do most of the thinking, writing, coordinating, and briefing. If, as a boss, you have a stable full of superb action officers, you are blessed in at least four ways.

1. You will learn a great deal from them.
2. They will help you in many ways.
3. You will establish life-long friendships with some of them.

4. They will uplift you with their enthusiasm and energy.

What is truly amazing is how fast new action officers can become deeply involved in making big policy and how soon they can brief and carry on important dialogues with top-level officials.

The trust factor. The best action officers are so good that bosses trust them to operate largely independently, except on the more sensitive issues. For instance, as director of plans on the Air Staff, I signed, on occasion, papers that were going directly to the chief of staff or the secretary of the Air Force without reading the entire package that supported the paper. I would read the one-page staff summary sheet, which is normally on the top of the package, read the implementer, check who the action officer was, glance over the coordination sheet, and sign my name in less than five minutes. Often, I would do this in the presence of the action officers to show them how much I relied on their judgment, maturity, careful consideration of the issues, and completeness of coordination. Sometimes I would ask, "How many sticks of dynamite are buried in this package?" or "Did you skip anyone important in the coordination process?" but sometimes I would not even do that. I trusted them, and I wanted them to know it. Of course, I did this only with the better and more mature action officers, but I did it often enough to signal to many how much I relied on them.

The creativity factor. One of the most meaningful expressions in the building is "Where were you when the paper was blank?" This is the action officers' way of telling their many critics, "With little help from anyone, I created, out of whole cloth, this package or briefing. If you want to criticize it, fine, but don't forget that it was my creativity and my hard work that got us from nowhere to where we are now." Pentagon actions are often supreme acts of creativity, for in very little time (a few days to a few weeks) the action officer must find the best solutions to generally intractable problems such as heading off a crisis, starting an important new initiative, or preventing something important from "falling through the cracks."

The game is serious—it is not just pertinent to U.S. national defense. It influences the defense of many other nations that are counting on the Pentagon to make the right moves, at the right time, and in the right areas. At no time and in no place in the modern era have the stakes been higher—not in the British colonial or military service in the nineteenth century; not in France, the Netherlands, or Spain in earlier centuries; nor in China or Japan or elsewhere. Except in periods of actual warfare, there has not been a situation in the past where so many nations had to rely on the good judgment of such a relatively small number of people working in a single building. As a Belgian general said to me many years ago, "We don't count, Perry; we are just a small country, but you count a lot and we are counting on you."

Many actions officers know intuitively that their work is of great importance. That is why they work long hours, endure short deadlines, take abuse in briefings, and accept setbacks with relative equanimity. Action officers learn rather quickly that if there is anyone in Washington who can think things through it is they. The colonels, generals, admirals, senior executive service (SES) civilians, the deputy assistant secretaries, the assistant secretaries, the secretaries of the military departments, and the secretary of defense are much too busy keeping many dozens of balls in the air. Only the action officer, who toughs it out with his or her three to six major issues, can ensure that each issue gets the careful consideration it deserves. Once an action officer understands the importance of his or her role, the psychic rewards of the job can become great indeed.

The evolution of the mindsets of action officers is a fascinating one. At first, they are convinced that almost everyone else is smarter than they are and better at identifying the important issues and how to get things done. This attitude lasts a few months until they begin to realize that they are as smart as most. Somewhere around the one-year mark, they begin to wonder why so few folks have as good a handle on the building and the issues as they do. How fast they evolve from neophytes to experts, from learners to teachers, is a fairly good indicator of how great they will be as action officers. When you overhear a flag officer saying, "Major X sure learned the ropes fast," and you are Major X, you should feel well complimented.

The roller coaster of morale. If you were to construct a morale chart of typical action officers you would find that their morale is quite high the first week or so. Having been selected from among many to serve in the Pentagon is an indication of the high esteem the military service has for the individual. In addition, the new action officer normally has a good feeling of self-worth and professional competence. Brand new action officers usually have expectations about how they might make things better out in the field by addressing some specific issues in the Building. Within two weeks, however, the morale of many new action officers begins to plummet. Whereas in the field the jobs have been quite well defined and performance criteria fairly straightforward, most new action officers in the Pentagon soon get the feeling that they are not trusted to do anything but make coffee and handle the most routine issues and actions. They also learn quickly that every bit of work that they do is closely scrutinized by dozens of people. Many of these people seem to take joy in criticizing and changing the words that have been so carefully crafted.

Their morale often stays quite low for a few months until one day an important action is assigned to them and they realize that the branch or division chief trusts them to take on the vital issues. Now they are going to work on really interesting and high-visibility stuff, and their self-esteem skyrockets. From that point, which usually takes place somewhere between the three- to six-month mark and the two-year mark, the morale of action officers is usually quite high. They do become frustrated about how hard it is to get things done and how much of their time is spent working to beat down dumb ideas or initiatives that come out of such places as the Office of the Secretary of Defense or Congress. However, in general, the six-month to two-year period is one of high morale and a renewed feeling of self-worth.

At about the two-year mark, morale begins to slide downhill again. This slide tends to be a gradual one. It normally begins when some action, idea, or initiative that the action officer has worked on before reappears in somewhat different form and is handed back to the action officer. The immediate reaction of many is, "I have already solved this problem." But, of course, few problems are ever solved permanently. It can be quite frustrating to address the same action time and time again as new bosses come in or new officials at higher levels in the Building, in the Office of Management and Budget, or in Congress want to take another look at your issue. This slow, downhill slide of morale normally continues until the action officer is reassigned to the field, at about the four-year point. However, as new hot actions are assigned, there is resurgent morale, so the slow slide in morale is interspersed with surges of enthusiasm and high energy.

Gaining respect. The action officers' life blood is trust. If they are trusted by fellow action officers to give accurate and unbiased information on a timely basis, if they are willing to drop everything to help someone in desperate need, they have found the secrets to success. It is my firm view that it is much more important in the long run to gain trust among hundreds of action officers than to impress your big bosses. It is a real kudo to be respected by peers within your own service or agency; it is a double kudo to be respected by peers in other services, staffs, and agencies. If you gain the reputation of being an untrustworthy or unhelpful action officer, your effectiveness will diminish quite rapidly. Unlike some jobs in other places, the most brilliant and hard-working action officer in the Building cannot thrive without lots of help from many others. That help will be forthcoming in wonderful quantities if you have earned the respect of others.

Figuring out the requirement. Action officers receive tasking in many ways. A top boss will grab you in the hall and tell you to do something, some key official will give you multiple taskings right in the middle of your briefing, and you will pick up taskings in staff meetings, in your in box, even at the athletic center, or at a social event. As soon as you hear the tasking coming, you should pull out your pen and start writing. If at all possible you should get answers to the following questions:

1. When is it due at various levels?
2. Who will sign it out (in other words, who are you writing for)?

3. Do we need a message, a letter, a briefing, or what?
4. What kind of specific guidance will you receive and from whom?
5. Can you run a draft by the person who tasks you to see if you are on the right track before you start the coordination process?
6. What are the key offices that will need to get involved in putting the action together?
7. To whom will we send the letter or give the briefing?
8. Are there any hidden agendas that you should be aware of?
9. Are there any special clearances needed?

As you are receiving the tasking, you should be very aggressive in asking these questions so that when you return to your desk and start to work you will produce what is *needed* in minimum time. If the person who is tasking you cannot answer some of these questions, think quickly and suggest some answers to your own questions. If you get positive responses to your suggestions, you are more likely to put together a package or a briefing that will "answer the mail."

Using the proper formats. There are a number of types of papers that you will be required to write; each one will have a specific format that you must follow. Hence, it is very helpful if you have a file of all these formats in your computer. Secretaries, fellow action officers, and others can help you, but it is much better if you can do this kind of work yourself so you don't have to bother others. Most offices in the Pentagon have these formats in a manual, office instruction file book, or on a computer. On computers, Truform and Filemaker formats are the most common.

The coordination process. A major portion of action officers' responsibility after the paper has been written is maintaining the coherence of the package during the coordination process. The coordination of a package often requires the concurrence of dozens of different offices. Since so many love to attack the substance or to nitpick (change "happy" to "glad"), it is awfully easy to allow the paper to slowly change and lose its focus, impact, and coherency.

Action officers soon learn where good, thoughtful, substantive help comes from and seek those people out *early* in the coordination process.

One approach that I found useful when I ran actions back in the early 1970s may still have some applicability. After I had written the message or letter that was the implementer, as well as the background papers, point papers, and staff summary sheet, I would take the following actions.

1. Ask an experienced and sharp action officer in my division to read it over carefully and critique my work.
2. Show the package to an action officer in another division that is one of the key offices on my coordination schedule.
3. Give it to my division chief for comments and suggestions.
4. Take the package to the toughest and most thorough "coordination stop" I know.

After receiving comments from these sources, I would redo the package, taking into account all useful suggestions that I had received during my informal coordination. Then and only then would the long process of full coordination begin. By this time I had thought through the action and had honed arguments to defend my position. If in the process of further coordination, someone convinced me to take another approach, I would redo the package and recoordinate through all the offices that had already agreed to support (signed off on) the package. In this case, the real challenge was convincing those who had liked the first version to agree with and coordinate on the newest version.

PITFALLS TO AVOID

Since much of the success of any action officer is measured in terms of avoiding mistakes, let me explain some of the many booby traps and detours that action officers should try to avoid. The following are some of the more significant ones.

Falling in love with his or her program. As a brigadier general, I was the deputy director of Air Force Plans and the chairman of the important Air Staff Force Structure Committee. An action officer came to see me to make a strong appeal that no money be removed from the program for which he was responsible. I asked him many questions and learned that his program had not met required specifications, had a large cost overrun, and was far behind schedule. I also learned that because of schedule delays, the program manager could not prudently spend all of the money allocated over the next couple of years. I told him that, as the head of the Force Structure Committee, I planned to recommend that some money be removed from his program in each of the next two years. He countered with the argument that if the Air Force went "soft" on his program, it might get canceled by the secretary of defense or Congress. When I said that I was going to recommend cuts anyway, tears welled up in his eyes. Gently, I tried to explain to him how important it was to maintain objectivity. I pointed out that we couldn't afford to have people who, because of their hard work and long-term commitment to a program, were not able to recommend that a program be modified, curtailed, or canceled when one of these courses of action was appropriate. I alluded to the British colonel who was the head of a large number of allied POWs in Burma during World War II in the Academy Award–winning movie of the late 1950s, *The Bridge Over the River Kwai.* He built the bridge for the Japanese and couldn't blow it up when the Japanese train arrived.

I am afraid that my discussion fell on deaf ears, yet the point is well worth emphasizing. Many people in the Pentagon become too committed to one course of action when there are almost always a number of courses of action that will serve the goal at hand. Many programs fail to live up to expectations, and those that fall far short should be restructured or canceled.

One of the most agonizing experiences an action officer can go through is the cancellation of a program that he or she was largely responsible for in the staff. A number of years of dedicated effort may go up in smoke in quick order when budgetary, congressional, international, or other factors cause a program to be canceled.

Well-known examples include the A-12 aircraft, the Seawolf submarine (SSN-21), the P-7A antisubmarine warfare aircraft, the Air Defense Anti-Tank System (ADATS), and the Tacit Rainbow autonomous vehicle. As a matter of fact, there are dozens of programs that are canceled each year, yet each cancellation is a spear in the chest of one or more action officers in the Pentagon as well as lots of people in the field or in the fleet.

It is awfully easy to react to the cancellation in a negative way. One common reaction is to assume that whoever canceled the program is stupid, parochial, shortsighted, or dishonest. Another common reaction is to assume that it was your fault that your program failed. Neither of these reasons is very healthy and seldom does either explain what really happened. Most programs are canceled because they fall short of expectations, have large cost overruns, are way behind schedule, are outclassed by other new or improved weapons systems, or fail to meet the challenge of an enhanced enemy threat. Stupidity on the part of the decision makers or incompetence on the part of the staff officers responsible for the program is only occasionally the reason for cancellation.

Program monitors in the Pentagon as well as program managers in the field must work very hard to maintain their sense of balance and perspective. They are expected to be advocates for their program, but if their program is canceled they should try very hard to be philosophical about the setback or they may become embittered and cynical. When that happens, their overall effectiveness in future Pentagon work diminishes considerably. Of course, most action officers are not program monitors for specific weapons systems, but that doesn't mean that they don't fall in love with positions they have so carefully crafted. Hence, all action officers must be careful about falling into the trap of having blinders on as far as specific programs, issues, or positions are concerned.

Excessive pride of authorship. Action officers who think that their prose is wonderful and who resist suggestions on how to improve their writing are in for a long and agonizing assignment. No matter how well they know the subject and how well they express themselves in writing, action officers must understand that others among the 23,000 workers in the Pentagon can improve the paper they have so carefully crafted. In fact, the Building is full of masterful editors who can take someone's writing, polish it, and improve its impact on the reader.

Inability to condense writing and briefings into short, crisp formats. Some action officers will say, "There is no way I can summarize this complex issue into a one-page staff summary sheet or a four-minute briefing." If they take this attitude, the boss will find someone who can and the really exciting and important actions will be assigned to others. It is harder to write a short paper than a long one; it is tough to find the four or five key points and put them into a three- or four-minute briefing, but it can and must be done, or the top bosses will never sleep.

Assuming you are wiser than the big bosses. Many action officers have opportunities to spend time with flag officers, SES-level civilians, and high-level political appointees in briefings, meetings, at an occasional social gathering, or at the athletic center. It is quite easy to fall into the trap of assuming that you are smarter, quicker, more tuned in, and more effective than one or more of these top officials. In the area of specific expertise, you are often right in this judgment. In fact, it is expected that the action officer is the one who understands a certain issue best, has the best files on it, and keeps up with changes that occur by reading the daily message traffic and keeping in close touch with points of contact.

You may well be smarter on certain issues, but the senior leaders often have a broader understanding of what is required to carry out the many responsibilities that fall on their shoulders. For instance, the official may have been the vice president of a large industrial company, or had a lot of combat experience, or spent many years in big jobs in Europe yet have very little background in your specific area. In addition, there is a high proportion of top leaders who are introverts and do not often reveal the talent and judgment that helped to get them where they are. Many of these bosses have their minds on something else when they are being briefed and therefore seem less bright than they really are. Finally, the demands of their calendar may cause them to nod off in the middle of a briefing. This can be enormously frustrating especially if you are about to give them the information they really need to make the correct decision.

If, in reaction to some of these proclivities on the part of his or her bosses, an action officer begins to demonstrate a degree of cynicism or arrogance, that officer will suffer. If in spite of yourself you find that you are becoming embittered, that is the time to ask to shift to another action, another office, or another location.

Assuming that the other services are doing better. It is a very common perception that somehow one or more of the other services is winning in the competition in the Tank, in OSD, OMB, or Congress. This is usually expressed along the following lines:

- "The Navy is eating our lunch on the Hill."
- "Those Air Force toads beat us again in OSD."
- "The Marines rolled us again in the Tank."

Certainly in the tough, competitive environment of the Pentagon, there are winners and losers on many issues, but over time, the balance of influence and performance among and between the services has been pretty good.

Although the Air Force did better than the other services in the 1950s and the Navy in the 1980s, the Marines and the Army have won lots of budgetary battles; in many cases, all the services were winners. When one service seems to be on top, it is often the result of technological achievements and changing national and military strategy, mission priorities, or threat patterns rather than the bureaucratic skills of the leaders of the ascendant service. But the service that does the best long-range planning, creating well-conceived master plans and strategies, does better over the long term. In the more than forty-five years since the Department of Defense was formed, all the services have done fairly well in developing coherent plans and programs.

When a military service has a setback, members of that service often feel that the other services will take advantage of the situation. This happens in some cases, but usually the other services don't try to kick their sister service when it is down. The leaders of these services know that there will be times when they will have setbacks and will want support from those who wear uniforms of other colors. For instance, in the late 1980s when General Welch, the chief of staff of the Air Force, and his personnel officer, Lieutenant General Hickey (who later retired as a major general), got in big trouble with Congress for allegedly ignoring congressional guidance on how to run promotion boards, the other services did not take advantage of this embarrassment. When General Mike Dugan was fired by Secretary of Defense Dick Cheney in September 1990 for revealing to the press many details of the planning for the upcoming Gulf War air campaign, the other services did not "turn the knife" in the Air Force. Nor did the other services try to take advantage of the Navy's embarrassment over the sexual harassment ("Tailhook") scandal of the early 1990s. My advice in this regard is to work hard to do your job and don't worry about how the other services may be doing.

Wasting everyone's time all the way up the line. Senior officials really appreciate action officers who take initiatives, work out happy compromises, solve problems, and come up with innovative solutions to tough problems. The action officer who keeps throwing the problem back to the bosses, who offers to hold the bosses' coats while they fight a battle that the action officer could have prevented, and who are problem creators rather than problem solvers normally fail. After a while the bosses begin to realize that this action officer is causing them lots of additional work and anguish and start asking some tough questions such as, "How come Major Y has got me into another fight with OSD (or General Y or congressional staffer Z)?" or "Doesn't Lieutenant Colonel Y understand that what I want him to do is solve problems—not create them?"

Becoming cynical after watching the slick careerists bamboozle their bosses with smoke and mirrors. Certainly there are lots of ambitious people working in the Pentagon, and some of them work overtime to further their own careers. A few are quite manipulative, but it has been my experience over the years that those with runaway ambition eventually drive themselves off some cliff. When flag officers have private discussions in the messes, their car pools, over the back fence at the Navy Yard, the Marine barracks, Fort Myer, Fort McNair, and Bolling Air Force Base, they very often talk about the folks they work with and are briefed by in the Pentagon. The following judgments are heard quite often:

- "That guy looks up much better than he looks down."
- "She sure works hard to get face time."
- "That AO seems to be unpopular with his peers."
- "I wonder why he seems more interested in pleasing me than in giving it to me straight."

Well-controlled ambition to accomplish important institutional and personal goals is fine, but burning personal ambition is normally detrimental to eventual success. Let's be completely frank: hyperambitious people often succeed in the short run. However, it has been my personal experience that the greatest numbers of action officers who have failed have been those who wear their ambitions on their sleeves and step on others as they try to fight their way up the greasy flagpole.

Giving up on a new idea too quickly. Action officers often come up with superb ideas and try them out on their colleagues and their bosses. If they meet resistance, they sometimes give up, bury the idea in the bottom of the safe, and go back to the same old way of doing things. Happily, within each major service or agency in the Pentagon there are clearinghouses for ideas, where good ideas are treasured, used, and entered into the decision-making process. For instance, there is a civilian official who has served in the Pentagon for many years and who many action officers come to see. They give him ideas, and he thinks of creative ways to use the better ones. He always does so with care, since he respects the chain of command and does not want to get action officers in trouble. I would love to list him in this book, but he has asked that his name not be mentioned. He feels that he can be more effective if he plays his role very quietly.

Not studying and understanding the role of congressional staffers. Pentagon staff officers normally can understand the roles congressional staffers on key committees play because they are similar to the roles played by the more influential action officers in the Building. These staffers often are the only people on the Hill who have expertise in a particular area. This expertise gives them power and influence since even the most experienced Senator or Representative must turn to them for advice and assistance. If the key staffer is not properly cultivated, the action officer and the entire chain of command may lose important battles without ever firing a shot. In many instances a member of Congress who has not had time to get into the details of a particular area will follow the recommendation of a trusted staffer no matter how senior or knowledgeable a representative the Department of Defense may have sent over to testify. Whereas the congressman may see a certain military officer a few times a year, he or she sees professional staffers on a much more regular basis.

Not keeping extra copies of the entire package when the action copy is going up the tape. Each package normally has a staff summary sheet, the implementer (usually a message or a letter), and a number of point papers, background papers, and other supporting documents. Every once in a while someone in the chain may ask for a copy of a background paper or attachment after they have finished coordinating on the package. It can be embarrassing when the action officer has to say, "I'm sorry, the only copy I have is in the action package." If this does happen, front offices can sometimes help (front offices usually keep on file everything the boss signs), but front offices rarely retain the back-up materials. Of course, if the package is saved on your computer, you should be in good shape.

Failing to follow a package through the entire coordination process. If an action requires the signature of a senior official, the action officer should not relinquish his responsibility once the package is in the front office of the next higher boss. Often, in the offices of top bosses, packages can get sidetracked or placed in the "do later" pile. The better action officers will monitor the progress of their packages through the executive secretaries, executive assistants, executive officers, or military assistants to ensure timely action. However, good judgment must be used about pestering top offices too much. If action officers bother front office people every day about routine packages, they will soon lose rapport with these key people. The care and feeding of top secretaries and military assistants is a subtle art that should be cultivated by all action officers.

Becoming too cozy with contractors. Many action officers have to deal with contractors on a regular basis. For instance, if you are deeply involved with a weapons system as the program element monitor for that system, you will be interacting with the contractor building that system and with the major subcontractors. The various contractor representatives at the factory and in Washington will give you lots of support and assistance. But action officers, like all officials in the Pentagon, must ensure that these relationships remain professional and that regulations and laws are not violated. If you are a superb action officer and do your job well, there may be a number of contractors who will feel that there is a direct relationship between your good work and their success. You must not let their appreciation be manifested in any gratuities, free dinners, or promises of employment after retirement.

If you would like to help a firm win a contract with your service because you are convinced that this contractor can build the best weapons system, you must not slip this firm any proprietary information from another contractor or in any other way diminish the fairness of competition. This can be particularly hard if you think the top bureaucrats may make the wrong decision or some powerful congressman may force the wrong decision to be made. Discipline, self-restraint, and integrity must be the rules of the game for anyone who deals with contractors.

Becoming careless about security. Everyone needs to be very sensitive about safeguarding classified material. Because many action officers deal routinely with highly classified and sensitive papers all day long, they may become complacent and too relaxed. Nothing can damage a promising career faster than a security violation caused by an open safe, classified material left in photocopiers or in a restroom, or a classified page hidden in the middle of a pile of unclassified material discovered at night by the security people. Believe me, security personnel check, and if it is there, they will probably find it. Big bosses do not like to get official letters from bigger bosses about security violations.

When it is time to lock up at night, the three-person check is recommended. Although a two-person check is normally all that is required, a third person is helpful, if available, as a final check. On weekends it is very wise indeed to ensure that someone else is in the office with you. This is especially true if you think you might be called to go down the hall to the office of a big boss, and a number of safes are open, and no one is around to cover the office.

As a final point, it may be useful to emphasize that how well action officers perform is a direct result of the environment in which they work. What happens in the branches and divisions is closely related to the leadership provided to these action officers. The next chapter discusses the second most important set of players in the Pentagon—the branch and division chiefs.

7
THE BRANCH AND DIVISION CHIEFS: A FORGOTTEN BREED

Leadership is the liberation of talent.

—PETERS AND AUSTIN

So much is said about the role of the action officer that the importance of the branch and division chiefs is often neglected. This chapter is written with three goals in mind. First, to help new branch and division chiefs do their important jobs well; second, to help new action officers and secretaries understand the vital role of their immediate boss; and, third, to help top-level officials understand the essential role that branch and division chiefs play in the policy-making process in the Pentagon.

Most division chiefs are colonels or captains or GS–15s; most have had some experience in the Pentagon before they are given the job. They normally have anywhere from 10 to 40 people working for them, with the average division being closer to the lower number. Branch chiefs are normally junior colonels or captains, senior lieutenant colonels or commanders, or GS–14s or –15s. Branches vary in size from about five to about 15 people.

The anatomy of branches and divisions. It is in branches and divisions where the rubber hits the road, where the actions get started, developed, and coordinated. It is the place of the blank page, the stubby pencil, and the short suspense. It is where an action officer has to create Hemingway prose and William Jennings Bryan oratory out of confused tasking, with limited guidance and in an unreasonable time crunch. It is a place of great activity and creativity as well as of terrible frustration.

Branch and division chiefs are managers; more important, they are leaders, and the leadership challenge is wild and wonderful. For purposes of discussion, let's assume that you are the chief of a division with sixteen people. You have a deputy, a lieutenant colonel who has been selected for colonel but has not yet pinned on his rank. Working for you are 10 action officers in the grades of 0–4 through 0–5; a civilian GS–13, who is a combination of analyst and action officer; and two secretaries (one grade 6 and one grade 4). You feel very fortunate for you have a better-than-average crew and you have one more secretary than most divisions have. Eight of your action officers are superb. They think, write, and brief well. They are not afraid of hard work and they know how to meet deadlines, coordinate packages, and stay tuned in. One of your very best action officers is having marital problems, but these problems do not seem to have a significant impact on his work. Another of your action officers is a woman; she is superb, the second-best thinker and writer in the office.

On the down side, two of your action officers are weak. One is brand new and, with a lot of personal attention on your part, may turn into an effective action officer. The other one is just not hacking it. He writes poorly, falls apart when senior people ask him tough questions, and doesn't seem to be able to identify the key issues in an action. Since you have been told that you must live with him until next summer, you keep him working on the less important stuff. As a result of his being given the lower-priority actions, he is having morale problems. Since he has great operational talent and experience, you are working on getting him a good job back in the field. One of your two secretaries is new, and it is already clear that she will not work out. The senior secretary is very competent and quite experienced, but you are concerned that she will be hired away by a more senior officer who can offer a GS–7 position.

You are pleased that you have such a high percentage of superb action officers, but that situation is not without its problems. Leading these superstars is a little like managing a stable of thoroughbred horses. They all want to race to the front of the pack, yet you don't have enough of the really hot, high-visibility actions to hand out to each of them. Much of the work in your division is quite routine. When a front-burner issue comes along and you select someone to take it, others are disappointed. You have another problem with this stable of thoroughbreds. One of your action officers, Major A, has caught the attention of your two-star general. The general so values this man's talents that he often suggests to you that Major A get some great new action. In other words, you don't have complete freedom to parcel out the actions in an equitable way.

You have other concerns. In the last six months, your division has had two security violations, and the pressure is on not to have another for the rest of your tenure. You know in your bones that one of the quickest ways to fail as a division chief is to have a series of security violations. The last violation was particularly gross—a safe was left open at night. As is often the case, it was your two top action officers who were working late that night. They were so wrapped up in putting together a hot package that they failed to notice that the safe they closed was not fully secure, even though they had both checked it.

Another big difficulty you face is a problem boss. He is a deputy director of a staff directorate and has four divisions and two branches working for him. His position is a designated one-star billet but is normally held by a senior colonel. Your boss is up for flag rank on the next promotion board, and promotion is clearly very important to him. He has been a workaholic and a micromanager (also a "micromangler") for a long time, but these proclivities have been exaggerated by his nervousness about being promoted. He greatly enjoys impressing his boss by getting actions done ahead of the normal suspense date. If the two-star wants the paper by next

Wednesday, your boss will insist that the completed package be on his desk by 7:30 A.M. on Monday. This usually means lots of unnecessary weekend work and shotgun coordination. Your action officers are wondering why you don't stand up to the boss and tell him to cool it. They want to take the time to do a better job on the packages and do a little less weekend work. You have raised this issue with your boss but with scant results. You haven't figured out a good way to readdress the problem without making the situation worse.

A candid look at division and branch chiefs. Each day in the life of a branch or division chief is a new ball game with new issues, fast-moving actions, unscheduled meetings, and coordination problems jumping up and grabbing you with little or no notice. Although there is lots of routine work to fill your in box every day, there is much that is not routine; this makes many days exciting and fast paced.

There is much discussion around the Building about the so-called iron majors running the place. But from my experience, it is the colonels and the branch and division chiefs who, in fact, establish and maintain the parameters for action and inaction in the Building. Unlike the majors, who look forward to one or more promotions and are often hesitant to take on their big bosses too often, many of the colonels and captains have a different perspective. Most of these people know that the rank of colonel or captain is the last rank they will achieve and a number are approaching retirement. If they think some idea is dumb, if they feel a flag officer is off on some wild idea, they will often find a way to keep things on a steady course. Hence, they are major forces of stability and prudence; it is the wise flag officer (and action officer) who listens carefully to their advice. The unhappy side of the iron colonels, however, is that they themselves are sometimes impediments to progress. They can quite effectively stifle useful ideas from above and below. I would therefore encourage branch and division chiefs alike to periodically take a look at themselves to ensure they remain mature progressives and do not become reactionary naysayers.

There are many secrets to success for branch and division chiefs. Those who subordinate their egos and their ambitions to the needs of the institution they serve have taken the first important step. If they are fully committed to giving praise and credit to their subordinates, if they worry more about the excellence of the staff work and less about face time with the big bosses, and if they are both good teachers and good listeners, they have a very high probability of success.

Branch and division chiefs must be ruthlessly introspective. Many of them think they meet the necessary criteria for excellence, when in fact they don't. Ambition, insecurity, inability to trust subordinates, and authoritarianism all tend to cloud the clarity of self-inspection. Branch and division chiefs need to ask themselves, "Would I enjoy working for me?" When they counsel their subordinates, which they should do at least every six months, they should ask, "What is it about me that bugs you? How am I wasting your time?"

One of the key challenges for branch and division chiefs is the leading and tutoring of their immediate boss and their bosses at higher levels. The opportunity to make an important contribution in this regard is enormous. The big bosses in the Pentagon have a great deal on their minds and on their plates. For instance, when I was director of plans in the Air Staff, I had 27 divisions working for me. Each division was responsible for at least a dozen important issues and many minor issues. With over 300 important issues and over 1,000 issues of lesser importance to deal with, I had to rely very heavily on my division and branch chiefs. Each of them taught me a great deal; almost all of them led me in the direction of the correct position and the right strategy on each issue.

On occasion, I would play a major role in forming an issue, but most of the time my role was modest. I would purposefully and explicitly tell my division chiefs that I did not want to give them guidance. I wanted them to feel free to look at all options objectively and pick the very best one for the nation. I also told them that if they wanted my ideas I would be happy to share them. But I didn't want them to treat my ideas as guidance for fear it would constrain their quest for the best possible solution to a problem or the most feasible plan for the future. Branch and division chiefs who seek guidance from their bosses are making a mistake in most cases. The better action officers don't want to be constrained by a tight leash. They resent having no flexibility in finding the best course of action.

Of course, there are a number of exceptions to this general rule. If the suspense is quite short, guidance may be in order so that little time is wasted putting the paper together. Also, if the top boss has such a strong feeling about (or he or she has already made such a firm commitment to) a particular course of action, it may be a waste of time to pursue other options. And, if the boss is clearly the expert on the subject, his or her guidance to the staff would be appreciated and appropriate.

A philosophy of leadership for branch and division chiefs. The staff structure in the Pentagon is quite different from line organizations in the fleet or in the field and somewhat different from other large staffs. The worldwide commitments of the U.S. military and the numbers of international negotiations that are taking place at any one time are large. This fact, in combination with the complexity of the service, JCS, OSD, OMB, NSC, State, Commerce, Treasury, and Congress interrelationships give division and branch chiefs great opportunities for leadership. Why? Because their bosses are caught up in activity traps to a greater extent than elsewhere in the military. These big bosses must rely on their branch and divisions chiefs as well as their action officers to do most of the thinking, planning, and coordinating for them. Those branch and division chiefs who are unwilling to be creative and to run hard with issues, even when specific guidance is lacking, are great impediments to progress and thoughtful decision making. How sad it is when some of these people are afraid of their own shadows and accomplish nothing but pushing papers around on their desks and frustrating their subordinates.

Let me relate a personal story in this regard. As a new colonel, I was a branch chief who had been in the Pentagon only a couple of months. I was sitting in the briefing room of the three-star operations deputy of the U.S. Air Force Dutch Huyser. Having just returned from a JCS meeting, Huyser was debriefing in his normal colorful style with lots of humor, lots of "who said what to whom," and lots of interaction with the staff. The room was full (perhaps 40 officers). General Huyser had just articulated his view on how the military ought to be restructured throughout the world. He wanted, for instance, a Northeast Asia Unified Command (commanded by an Army four-star general), a Southwest Pacific Unified Command (commanded by an Air Force four-star general), and a Specified Naval Command in Hawaii (commanded by a four-star admiral). After his monologue on this subject, he asked if anyone in the room had any objection to his grand design. There were a number of people in the room who were clearly not comfortable with some of his ideas, but since he was expressing them with such conviction, none of my colleagues spoke up (in the Pentagon vernacular this is called "checking your shoe shine"). Although I was so new that General Huyser didn't know who I was, I knew quite a lot about the Unified Command Plan and I felt *somebody* ought to speak up. So I held up my hand and said that I thought that some changes were needed but that some of his ideas would be bad for the Air Force and for the nation. He flushed slightly, asked what my name was, and walked out the door.

The next day, I was assigned as team chief for an ad hoc group that was to put together an Air Force position on a revised Unified Command Plan that would be briefed to the chief. Over the course of the next few months, I learned much more about the intricacies of the U.S. military command structure throughout the world. My team was able to teach many of our superiors across the entire Air Staff that reorganization of the Unified Command Structure is fraught with many more difficulties than most of them realized. Our alliance structure and the command structure that supports it is extraordinarily complex. This is especially true when the impact of organizational changes on other nations, all of the military services, and the U.S. Congress is considered. The bosses were willing to listen when they realized how deeply we had researched and understood the subject. We were also able to develop some excellent options because we were not constrained by specific guidance from General Huyser or anyone else that would have limited our vision or restricted the options we could examine.

My point is that division and branch chiefs should view themselves as much more than people who answer the mail and solve the problems. They should consider themselves to be important leaders in the Pentagon with a major responsibility in ensuring that the best defense is provided to this country and its allies and friends. They should be willing to stand up for what is right, challenge conventional wisdom and outdated policy, and come up with new ideas and initiatives. If the tasking they receive is misguided, they should elevate the issue quickly (the general rule is the dumber the tasking, the faster the elevation). The better bosses at the top know that they pass out poor guidance on occasion and welcome somebody who quickly challenges them so that they don't waste people's time on unwise things.

Branch and division chiefs also have a special obligation for the professional growth of the action officers who serve them. They should "cross train" action officers for a number of reasons. First, it will broaden the experience and horizons of these future leaders. Second, it helps to even out the work load so that some action officers are not working 14-hour days while others have barely enough to keep them busy. Third, it provides much more flexibility in times of crises. Fourth, it is a helpful way to build teamwork and enhance morale. And last, but not least, it reduces the number of times you will have to cancel vacations and leaves on short notice.

As a branch or division chief, whether you are in your last tour before retirement or on the way to many more assignments, you should provide the kind of uplifting leadership that your people want and deserve. You should be the "heat shield" that protects your people from some of the poor guidance and unreasonable pressures from above. You should work hard to help give your action officers both the freedom and the visibility that they desire and deserve.

Branch and division chiefs should look out for the welfare of their people. They should be good listeners and supporters; they should be part coach and part cheerleader; they should arrange for social functions a couple of times a year so that families can get to know each other. They should be especially mindful of making the newly assigned individuals feel welcome. Welcome letters, help with house hunting, solid orientation sessions, and careful nurturing until the individual is ready to race down the corridor with a hot action are all part of the chief's responsibility to the newest members of the branch and division team. When officers are finishing up their Pentagon tours and are coming up for reassignment, branch and division chiefs should do their best to ensure that the personnel system is not "screwing them over." If you help your people get really good jobs when they leave, you will find more and more good people will want to work for you.

Finally, let me share a bit of advice from a trusted friend who served in the Pentagon on many occasions and prior to retirement was a commander-in-chief in the Unified Command Structure of the U.S. military. After reading this chapter, he agreed with my emphasis on the importance of branch and division chiefs. He worked for a division chief in the Pentagon more than 30 years ago whom he greatly respected and whom he still thinks about with affection. This division chief gave him the following advice when this general was a young action officer in the 1950s:

> You are on a fast track, working the biggest and hottest issues. If you get tasking from the general officers, respond to it with the speed of light—you do it and do it well. Don't think you have to run everything by me and slow up, but I do ask that you keep me filled in on what's happening. I'm not going to be part of the problem; I am going to be part of the solution.

This reflects the kind of philosophy that action officers admire in their branch and division chiefs.

8

FLAG OFFICERS, SENIOR CIVILIANS, AND POLITICAL APPOINTEES: THE NEED FOR LEADERSHIP

Some people live in the present, oblivious of the past and blind to the future. Some dwell in the past. A very few have the knack of applying the past to the present in ways that show them the future.

—RICHARD NIXON

The purpose of this chapter is to assist people who are moving into senior leadership positions. A number of top leaders come to the Pentagon without previous experience in the Building or, in many cases, previous experience in the Washington environment. The Building is a fast track for any newcomer; it is a *very* fast track for a political appointee, SES, or flag officer who has not served in the Building before. Within a week or two, you may be attending important policy meetings and making recommendations and decisions without the deep understanding of either the bureaucratic realities or the issues that your colleagues around the decision table will have.

But this chapter is not just for the new high-level official. This chapter is also designed to help the less-senior officials understand the demands and pressures that their bosses and bosses' bosses face. Anyone who can gain an appreciation of what it is like to be a top official can serve that boss better.

Too many senior officials in the Pentagon are victims of their in boxes, their telephones, and their meeting and travel schedules. As a result, they fail to provide the visionary leadership that this country needs. Top officials should be in the planning and policy making business, helping their departments, services, and agencies formulate a vision and ensuring that day-to-day decisions are formulated and implemented in pursuit of this vision. In the hopes of making top leaders in the Pentagon more efficient, more effective, and most important, better long-term thinkers and planners, the following rules of thumb are suggested.

ITEMS TO CONSIDER BEFORE YOU CHECK IN

Do a little reading. You probably will not have much time to get prepared for the major responsibilities that you are soon to undertake, but if you do have a few spare days or hours, use them wisely. There is a marvelous book that seems as if it was designed to help people in high positions in Washington. Written by two marvelous people, Ernie May and Dick Neustadt, it is rich with insights for the higher-level official in the national security arena. *Thinking in Time* (New York: The Free Press, 1986) is must reading. If you don't have time for the whole book, read chapters 1, 3, 4, 5, 8, 13, and 14.

Put together a transition plan. Too many high officials arrive on the scene, dive into their in box, and never take a strategic view of their responsibilities and opportunities. May I suggest that you read the transition chapter in my book on leadership of large and complex organizations, *Taking Charge: Making the Right Choices* (Garden City, N.Y.: The Avery Publishing Group, 1988).

THINGS TO DO THE FIRST FEW MONTHS

Take control of your schedule. This is much easier said than done since you probably are a member of many committees, steering groups, study efforts, working groups, and ad hoc groups. You are chairman of some of these committees, and you are expected to attend every meeting. In addition, you are a principal on many other committees, and your attendance is also expected. Yet top officials must be ruthless about freeing themselves from involvement in unimportant meetings and commitments. Lots of techniques are available. If you are chairman and the committee is no longer serving a useful purpose, take action to close it down or fold it into another committee. If these avenues are not available, another technique is to quit calling meetings and let the committee fade into disuse. A third technique is to stretch out the time between meetings. A fourth technique is not attending and not sending a substitute. Sending a substitute on a regular basis is an approach worth considering if there is no way to close down the committee or to have your office totally ignore the meetings. The weak approach is to continue to attend every meeting on your schedule. Top-level officials have to be very tough-minded about meetings. They should require agendas ahead of time as well as demand to know the purpose and desired outcomes of meetings. If these are not available officials should politely decline to attend.

Whenever someone comes up with the idea of forming a new committee, ask some very tough questions:

- Why a new committee?
- Why should I be a member?
- Why can't the issue be handled through normal staff action?
- Why can't this issue be handled by a committee that is already constituted?

In the business world, the top executives spend, on average, 17 hours a week in meetings. Most management consulting firms feel this is an excessive amount of time. If you can hold the number of hours per week in meetings in the Pentagon to fewer than 15, you will be doing quite well. Don't contribute to this problem by calling a lot of unnecessary meetings. Don't waste your time and the time of your talented subordinates.

Learn how to dictate and use the skill often. This is by far the most useful skill for top officials. It is easy to learn and to do, it is fast, it is efficient, you can do it almost anywhere, and the result is often better than the long, involved sentences that are written in longhand or on a word processor. If you have never given dictation before, you might try writing down a short outline of what you want to say so that when your secretary comes in to your office, the dictation is well organized and goes quickly. Having written books using all three methods (dictation, longhand, and word processor), it is clear to me that through the dictation technique your writing is more likely to shine with clarity, brevity, and punch. We all tend to speak in short declarative sentences. We use the present rather than the past tense in speech. We use fewer fancy words. Dictation can also save you the most precious resource—time. Through dictation, I saved about an hour a day when I was in a two-star position in the Building.

Buy a personal computer and use it at home. This is a wonderful way to keep up with perhaps the most important technology of our times: the personal computer in combination with easy-to-use, sophisticated software. If you are computer literate and understand the lingo of the computer world, you will do a much better job in the Building. This was one of my major mistakes: I didn't buy a personal computer (PC) until after I retired from the military. I thought I understood all those computer terms and concepts that I was constantly getting briefed on, but I didn't. It was an exercise in self-deception that many senior people are still going through.

Choose a personal computer that is compatible with the system in your office so you can work at home and bring the diskette to work. In the Building today most of the three-star officers use electronic communication in their offices, and many other top officials are following their lead. Hence, to remain computer illiterate in the 1990s is to fail. Don't wait until next month or next year for a new model to come out. Buy one by the end of this week. If you own an old computer that you no longer use, buy a new one. The newest ones are much easier to use than those that came out just a few years ago.

Take the DoD Computer Institute's three-day executive course. Within your first few months, take this fine course. Given about four times a year to 15 or 20 flag and general officers (and those who have been selected for flag rank) and SES civilians (there are no exceptions to these qualifications for attendance), this course is entitled "The Automated Information Systems Management Course for Senior Executives." In three days you will be updated on the latest developments in computers, software, computer graphics, artificial intelligence, and expert systems. It is held right here in town and is aimed at the proper level for you. You will learn a lot from the professors and outside lecturers, meet some other top officials around town, and learn from their questions and comments. The director is a Navy captain (telephone 433-3000), and the classes are held at the Washington Naval Yard in southeast Washington (10 minutes from the Pentagon).

Choose your executive officer from your current staff. Don't bring in a crony from outside. Choose someone whose background is quite different from yours so you can learn from each other. Pick someone who is both well respected and well liked by his or her peers and who is within about a year of moving on. Every year bring in a new person. Teach each executive officer your job. If they fully understand what you do and how you make decisions, they can be very helpful to the staff in explaining your viewpoints, hang ups, priorities, and points of emphasis. Also, when these people return to the Pentagon (which is very likely), they will be able to move into big jobs like yours and, with the experience and wisdom that you have shared with them, serve with distinction.

Don't allow your executive officer or military assistant to wear your rank. Although this is not a common problem in the Pentagon, big bosses need to ensure that the role of the executive officer or military assistant is kept in the proper perspective. The best bosses in the Building use their outer offices to serve them while not allowing themselves to be steered or dominated. The outer office people have a responsibility here, also. They should be unselfish in their service and avoid self-aggrandizement and power trips. If the big boss tries to delegate inappropriate tasks (such as writing effectiveness reports on officials who are more senior than the executive officer or telling some senior official it is time to move on), they should gently remind the big boss of the dangers of such inappropriate delegation.

Provide a philosophy letter for subordinates so that everyone can play from the same sheet of music. I strongly recommend that all senior officials who are in charge of large numbers of subordinates (directorates, deputates, and the like) write a short (5- to 10-page) philosophy letter explaining their long-term goals, priorities, and areas of emphasis and concern. Before publishing and distributing this letter, it should be coordinated with each of the immediate subordinates to be sure it covers all the key elements, conforms with the long-range plan of the larger institution they serve, and does not mislead anyone. This letter should emphasize the importance of integrity, of concentrating on what is best for the nation (rather than what is best for the service or agency), of innovation, and of magnanimity toward other agencies, departments, services, and directorates. Once it is finalized, it should be distributed to every individual who serves under the flag officer or senior civilian and should be included with the welcome letter that is sent to each new assignee.

Write a welcome letter and send it out to all new people. You should make your final decisions on each new person you will hire about six months before the person actually arrives. A letter from you should go out very soon after the personnel system has informed each individual of the upcoming assignment. This welcome letter should be a warm one and should stress the importance and the excitement of the work. It should also include a very short reading list. See appendix B for a sample welcome letter.

Establish a "no nonconcurrence through silence" policy. One of Dwight Eisenhower's greatest contributions to posterity was his carefully developed and nurtured policy of "no nonconcurrence through silence." This is how it works. Soon after you take over your big leadership job, you call in your staff. You explain to them that when you are making a decision, it is imperative that you receive, from each one, candid comments on the thrust of your tentative decision. In other words, it is the responsibility of staff members to speak up strongly if they don't agree with your decision. They must do so now rather than six months after the decision is made. Silence on the part of a staff officer must mean consent, not quiet nonconcurrence. Of course, as the boss, you must be open to criticism. In fact, you should actively seek it out. If you do not establish this rule explicitly and if you do not reemphasize it periodically, there will be some quiet individual sitting over in the corner with a marvelous reason for not liking the decision you are about to make (or who has a better answer to the problem) who won't speak up.

RULES FOR ALL SEASONS

Don't ask or permit your outer office people to lie or cover for you. It is quite important that the relationship that you have with your secretary, executive officer, and any others in your immediate outer office be a warm one. On the other hand, it is also important that these people fully understand your strong commitment to integrity; do not allow them to cover for you. If you are enjoying your once-a-month (or once-a-year) golf game or your once-a-week trip to the athletic center, don't allow them to say you're in conference. If standards of integrity are low as far as these small points are concerned, other ethical standards will also degenerate over time.

Avoid the Paul Principle. Many top bosses move into their jobs with superb backgrounds, lots of energy and enthusiasm, and some important goals to accomplish. However, over time, some begin to lose touch and slowly but surely become less effective as leaders. They often fail to recharge their intellectual batteries with outside reading or with discussions and seminars with creative individuals in the better think tanks, industry, or academia. (One of the best Saturdays I spent in the Pentagon was a full-day seminar with four superb long-range thinkers: Herman Kahn [a few weeks before his death], George Heilmeier, Norm Augustine, and Colin Gray as we examined the long range future of the Air Force). Sometimes leaders fail to keep up with the changes out in the field or the fleet, and some fail to keep up with changes in technology and with new and important conceptual developments. Bosses who are only as smart as their in boxes, their staff, their personal experiences, and their TV sets are not wise enough to be the kind of visionary leaders this country needs in the top jobs in the Defense Department.

Take a broad view of public service. A few top bosses in the Pentagon push a parochial political point of view or a self-serving personal agenda to the detriment of the nation as a whole. Political appointees must be careful in this area since they can do great damage without realizing it. New political appointees should listen very carefully to their staffs, particularly when trying to take major new initiatives. The idea they are pushing may be an excellent one; then again, it may not be. If you are a political appointee with very little experience in Washington, work hard to be a good listener. An idea that may have seemed superb in your last job in an aerospace company, on a university campus, or in a state capital may not serve the nation well. Just because you are fortunate enough to have been picked to serve at a high level within the Department of Defense doesn't mean that all your ideas are wonderful.

Military officers at the flag-officer level have a different problem; their greatest challenge is rising above service parochialism. At times they must be willing to take on their own services. The role of the chiefs here is crucial. If chiefs reward parochialism on the part of flag officers who serve in the various jobs around the

Pentagon, they do their nation a great disservice. Instead of getting mad at the generals in the Office of the Secretary of Defense, in the defense agencies, or on the Joint Staff who are opposing his position, a chief should reward them for having the courage to raise important issues. The key motto for public service in the U.S. military is not "Duty, Honor, Army," "Duty, Honor, Navy," "Duty, Honor, Air Force," or "Duty, Honor, Marines"; it is "Duty, Honor, Country."

Do your homework. Here is the scene. An action officer has spent the last two weeks putting together a package on an important and complex issue. The package has been carefully coordinated, and the action officer has built a number of horizontal and vertical alliances to ensure the positions recommended in the package have an excellent chance of acceptance at the key meeting. You fail to read the package before going into the big decision meeting and you get blown away by a well-prepared individual who has great arguments for a less prudent decision. Guess how that action officer, the branch chief, and lots of others feel about you? Yet this kind of thing happens quite often. You may not have the time to read the whole package, but, at a minimum, spend a few minutes studying it and drawing out the main issues and arguments.

Before making each decision, go through six decision checks. These checks are the systems, sanity, integrity, dignity, media, and long-term implications checks.

1. Does the decision you are about to make fit together nicely or have you and your staff constructed a camel of many humps? In other words, does this decision have internal consistency?
2. Does this decision make sense? Would a family member if asked, say, "It doesn't make much sense to me."
3. Will this decision enhance or diminish the integrity of your organization?
4. Will this decision enhance the dignity of your organization?
5. When the decision is looked at critically by unfriendly members of the media, will they crucify your organization publicly?

6. Does the decision conform with our long-range plan? Are you solving today's problem but building bigger problems for the future?

Compliment often your people and others who help you. If you are not passing out compliments every day, you are missing a wonderful opportunity to thank the many people who are working hard to help you do your job and help you look good. Short notes, written in your own hand, that you stick on to packages that say, "This is a great package—better than I could do!" or "This is just what I needed; thanks for getting it to me in time for me to study it and use it" or "We lost on this one, but the fault was mine; your package was excellent" are wonderful morale builders. If the package does not meet your needs, try to criticize it gently. For instance, "This is a first-rate approach—I give you high marks for making your case well. Next time, may I suggest a more visionary approach—a paper that may be harder to coordinate but will make a bigger difference in the long run."

Hold one-on-one sessions every six months with each official who works directly for you. These sessions can be very helpful to you and to each subordinate. In addition, they will encourage your subordinates to do the same thing with those who work directly for them. One of my favorite questions is, "What am I doing that is wasting your time?" Another is, "Is there anything going on in your personal or professional life that you would like to share with me?"

In answer to the second question, one of my division chiefs in the Pentagon once told me, "Now that you asked, sir, there is one thing—I am dying of degenerative heart disease." It turned out that high-pressure work was shortening his life considerably. The forecast was death in five years or less. I am sure glad I asked. I moved him to a less taxing job, and more than ten years later he is still alive and doing quite well.

A third question that I love to ask is, "What bugs you about me?" The answer gives me great insight into my leadership style, and I learn a lot about how confident the person I am asking is in telling me things straight.

Take your key subordinates on an annual two-day retreat. Every year, preferably in the early autumn, you should take your top 20 or so subordinates to Fort Ritchie, Annapolis, Airlie House, the Xerox Conference Center, or some other convenient location for an informal off-site seminar. Subjects to be covered should be a review of the past year, upcoming issues for the next year, and a long-range look at your organization. No outside speakers should be used, with the exception of a futurist who would stretch the minds of you and your staff. Housing should be set up so that old heads are doubled up with the new folks (no spouses should be included). Two or three hours should be set aside for informal sports activities in the late afternoon—a softball game, a tennis round robin, a nine-hole golf tournament, or a volleyball match. The best time for such an event is probably on Friday to Saturday, to avoid the appearance of a boondoggle. The dress should be casual, no uniforms. This is a great way to communicate with your people, to get to know the new folks, and to give the new team the opportunity to get to know each other early in the season (after the summer turnover is complete).

Read a good book on defense policy, foreign policy, technology, or economics every month. You will have some dead time in your schedule. When you are cooling your heels outside some senior official's office, on a long flight, spending a quiet weekend afternoon, when your spouse is at choir practice or playing bridge (or poker) somewhere, or when you wake up in the middle of the night and cannot go back to sleep—take these times to read that new nonfiction book that is getting such great reviews. To save time, read the table of contents and the first and last chapters and then decide if you want to read the whole thing. If you read good books, others will be encouraged to do so too, and the quality of the thinking throughout your staff will improve. Be sure to mention in staff meetings the books that have especially impressed you lately and occasionally ask your staff what good books they have been reading. If you are willing to demonstrate by your personal behavior that a breadth of knowledge is a vital quality of top leadership, you will encourage others to look beyond their in box.

Lend support to the long-range planning process. If there is an on-going long-range planning process, give it strong support! If there is no long-range planning process, take some action to get something started. The great Pentagon leaders of the past, George Marshall and Hap Arnold, to name a couple, were committed to long-range planning and supported a strong institutionalized strategic planning system. You should be similarly committed. With every decision and at every briefing, you should ask the key question, "What are the long-term implications of this approach?"

Maintain a sense of outrage. If the system isn't working for your people, get mad and do something about it. Of course, keep your emotions under control and don't fly off the handle, but controlled anger and outrage can be powerful tools in the Building. Please remember, there are many people in the Pentagon, and lots more out in the field or in the fleet, who are counting on you to make sure things come out right. So step in and do something when the bureaucracy has lost its way, or its heart, one more time.

Fight cronyism whenever you observe it. Although the Pentagon operates generally as a meritocracy in which the more energetic, talented, and innovative people rise to the top, there is still too much of a "good old friend" approach to hiring people to work in the Building. Just because someone was a neighbor, in your old unit, a friend of the family, with you at one of the academies, or a roommate in college doesn't mean that this person is the right one for the job.

When I first took over the directorate of plans in the Air Staff, I took a close look at the 250 people who worked for me. The first thing I noticed was the talent that had so impressed me in this same directorate five years earlier seemed to have deteriorated during my long tour in Europe. I asked to see the records of all the new people who were headed to the directorate. Next, I called in each member of my top staff and went through the names of the inbound people whose records didn't look very strong. In most cases, I received this rationale: "I knew this officer at base X and was impressed" or "My division chiefs know these people and vouch for them." When I would follow up and ask, "What specific-ally impressed you?," I often found out that the talents they had perceived had little to do with being an excellent staff officer in a high-pressure policy arena. When I would ask, "Yes, but how does this officer think, conceptualize, and write?," I sometimes got un-satisfactory answers. I soon set a new hiring policy: no one made a final decision until I looked over the personnel file of the individ-ual who was being recommended. I very seldom overruled a rec-ommendation, but since the intermediate bosses knew I would be checking, they quit hiring cronies of mediocre talent. Within a year or so the talent level had risen appreciably and the quality of work had improved. Just before I left that job, one of the strongest critics of my hiring policy (a general officer selectee) came up to me and said, "You were right and I was wrong. This place is much stronger now that you have stamped out cronyism."

Steer a steady course between being cynical and being a Pollyanna. Top leaders in the Pentagon who keep making the "ev-erything is wonderful" speech are almost as bad as top leaders who become cynical about ever accomplishing anything of importance. If you find yourself drifting in either direction, try to catch yourself and force yourself back to that middle ground of realistic optimism.

If you choose to use profanity, use it with discretion. The language of the locker room is not appropriate in the higher offices of the Building; it diminishes the dignity of the office and the individual. However, there may be times when a little profanity is helpful in making your point strongly, letting people know you are really concerned, or expressing your sense of outrage. If, however, every fourth word is profane, style, grace, and impact are all lost.

Don't take on too many heavy hitters at the same time. One of my big mistakes as a general officer in the Pentagon was to confront some very senior officials who were, in my judgment, taking paro-chial positions that would not serve the Air Force or the nation well in the years ahead. On many occasions, I was able to gain the support of the chief of staff and the secretary of the Air Force, and often my position prevailed. But over time I gained the reputation of being too critical of the major commanders in the field. When I was reassigned, some of the more enlightened policies that I had helped develop reverted to the old ways. In retrospect, I would have accomplished more in the long run if I had been a bit more modest in my objectives and less aggressive in attacking the parochialism that I perceived.

Be candid with your bosses. You were not brought to the Building to serve in a senior position in order to compete for the "wimp of the year" award. There are times when it is important to tell your secretary, your chief, or other high officials that they are standing on thin ice. Let me relate a specific example. In early 1982, I was preparing to give an important briefing (probably the most important briefing I ever gave) to then Deputy Secretary of Defense Frank Carlucci. A couple of days before the briefing, I had the last of many meetings I was having with Secretary of the Air Force Verne Orr. In the privacy of his office, Secretary Orr told me that he was going to postpone the R&D program for the C-17 four years and cancel another program that was designed to upgrade some commercial airliners to carry military cargo in bulk and oversize configurations. I felt strongly that these decisions were unwise. I immediately said, "Sir, if you do that, I suggest you fire the commander in chief of MAC [the Military Airlift Command], for you will have destroyed his credibility with his people, with the other services, with the defense industry, and with Congress." A few minutes later as I was walking back to my office, I said to myself, "Did I really talk that way to the secretary of the Air Force?"

There are two happy parts of the story. He took my advice, at least in part, and General Jim Allen kept his job as the MAC commander as well as his credibility with his various constituencies. Also, from that time forward, Secretary Orr asked my advice often, for he knew that I would always tell him what I thought—straight.

Watch out for the "low integrity once removed" problem. One of the secondary lessons of the Pentagon procurement scandal of

1988 may be that people are less vigilant about integrity when there is no obvious violation of recognized rules of the game. Let me explain how this almost occurred in my personal experience. When I put together the briefing for Mr. Carlucci, I was able to demonstrate conclusively that the Air Force should immediately develop (and procure as soon afterward as possible) a new airlift aircraft, the C-17. As I worked on the briefing, it became clear to me that the best contractor to build the C-17 was not very effective on Capitol Hill, while the competing contractors were much more skillful in gaining broad congressional support for their various programs. I was tempted to help the better contractor put together a more persuasive case for the C-17. I knew that getting a favorable decision on the C-17 in the executive branch depended, in part, on how much congressional support could be gained for the program. I resisted this temptation and did not help the contractor, McDonnell Douglas. In late January 1982, a decision was made to build 50 C-5Bs, made by Lockheed, and to slip the procurement of the C-17 for several years. It would have been unethical for me to help McDonnell Douglas or any other contractor before a final decision was made in the Pentagon even though the C-17, in my opinion, was the best airplane.

Once someone crosses the ethical barrier to help a company during the competition phase, the temptation to take the next step and provide proprietary information to the favored contractor is great. The third step—to receive money or other compensation for such activities—is particularly unconscionable. It is a clear demonstration of the slippery slope of low integrity playing itself out. One bad step leads to another. A few scumbags come out of the woodwork and start accepting money for their already unethical behavior.

Stay in touch with your people. Don't let the power and prestige of your position let you slide into an attitude and a posture of imperiousness. As Kipling wrote, "Walk with kings but do not lose the common touch." To a large extent, you serve the people that work for you. Don't let your attitude or your work disappoint them. If you hold them in great respect, encourage them to be creative, and know their names and a little bit about their lives and their families, they will walk off cliffs for you. When I worked with my subordinates in the Pentagon, I would try to remember the words of George Patton: "Never tell people how to do things. Tell them *what* to do and they will surprise you with their ingenuity."

Learn how to deal with Potomac fever. Many families sink deep roots into the soil of Northern Virginia, Maryland, or the District of Columbia. When the next assignment comes and it is time to leave the area, one or more family members want badly to stay. This can lead to lots of anguish not only within the family but also on the job. As a senior official in the Building, you need to emphasize to your military subordinates the need for them to remind their family members periodically that they can expect an assignment within three or four years and that they should try to avoid sinking deep roots.

This is a much bigger problem than meets the eye. I can vividly remember suggesting to a colonel who had served for ten consecutive years in various jobs in Washington that it was time for him to move back to the field. He could not understand why I could not support his request to the personnel system for just one more year or one more assignment in the Washington area. One of the great strengths of the Building is that there is a good flow of people to and from the field. Unlike many other Washington departments and agencies, the Pentagon does not get too isolated from the real work in the field: the world of military capability, ships, tanks, and planes. If too many military people hang around the Building for years on end, the Pentagon will slowly lose touch with the operational world. Also, it is important that throughout the military there is a healthy percentage of people who know how the Building works and who can effectively articulate important viewpoints back to the Pentagon. One option for those who have strong feelings about not moving their family but wish to continue a military career is a one-year remote assignment followed by an assignment back to the area.

When it is time to step down, do it with dignity. There may come a time when you feel that it is time to depart the scene. It may be because of poor health, family considerations, a pass over for promotion, a great job offer in the business world, a change of administration, disgruntlement with a major decision by your boss, or burn out. Whatever the reason and no matter how embittered you may be, remember to do what you have done for years: put institutional goals first and personal considerations second. Leave with style, grace, and dignity. This does not necessarily mean that you should remain silent about your reasons for leaving. But, when in doubt, silence is the best choice. Don't let your anger, cynicism, ego, or disappointments stand in the way of respect for the institution that you have served so well.

Many of the best leaders in the Pentagon are those who have failed, often more than once. Those who have had some major setbacks and faced them were strengthened by the experience. They tend to be more tolerant of failure in others. The catharsis of risk taking, failure, and comeback is the stuff of great visionaries and leaders. What is needed for the 1990s and beyond is not efficient functionaries in high places who cleverly push papers, always trying to impress the boss. What is needed are men and women of passion with the courage to ask Why not? rather than Why? and who are challenged and motivated to action by bureaucratic barriers to progress. It saddens me to say that too many efficient, risk-avoiding, cold fish have oiled their way to the top in recent years. They tend to select clones to replicate and replace them. This is not a healthy trend. What is clearly needed at the top are people who dare to dream, who have fire in their bellies, who are frustrated by the sterile logic of "We have always done it that way" and who say, in return, "There must be a better way." Generals, admirals, and high-level civilian employees of the future must avoid the seductive aspects of good-natured pragmatism with no visionary content and no sense of towering integrity.

We need in the Pentagon more leaders who, despite years of working in a vast bureaucratic structure, are willing to take steps that fundamentally change and modernize the institution. Today leaders are needed who are interested in walking out the door in the future with head held high for having maintained their integrity and for having tried great things. The name of the game for too many is "risk avoidance," "damage limitation," "survival," and "turf protection." Let us hope in the future that there will be no one in a key position who, in the course of a Pentagon assignment, compromises a thousand times to satisfy the forces of the past and policies and systems grown obsolete.

9
DIFFICULT BOSSES

One of the paradoxes of an increasingly specialized bureaucratized society is that the qualities rewarded in the rise to eminence are less and less the qualities required once eminence is reached.

—HENRY KISSINGER

Although the quality of leadership in the Pentagon is quite impressive, there are a few people at the branch and division chief level and higher that are just plain tough to deal with. The most agonizing year of my 30-year Air Force career was working for an ambitious, hard-working, and insecure boss on the fourth floor of the Pentagon. As a division chief, I worked directly for this person. I learned a great deal that year about what not to do as a leader in a staff setting as well as how to deal with a difficult boss in the Pentagon.

Many readers may wish to skip this chapter since most of you will not have to deal with a difficult boss and will not find this discussion useful. However, those who do face a difficult situation with their immediate boss or the boss at the next higher level may wish to read on. I would like to discuss each type of difficult boss that I have observed in the Building and my best advice on how to deal with each. (For those interested in pursuing the subject of difficult bosses in greater detail, may I recommend a paperback book entitled *Problem Bosses: Who They Are and How to Deal with*

Them by Marty Grothe and Peter Wylie [New York: Fawcett Crest, 1987].)

The loose cannon. This individual tends to be very bright, full of ideas (some of which are quite good) and energy, and anxious to explore uncharted waters. In general, this person is very critical of the Pentagon bureaucracy and is convinced that only through radical action can anything of significance be accomplished. Unfortunately, these individuals don't listen to good advice from subordinates and are generally unwilling to go through the slow and deliberate coordination process to be sure that all factors affecting the decision and its implementation are considered. They also don't understand the need to build horizontal and vertical alliances to ensure that the correct decision is made and, much more important, that the decision is supported and implemented rather than resisted. If these individuals are high enough in the organization or have the ear of a really big boss (such as a chief of staff or a secretary of a military department), they can do considerable damage.

Dealing with a boss who is a loose cannon takes a great deal of creative work. Giving these bosses lots of support and encouragement when they come up with really first-class ideas or initiatives can work well. Heading off disaster when the boss's latest idea is a guaranteed loser is much harder. One of the most useful approaches is to give these bosses good ideas in hopes that they will jump on some of them and spend most of their time pushing the better ones. Although these bosses may soon forget that the idea was yours, being magnanimous is a small price to pay to keep them on track.

Where the difficulties arise, of course, is when these bosses go off with great momentum in a wrong direction. Here, the challenge is a severe one. Rather than approach the problem directly and have your legs cut off, the indirect approach is often best. One useful method is to suggest full study and coordination and to argue that the idea is so radical that the only way to succeed is to build lots of alliances within your organization and in neighboring organizations. If it is truly a terrible idea, one argument worth trying is, "If you push that, sir, you will destroy your credibility around here for a long time," and then explain why. An argument that is not very useful in dealing with the loose cannon or hip shooter is, "Sir, we tried that last year, and it really bombed." He or she will immediately assume that you are part of the problem and will be even more reluctant to listen to your advice. A more subtle approach is to say, "That was tried last year, and it ran into a few problems. Before we try it again, let me explain what we all learned from that experience." Then, as dispassionately as possible, explain how and why the idea bombed.[*]

The micromanager. Often the micromanager and the workaholic are housed within the same mind and body. These people are often insecure. They work very hard and get into the details because they are afraid of their boss, lack confidence in their abilities, or both. I have found that it is almost impossible to help senior officials who have been micromanagers for many years. One technique that can be effective, however, is to allow the system to overwhelm these individuals with so many issues, briefings, and data that they finally come to the realization that they cannot accomplish everything themselves. When you see signs of the boss reaching a saturation point, you can volunteer to sort out the issues and suggest to the micromanager boss which ones he or she may wish to get deeply involved in. Conversely, you can suggest that the boss not get involved deeply in other areas. If you can steer bosses into areas where they really can make a contribution based on their interests and background, you are well on the way to reducing the problem considerably. All this may sound like crass manipulation of your boss. It is not. Rather, it is a subtle and often very effective approach to one of the very biggest problems in the Pentagon. Since the relationship between leader and subordinate is a two-way street in any democracy, it is not inappropriate for the subordinate to try to help bosses overcome some of their weaknesses (and vice versa).

---

[*]I recommend a wonderful book about the British political system entitled *The Complete Yes Minister: The Diaries of a Cabinet Minister* edited by Lynn and Jay (Harper and Row, 1988).

Retired-on-active-duty (ROAD) boss. Although these bosses are
not common at the highest levels in the Pentagon, there are a number of them in the middle-level leadership jobs. Old timers who
have fought the good fight in the Building for many years finally
begin to run out of energy and enthusiasm. When a hot issue hits
their desk, they are likely to say, "Oh no, not that issue again; let's
pass it off to some other division, study it to death, wait out the
boss, or stonewall." It may be a marvelous issue that you would
enjoy sinking your teeth into, yet your boss won't let you run with
it. This can be very frustrating to a hard-charging person who
would really like to make an impact on the development of policy
in that area.

There are a number of ways to deal with this type. If you can
convince these bosses you will do all the work and that they will
not have to expend any of their effort or overtime, they will often
let you run with the action. However, this argument is sometimes
unconvincing to the retired-in-place bosses since they will be responsible for the end product. If this approach seems infeasible,
you might try the "If we hand this hot potato off to those folks
down the hall, they will mess it up and it will end up back on your
desk with a short suspense" approach. This "we pay now or we pay
later" argument can have impact on a boss who has great regard for
you and much less regard for the weenies down the hall. Another
approach is to try to keep these bosses on the road a lot and, when
they are gone, to secure as much of the important and interesting
work that you can for you and your colleagues. By the time the boss
gets back, you have the action, and there is no way to hand it off
(actions in the Pentagon once assigned usually stay where they
were first assigned). This approach may sound a bit disloyal but
loyalty to boss and loyalty to institution must sometimes be
weighed together.

The hyperambitious boss. These bosses tend to judge all activities
in terms of effect on their careers. The very worst boss I ever had
was this type of person, and I found it extraordinarily difficult to
deal with him. These bosses normally want to have a lot of face
time with the big bosses and anything positive having this result is

normally welcomed. Some of the best actions that a staff officer is working on will be grabbed by that individual when it appears that it is something the big boss is particularly interested in. If you are a staff officer, it can be very frustrating when bosses grab some of your good staff work and research and use it to serve their own ambitions. However, sometimes you can use this proclivity to serve the purposes of the institution, for instance, when there is an important issue that has not been receiving proper attention from your boss. If you can convince him or her that the big boss is really excited about the issue, you may quickly get needed support. Also, you can turn off bad ideas from the boss if you can demonstrate that pushing these ideas may make the big boss mad and hurt career prospects.

The wimpy boss. This boss is often unwilling to take a strong position on issues. This can be very frustrating. Although it is important for bosses to be cooperative with other agencies and services, if they *never* stand up and be counted, especially on very important issues, they are not serving the institution or the nation well. Your job is to stiffen the resolve of these bosses by presenting strong arguments and demonstrating that the wimpy approach will not only hurt your institution but will also hurt the boss personally. Another approach is to try to convince the boss that the big boss (or some very important player) feels strongly about the issue and to fail to stand firm at a key meeting will lead to bigger problems in the long run than accepting a weak compromise.

The interruptaholic. These bosses love to jump from issue to issue in rapid order; the more balls they can keep in the air simultaneously, the happier they are. It is very difficult to get these individuals to stay with an issue long enough to reach any kind of closure. They not only thrive on distractions, they regularly create them. These are people who will try to run a meeting while talking on the telephone, or enjoy starting things much more than finishing things, or ask a question, and before you have a chance to answer it, ask the next question.

Dealing with this type of boss can be quite frustrating since the

Pentagon environment seems to encourage this behavior. One approach is to work with the boss, the boss's deputy, the executive assistant, and the secretary to try to reduce the load in the in box, the number of phone calls when the boss is chairing a meeting, and the meeting schedule itself. Try to schedule meetings in places where no phone is available.

In dealing with problem bosses of various types you may find opportunities to let them know they are part of the problem. For instance, if bosses ask you for advice on how to improve performance throughout the organization, you might wish to point out where they have caused the staff problems. You should be ready for some specific ideas and some good rationale for each criticism and each suggestion.

In summary, difficult bosses are not a problem for the vast majority of people who work in the Pentagon. They are, however, a big problem for enough people in the Building that, after some hesitation, I decided to include this chapter.

10
OPERATING IN THE TANK: A VIEW FROM THE INNER SANCTUM

It is never too soon to do the right thing, for too soon can quickly become too late.

—ANONYMOUS

During my tour on the Air Staff, I spent many hundreds of hours in the Tank. The Tank is actually a room where the Joint Chiefs of Staff meet. According to folklore, the name "Tank" originated during World War II. At that time, a forerunner of the JCS, the Combined Chiefs, met in the basement of the Public Health building. While entering through a narrow hallway with hanging lights, one of the generals said he felt like he was entering a tank. The name stuck. Although the formal protocol name for the meeting area is the "Gold Room," everyone calls it the Tank.

The Tank is on the second floor of the Pentagon, very close to the River Entrance. The Tank was completely renovated in 1988 and was used for the first time during the historic visit of Marshal Akhromeyev of the former Soviet Union. The carpeting and drapes are a shade of gold. And the art work is of a joint nature as each service is represented by a painting.

When I served on the staff, there was a bureaucratic process surrounding the whole joint system. At that time, the Joint Staff

122

worked for the corporate JCS body. In other words, all Joint Staff action officers worked for the Joint Chiefs. The chairman had a small staff group and personal staff to support him. Without fail, Tuesdays, Wednesdays, and Fridays were very busy days in the Tank. The chiefs of staff of the services, together with the chairman and the vice chairman of the Joint Chiefs of Staff, met on Wednesday and Friday afternoons.

On Wednesday and Friday mornings, the three-star deputies of each of the four services, or operations deputies, and the three-star director of the Joint Staff would meet. These generals would also join the service chiefs at their meetings. The director of the Joint Staff is the most powerful of the three-star officers in the Joint Staff. He chaired these meetings of the operations deputies.

On Tuesday mornings in the Tank, a group of two-star officers met. Known as deputy operations deputies, they included the chief planner for each of the services plus the vice director of the Joint Staff, who is the chairman. These deputy operations deputies tried to solve as many joint issues as possible in order to reduce the agenda for the three-star group. It was in this position, as the Air Force deputy operations deputy, that I served in the Tank for a little over two years.

The Defense Reorganization Act of 1986 (Goldwater–Nichols) drastically affected the activities surrounding the Tank. Although it took some years for the act to mature, the new culture is firmly in place. Since my tenure in the Building, these groups of general officers meet less frequently in the Tank. This doesn't mean that important military business is not being done in a joint manner. Rather, it is simply being done differently.

When I was on the Air Staff, any service could introduce an item into the Tank, and the Joint Staff, which worked for the corporate JCS, would staff and coordinate the action. Under Goldwater–Nichols, the Joint Staff now works for the chairman in his role as the primary military adviser to the president. In other words, the staffing power now lies in the Joint Staff, which works the issue for the chairman and coordinates with the services. This means that there is no longer a need for a vote. Consequently, the formal business of the Tank has atrophied.

Another factor contributing to less Tank activity is the personal style of General Colin Powell. General Powell's predecessor, Admiral Crowe, started to wield the power of Goldwater–Nichols, and General Powell completed the process. Rather than hold scheduled Tank meetings, General Powell brought the chiefs together without the formalities associated with the process before Goldwater–Nichols. Obviously, General Powell's political savvy in Washington and his charismatic leadership combined to make him a very powerful chairman. Even when the chiefs disagreed with him, they were hesitant to confront the chairman or to go around him to the secretary of defense or the president. Since future chairmen are unlikely to have the same power as Colin Powell, the services may gain back some of the power they lost during the Powell era.

Regardless of the ebb and flow of service power, some things have remained constant. The actions handled in the joint arena bring together participants who are captives of their experiences and background. It is natural and healthy for a Navy admiral and an Air Force general to have different views on strategy, doctrine, war fighting, tactics, or weapon system effectiveness. In addition to conflict, there is also cooperation and compromise in the meetings. Equally important, the participants learn from one another and form deep friendships that will pay off in future crises. My experience is that specific issues have one or two "honest brokers" who don't have strong interests in the issue at hand and who serve as catalysts for effective solutions and meaningful compromises. Everyone wants what is best for the country, and there are very few ideologues at this level.

The natural alliances. In general the Army and the Air Force agree on most issues, and the Navy and the Marine Corps find themselves in agreement most of the time. As a result, it is quite common to find a two-two split among the services. The harshest rivalry through the years has been between the Air Force and the Navy. But even that rivalry is muted on issues such as nuclear strategy (but not on nuclear force structure), where the Navy and the Air Force have more in common with each other than with the

Marines and the Army. The Army and the Marine Corps find much agreement on many issues (the secretary of defense lumps these two services together when he discusses land forces in his annual posture statement), particularly when it comes to finding the proper balance between nuclear and nonnuclear forces. What is quite important is that today's enemy in the tough debate in the Tank may be tomorrow's ally. If you cut off someone's legs, he may try to do the same thing to you later.

Until the passage of the Goldwater–Nichols Act of 1986, the chairman's power was quite limited. If he couldn't get the chiefs to agree unanimously, the issue was often postponed without resolution. This exercise in postponement is often called "kicking the can" (in other words, if you can't resolve the issue, you kick it down the road a few months in hopes that you can solve it later). The Goldwater–Nichols Act took a major step to change all that by not only giving the chairman much more power but also establishing the position of vice chairman, who is number two in the military hierarchy (in other words, the vice chairman ranks above the chiefs—he is number two rather than number six). Having a vice chairman as the number-two man rather than the number six has not been easy for the chiefs to swallow. However, the first two vice chairmen, General Bob Herres and Admiral David Jeremiah, both did a good job of providing legitimacy to this new and extremely important position.

Different talents, backgrounds, and capabilities among the participants. Like all committees at every level throughout the Pentagon, not all participants are equally experienced and talented. At any one time, there may be one of the operations deputies or one of the chiefs who is not as skilled in debate and discussion as the others. In some cases, this is a person who is worn down by the extraordinary demands of the job and no longer has the energy, the drive, or the temperament for the negotiation process.

In other cases, the weakness comes from the lack of experience in certain areas of military affairs. Occasionally, someone may be less endowed in either common sense or intellect than his colleagues. If one of the participants from your service is the least effective among his colleagues and you work for him on joint matters, you are in for some difficult times. He will not enjoy going to the Tank, will be rolled by others, will tend to claim more in the debriefing after the Tank sessions than he actually accomplished, and may miss some of the important subtleties that take place around that big table. In the many years that I was involved in the JCS process, I watched with admiration the skills and the intellects of a number of very impressive people. Only a small number of participants fell short. However, in the environment of the Tank, those weaknesses were accentuated and highlighted.

Briefing in the Tank. Most Tank briefings are presented by officers assigned to the Joint Staff, but others, on occasion, also get a chance to brief in the Tank. It can be both a heady and scary experience. The scene is awesome. With all those stars shining back at you, it is easy to get a bit nervous. If you are briefing the chiefs (with the operations deputies in attendance), you will be looking out over 60 stars on the shoulders (or collars) of 12 flag officers (remember that in addition to the chiefs, chairman, vice chairman, and the operations deputies of each service, the director and vice director of the Joint Staff will also be there). On your immediate right will be the chairman, the vice chairman, and the director of the Joint Staff. On their right will be the Air Force chief and his operations deputy. Directly opposite you, at the end of the table, will be the Marine Corps commandant and his operations deputy. At the far lefthand corner of the table will be the chief of Naval Operations and his operations deputy, and on your immediate left will be the Army chief and his operations deputy. There will usually be one or two chiefs missing, and they will be replaced by their vice chiefs. Vice chiefs are seldom as vocal or as strong on issues as their chiefs, so the absence of a key chief can be terribly important to you and your success with an issue. In any case, you should find out in advance who will be there and what their positions are likely to be on the issue you are raising.

Along the wall on your right will be a few additional officers. They will be members of the chairman's group (colonels or captains who work directly for the chairman and are often in line for promotion in the next two or three years) and a Joint Staff officer who works directly for the director and schedules the Tank briefings. In the far lefthand corner sits the secretary of the Joint Staff. Along the wall to the left are about six chairs for visitors for your briefing. That is where your boss or bosses usually sit, as well as one or two of your fellow staff officers who may be there to lend their expertise to the discussion period. Representatives from other Joint Staff directorates often occupy the other chairs. When questions are raised by those sitting around the table, you should be prepared to answer them, but you should quickly defer to your boss if he or she wants to jump in and answer the question or make a point in the discussion. You will always remember the events of your very first briefing in the Tank.

In summary, let me relate my most memorable experience in this inner sanctum of the U.S. military leadership. In the early 1980s, the Reagan presidency was in its infancy, but it was crystal clear to all that a great deal of additional money was going to flow into the Department of Defense and, in turn, to the military departments over the next few years. On the urging of the chairman of the Joint Chiefs of Staff, each service agreed to provide a briefing in the Tank, before the chairman, the chiefs, the operations deputies, and the director to the Joint Staff. This briefing was supposed to cover the highlights of the upcoming program (the program objectives memorandum, or POM) that would be submitted to the secretary of defense later on in the spring.

I was asked to give the first of the service briefings. I was chosen, I think, to give the first briefing because I had spent a lot of time in the Tank, knew the chairman and all the chiefs, and was intimately familiar with the United States Air Force POM for fiscal years 1984–88. I gave a 30-minute briefing using about 20 slides. I used notes but did not use a scripted briefing. At the end of the briefing, the chairman said something like: "I have been sitting in the Tank for the last seven years, four years as a chief and three years as the chairman and that is the worst briefing I have ever heard!"

As far as I could tell no one in the room agreed with the chairman (although no one came to my defense) and having heard dozens of briefings there myself, I knew my briefing was not even in the bottom half. What the chairman was trying to say—and he might have found a somewhat kinder way to say it—was that my briefing did not give enough details and that future briefings on the various department programs must be more complete. My reaction, having known the chairman for many years, was to smile at his comment and admire him for realizing that some of the important issues in our program had not been highlighted adequately. Of course, it served his purpose to beat up on me (I think he knew that my skin was tough enough that I would not be destroyed by his criticism). This story tells a lot about what the Tank is all about.

1. It is a tough environment.
2. What appears on the surface is not the only thing that is happening (in other words, there are many hidden agendas).
3. There is much signaling and bargaining going on.
4. Only those who listen carefully will have a real understanding about what really happened in the Tank and what follow-up actions are needed.

There is no doubt that the Tank is a less important arena than it once was. Nevertheless, you never know when your boss will direct you to brief in the Tank. When you are selected to brief in the Tank, remember that you probably know as much about the subject as anyone in the room. After all, you will likely be the expert on that subject while the general officers must be familiar with a wide range of issues. I also recommend you visit the people responsible for the room to find out the idiosyncrasies of the sound and projection system. Most important, go into the Tank and dry run your briefing. Briefing the JCS in the Tank is what the action officers refer to as "logging major face time."

11

THE JOINT STAFF

*We must indeed hang together, or, most assuredly, we
shall hang separately.*

—JOHN HANCOCK (4 JULY 1776)

This chapter was specifically designed to help those who are
headed to the Joint Staff. If your assignment is somewhere else in
the Building, you may wish to skip this chapter. However, if you
think you may work some joint actions or have dealings with the
Joint Staff, then you may wish to read on. Of all the various staffs
in the Pentagon, the Joint Staff has changed the most in recent
years. Because the Goldwater–Nichols Act has given the chairman
of the Joint Chiefs of Staff so much power and because General
Colin Powell institutionalized this power with such skill, the Joint
Staff has become the most powerful staff in the Pentagon and probably the most talented large staff in our federal government.

So you have been assigned to the Joint Staff. You ask around
among the people who seem to know something about the Building, and these are some of the things that you hear.

"The Joint Staff is the pits. Sure, you get lots of visibility but
with the wrong folks. It is much better to go to your service staff,
where you will be working on issues you understand and if you do
well the big bosses will notice and take care of you."

"You're lucky, my friend, the name of the game has changed,
and the Joint Staff is the best place in the Pentagon to work; the

personnel system is sending you a strong message and it is a good one."

"If you go to the Joint Staff, there is no way you can get out in less than three years—maybe more."

So what are the similarities and differences between the Joint Staff and the service staffs? Can you accomplish anything there or is it just lots of papers and briefings that go nowhere? Will you just get in trouble with your own service? Will you work in areas that you know something about, or will it be a whole new ball game?

There are eight directorates in the Joint Staff. Your level of responsibility, depth of learning, and even work hours will be determined by the directorate to which you are assigned. Some divisions work normal eight-hour days, while others work much longer hours and often spend Saturdays at their desks. It may not be fair, but the busiest divisions are usually the ones that do the most important work or have the highest visibility. For example, the action officer with the responsibility for Kuwait was a very busy individual after the Iraqi invasion in August 1990. Similarly, a coup or hot spot can result in your time in the barrel. In the next few pages, I will explain the culture of the Joint Staff and discuss some skills that will help make you a more effective Joint Staff action officer.

MAJOR DIFFERENCES

First, let's address the question of what the Joint Staff is and what makes it different.

Your peers will generally be a terrific group. The Joint Staff is composed of approximately 1,300 people. Most are military officers, often referred to as "purple suited" since they work on a Joint Staff and theoretically have left their service biases behind. Since the Joint Staff works for the chairman of the Joint Chiefs of Staff (CJCS) the services usually send the best talent they can find. The services understand that superior talent will represent their uniform well and will do what is best for the country.

The Joint Staff budget has grown considerably since Goldwater–Nichols. Although not nearly the size of the services that must

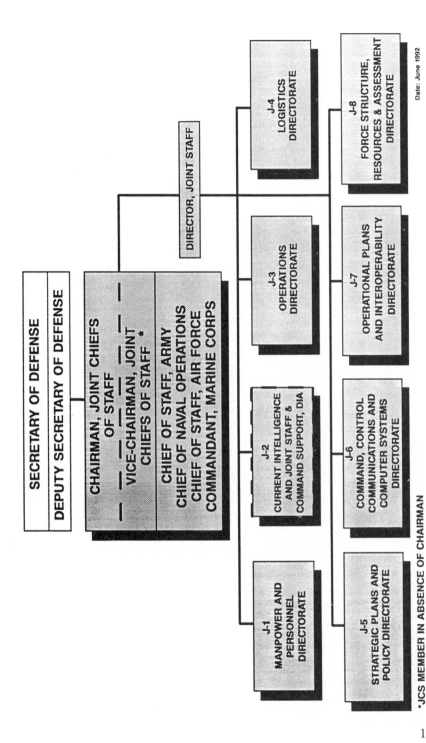

FIGURE 2. Organization of the Joint Chiefs of Staff

SECRETARY OF DEFENSE

DEPUTY SECRETARY OF DEFENSE

CHAIRMAN, JOINT CHIEFS OF STAFF

VICE-CHAIRMAN, JOINT CHIEFS OF STAFF *

CHIEF OF STAFF, ARMY
CHIEF OF NAVAL OPERATIONS
CHIEF OF STAFF, AIR FORCE
COMMANDANT, MARINE CORPS

DIRECTOR, JOINT STAFF

J-1 MANPOWER AND PERSONNEL DIRECTORATE

J-2 CURRENT INTELLIGENCE AND JOINT STAFF & COMMAND SUPPORT, DIA

J-3 OPERATIONS DIRECTORATE

J-4 LOGISTICS DIRECTORATE

J-5 STRATEGIC PLANS AND POLICY DIRECTORATE

J-6 COMMAND, CONTROL COMMUNICATIONS AND COMPUTER SYSTEMS DIRECTORATE

J-7 OPERATIONAL PLANS AND INTEROPERABILITY DIRECTORATE

J-8 FORCE STRUCTURE, RESOURCES & ASSESSMENT DIRECTORATE

*JCS MEMBER IN ABSENCE OF CHAIRMAN

Date: June 1992

131

organize, train, and equip forces for the warfighting commanders in chief (CINCs), the Joint Staff budget is still quite significant. For example, the chairman's exercise program funds the transportation necessary to deploy and employ forces and to conduct joint readiness training. There is also the CINC Initiatives fund, which allows the chairman to respond to CINC requests for additional limited funding in specified areas. Like other areas of the Joint Staff, the comptroller is growing in size and importance.

You are likely to be involved in the PPBS process. This is because the CJCS is the principal military adviser to the president, National Security Council, and the secretary of defense. In addition, Congress will seek the chairman's advice. Further, the Joint Staff plays a large role in developing many of the joint planning documents that provide a basis for the *Defense Planning Guidance*, the Future Years Defense Plan (FYDP), and the defense budget.

Another area where the Joint Staff is a big player is the responsibility of the Joint Chiefs of Staff to provide strategic direction and planning guidance to the combatant commands. The chairman provides the channel of communications for instruction between the National Command Authority (NCA), consisting of the president and secretary of defense, and the combatant commanders. The chairman is the spokesman for the commanders in chief of these combatant commands to the NCA. The chairman advises the secretary of defense on the extent to which service and other defense agency programs meet the warfighting priorities of the CINCs. Therefore, the Joint Staff emphasizes missions rather than functions. (Services are more involved in the latter.) The Joint Staff must focus on effective integration of forces, interoperability, and readiness. For example, the Joint Staff (J-7) is developing joint doctrine to synthesize individual service doctrines into one cohesive whole. This process of developing joint doctrine is an enormous challenge and will require more years of hard work.

The JCS are placed in a strategic position between the highest civilian authorities (executive and legislative) and combatant military forces. This requires that the Joint Staff work with the civilian staffs supporting cabinet-level officers and Congress, which continually call upon the JCS to explain military requirements, capabilities, and limitations. The Joint Chiefs must also transmit to combatant commanders the guidance and direction necessary for military planning and execution of operations in exercises, in support of civil authorities (e.g., humanitarian assistance), and to deploy and employ forces to counter threats to U.S. security interests during periods of crises and war.

In summary, the unique features of the JCS and chairman's responsibilities that will affect your role are their involvement in planning for integration of forces as opposed to the services' role in organizing, equipping, or training forces. The JCS are deeply involved in the planning part of the PPBS and in providing military advice during the rest of the PPBS process. Providing strategic direction and planning guidance to the CINCs and working with many other governmental departments in the process will also affect many action officers' jobs. Finally, the Joint Staff works with similar military organizations in other governments, primarily those of our allies.

If you thrive on variety and complexity and if you enjoy the challenge of dealing with tough but important issues, the Joint Staff is just the place for you for the next few years.

THE FIRST FEW DAYS

Shortly after receiving the assignment, you should receive your directorate's welcoming letter and one from your sponsor. They both will invite you to call and write for help. Take them up on it, whether it involves housing, transportation, professional responsibilities, books to read; don't be afraid to ask for assistance.

Upon arrival, be comforted by the fact that everyone else that preceded you was also bewildered. Your sponsor should meet you for the check-in process. The Joint Staff offices are on the first and second floors. You will notice the additional security requirements: security guards at all the interior JCS entrances and an extra clearance process to get a JCS pass. Incidentally, if you are assigned to the Defense Intelligence Agency (DIA) staff or J-2 support office (DIA's interface with JCS) in the Pentagon, they require a third badge. To complicate the security issue a little more, if you are assigned to the National Military Command Center or need frequent access, special clearance procedures will be needed to enter that center. Security will play a big role in your life. Give it your attention. Failure to do so can lead to trouble—fast.

After you have in-processed and met your bosses, you will attend the Joint Staff Officer's Training System (JSOTS). This is a short, state-of-the-art course designed to introduce you to the Joint Staff. The course is a self-paced computer course lasting approximately one day. It will quickly introduce you to the key players on the staff and to some of the more common staffing procedures. At the end of JSOTS you will gather in the Tank to learn more about briefing the JCS.

Following JSOTS, you will attend a course designed to teach you some basic word-processing and computer skills. Some time ago, the Joint Staff gave up many of its secretarial positions to retain action officers. For better or worse, you will become familiar with the Joint Staff computer system. Although you will find it frustrating at first, word processing is a modern communication skill that is extremely handy. Many former wing, brigade, and ship commanders pound away at their word processors as they develop staff positions or build briefings.

Both JSOTS and the computer course should not be avoided. Some directors of the Joint Staff have placed great emphasis on the courses while others assume you will go because it is in your own best interest. Additionally, some division chiefs will immediately pile work on you, and before long, you will feel you are too busy for some simple course. Trust me, attend these courses *immediately*. They will make you an effective action officer more quickly than the school of hard knocks, and it is easier.

Within six months you will be an expert in a number of areas. By now you may have realized that your previous service background may be totally unrelated to your Joint Staff assignment. Like you, many others have faced the same challenges and opportunities, and they have learned quickly and succeeded. In the Joint Staff you will be operating basically on your own. You have to be a self-starter and do many things that you might have delegated to others in the last assignment. On the Joint Staff, general-officer and flag-rank selectees are some of the best typists and slide builders because they understand the importance of the issues and have the required skills.

PROMOTION POTENTIAL AND TOUR OF DUTY

In a nutshell, promotion potential here is, in most cases, better than anywhere else in the Pentagon. Although your effectiveness reports may be prepared by an officer of another service, they will be endorsed by a flag officer of your service. A three-star flag officer will always be available within the Joint Staff to provide the exceptional endorsement and extra push when required. You can expect to be in the Joint Staff for at least three years. Only a few leave sooner.

WHAT KIND OF ACTIONS WILL YOU BE EXPOSED TO?

Fortunately, you will no longer have to contend with the old Joint Staff process of JCS papers. That process was the cumbersome and bureaucratic method of paperwork designed to produce service consensus. The buff- and green-colored papers with terms like *red-striped* were a lot of work and often were very frustrating.

Since the Joint Staff now works directly for the chairman, it operates like most other staffs. That is, it responds to taskings and to the needs of its boss, the chairman. Some of the actions you could be involved in are international conferences, Joint Staff talks with allies, international negotiations, and interdepartmental studies on such issues as logistics; command, control, and communications; and intelligence. Since the chairman, vice chairman, and commanders have become more involved in the planning, programming, and budgeting system (PPBS) in recent years, action officers have also found themselves involved in net assessments, preparing position papers for the chairman's and vice chairman's participation in DPRB meetings, and other budget deliberations.

Many action officers represent or accompany their principal (superior) to interagency and other interdepartmental meetings, where these superiors will present the JCS position on a particular topic. You will be expected to prepare accompanying books containing position papers on all expected topics of discussion. Full coordination of these papers is necessary to ensure that your representative is fully empowered to speak authoritatively rather than to present a personal opinion. Most Joint Staff action officers become involved in coordinating or preparing position papers for these books. In fact, this is a big part of the life of many Joint Staff officers.

The CJCS and senior officers of the Joint Staff will host or participate in formal and informal military staff talks with allied nations. Your action will be to prepare for and, on frequent occasions, participate in those talks.

Similarly, when the CJCS and other senior officers travel, you may help in that preparation including the ever-present "book," which includes the travel schedule, background papers, issue papers, and point papers. In many instances, an action officer will accompany the traveling party.

One of the most important, pervasive actions that involve Joint Staff action officers is in support of the Joint Planning System. This involves providing input to the major planning and force structure documents and refining concepts of operations, operations plans, and supporting plans in preparation for deployment and employment of forces.

Many action officers will become involved in reviewing existing operational plans for supportability. This process is part of a review cycle that might have begun years ago with a JCS decision to task a CINC (or a CINC request for authorization) to prepare an operational plan for a certain situation. The CINC is responsible for developing his plan, and he submits it for JCS review, where it is tested for supportability and feasibility. Since resources are seldom adequate for a major operational plan, it is periodically revised to accommodate the changing threat, U.S. force structure, and support capabilities.

A couple of times a year, action officers will participate in exercises centered in the National Military Command Center (NMCC) on the second floor of the Pentagon or the alternate site in the Maryland hills. Actual force deployments and employments may also cause formation of crisis action teams at the NMCC that require support of many of the eight directorates. In addition, response cells may be formed in applicable directorates (e.g., J-4, J-5, J-6, and J-7).

Though a crisis is not an everyday occurrence, it is worth discussing how the Joint Staff organizes to react. Many officers will be involved because of the requirement to set up shifts permitting 24-hour operation. As the crisis begins, the director J-3 will likely form a response cell composed primarily of J-3 officers and NCOs with some limited representation from other directorates. The response cell augments the National Military Command Center staff responding to increased requirements for reporting and responding to initial CJCS taskings. As the crisis escalates, a crisis action team (CAT) may be formed. A J-3 planner directs the team's effort and the services, and J-Directors usually provide full-time planners (colonels/captains) and action officers. The State Department and OSD may also be represented. The J-Directors may form their own response cells as well to react to fast-breaking actions. The CAT will prepare staff actions necessary to direct preparation of warning orders, operations orders, and execution messages directing readiness, deployment, and employment of forces. The CAT may also prepare briefings and papers for JCS consideration in the Tank as well as position papers for NSC meetings. As the crisis winds down, the director J-3 may disband the CAT, reverting to the smaller J-3 response cell.

In addition to the above, you will encounter the usual assortment of administrative actions such as Freedom of Information requests, requests for declassification of documents, and many more similar actions—all time-consuming but part of the job.

All of the actions discussed above require survival skills that are common to many actions. I have already alluded to many of them, but it is worth taking a more detailed look at them in the context of the Joint Staff.

SURVIVAL SKILLS

Building contacts. Building and maintaining good contacts is critical to your success in the Joint Staff. These contacts will warn you of impending tasking, which will permit you to anticipate fast-breaking actions. They will broaden the knowledge base needed to create many of your papers; they will expedite coordination of your paper and advise you when you're off track or when your paper is about to be attacked from a blind side. It takes time to build and maintain these contacts, but it is well worth the effort.

Who are these contacts? They are officers (military and civilian) in the Joint Staff, the services, OSD, defense agencies, CINC staffs, State Department, NSC staff, and other governmental departments that can help you prepare a better action. They are people who can assist you in understanding the big picture. Within the Joint Staff, the director's and chairman's offices and military secretaries of the J-Directorates are extremely important to you because they control the actions and suspenses. Ask your peers or branch or division chief if you need an introduction. Make a list of their names, organizations, and phone numbers; keep it handy, current, and call on them periodically.

Writing. Formats are unique here as they are in many staffs. The *Joint Staff Officer's Guide* has sample formats. Your peers, division chief, and military secretaries are a great resource for help and to answer questions. Additionally, there are editors on the Joint Staff affectionately known as "comma mamas." They know the style of the chairman or director and can help you write correspondence correctly the first time.

Above, I discussed well-coordinated joint papers that result in a chairman's or director Joint Staff's signature on a JCS memorandum. However, many of your actions may involve correspondence for the chairman, vice chairman, or director's signature that do not involve formal service coordination. These memoranda by the chairman and others (including messages) are processed using a coordination cover sheet called a *Form 136.* The Form 136 contains essential background information and recommends action on the attached implementer (action paper) and indicates coordination obtained. (Coordination can include services, if appropriate.) In light of the chairman's increased clout since 1986, there is an increased emphasis on actions carried by a Form 136. As in briefing your superiors, the Form 136 must contain essential information, identify key issues clearly, and recommend specific action.

Running meetings. Chairing action officer meetings is another important responsibility. These meetings may be necessary on any action requiring service or Joint Staff coordination in which you are trying to resolve issues or to obtain concurrence or opposing views on several complicated issues. The meeting should be planned carefully so that you maintain control of the meeting. Do not permit participants to emasculate your paper. Under current guidance, your paper should present your best recommendations. If you do not have a consensus, after a serious effort to resolve differences, then move the paper up the chain of command. In the past, the Joint Staff has been forced to delay some papers due to a lack of consensus or "foot dragging" by one or more services. This is no longer true since the 1986 reorganization act. The Joint Staff works for the chairman, who is now vested as the principal military adviser to the NCA. In the past, the corporate JCS provided the advice and the chairman was simply their spokesman. Since the chairman now has lots of power, you also are in a powerful position. Use your power carefully in these meetings. The more consensus you can build, the better.

Networking and research. Information is the medium of the Pentagon and Washington in general. Without it one is isolated. In the Joint Staff, the historical section maintains a database on all prior joint actions. Take time to visit the section and understand its capabilities before you are assigned a fast-breaking action. Another valuable source of information available to each action officer is reviewing daily message traffic and intelligence reports available from all military sources as well as other departments. Also review the early bird newspaper clipping service and other periodicals including defense-oriented publications. Some fast-breaking actions or calls from your bosses can be anticipated by catching an early morning newspaper article. A newswire service can beat the intelligence reports to your desk. CNN television and CNN radio have gained credibility as organizations that seem to get the story first and with reasonable accuracy and objectivity. Further, your division or branch maintains files of recent actions (for at least the past two years) and current joint publications. Familiarize yourself with these. Your sponsor or division chief should provide a training program to include a reading list that includes this documentation. JCS Administration Publication 1.1 will describe the functions of your organization. It is a good place to start.

GENERAL COLIN POWELL'S TENURE

To understand the workings of the Joint Staff, it is not only important to know the Joint Staff's subculture and its procedures, it is also important to understand the revolution carried out by the most powerful military man in the Building since George Marshall in the 1940s. General Colin Powell—chairman of the Joint Chiefs of Staff in the late 1980s and early 1990s—took the authority that was given to the chairman as a result of the Goldwater–Nichols Act of 1986 and consolidated and institutionalized that power in a myriad of ways. For instance, during his tenure as chairman, he picked each of the chiefs of staff. He chose people who could work comfortably with him and who understood how important it was for the chairman to be the key decision maker within the military. He also changed the decision-making process by making many important decisions through the use of a small number of key staff members from the Joint Staff rather than involving large numbers of staff members from the Joint Staff and the service staffs.

Although these changes in the influence and decision-making power of the chairman are quite dramatic, it remains to be seen if future chairmen will retain this power. If this extraordinary power remains with the chairman, key decisions in the Pentagon will be made by a small group of people who are close advisers either to the chairman or to the secretary of defense. The rest of the Pentagon will coordinate and implement policy but will not make policy on the more important issues. The great advantages of this approach to decision making are that there is decreased infighting and less delayed decision making. Also decisions are not watered down the way that they were prior to the late 1980s because of the need to accommodate the disparate views of all the chiefs.

On occasion an individual service chief or commander in the field will emerge as an important figure for a period of time, but the chairman will remain preeminent among all military men in the Pentagon and in the field. General Norman Schwarzkopf wielded extraordinary power prior to and during the Gulf War of 1991, but Schwarzkopf knew who his boss was and always deferred to General Powell. The Air Force Chief of Staff, General Tony McPeak, briefed President Bush in December 1990 on the upcoming air campaign over Iraq and Kuwait and told him that a sustained air campaign could so paralyze the Iraqis that the coalition forces could win the war with very few casualties in less than two months. When McPeak's predictions came true and when President Bush's popularity hit an all time high in the polls, McPeak's star rose to great heights. His star rose again when he was the first of the chiefs of staff in the post–cold war era to radically reorganize his service. (Among other changes, McPeak disestablished Tactical Air Command, Strategic Air Command, and Military Airlift Command—the three largest operational commands in the Air Force). But even then, it was Colin Powell who retained both the ear of the president and the power to make decisions for the chiefs and the commanders in the field. Like Schwarzkopf, McPeak knew that Colin Powell, who had picked him to be the Air Force chief, was his superior.

Whenever a particular position in a bureaucracy gains great power, other positions lose power. The service chiefs have lost power to the chairman, and the service secretaries have also lost power. In fact, in the years ahead, I expect that an effort will be made to do away with the service secretaries and their large staffs. George Marshall's great dream of unifying the military, which was so successfully thwarted by Secretary of the Navy James Forrestal immediately after World War II, has made a major step forward under the skillful leadership of General Colin Powell. Although the individual military services should remain separate entities in the years ahead, the powerful service fiefdoms that predominated American military history since the late 1800s are no more. Many people decry this change in power relationships and the decline of the power of the individual services. However, with the military being reduced in size dramatically throughout the 1990s, these cutbacks can be made more rationally in an era where cooperation with the chairman is standard.

12

THE OFFICE OF THE SECRETARY OF DEFENSE

If we plan to defend only North America, one day we will have only North America to defend.

—JAMES SCHLESINGER

Anyone who has worked both on one of the service staffs and in the Office of the Secretary of Defense (OSD) understands that there are many differences in approach, attitude, and administrative procedure in OSD. Since the staff of the secretary of defense is smaller than that of the service chiefs and since the OSD staff is considered the enemy by many of the other staffs in the Pentagon, the OSD staff, at times, has more of a feel of an embattled small town that joins together to deal with all the outside criticism than do other staffs in the Pentagon. This is especially true when the secretary of defense himself has not established a close and warm relationship with the key leaders in the military departments and in the Joint Staff.

In OSD, the staff coordination process is less complex and the people who have direct access to the secretary and the deputy secretary can move paper quickly and get decisions in reasonably short order. This is both a strength and a weakness. OSD can make decisions fast but sometimes fast coordination leads to a bad decision or a decision that must be changed once the military departments, the Joint Staff, the White House, or Congress learn of it and its full implications. The executive secretariat of the secretary of defense plays an important role here in ensuring that good staff coordination takes place. If the secretary and the deputy give the secretariat strong support, the coordination is normally quite good. If, however, the secretary and deputy secretary make lots of decisions without checking that there has been coordination through the executive secretariat, the coherency of the policy will suffer.

There is, of course, a higher percentage of political appointees in OSD than can be found in the military departments. Depending on the ideological proclivities of the president and the personnel office in the White House, OSD is sometimes filled with true believers of one bent or the other. These ideologues feel that they have a mission to push the Department of Defense in certain directions. The trouble with ideological litmus checks for political appointees in the Pentagon is that the people who pass the litmus test and are appointed are often guilty of group think and don't examine all options as objectively as they should. The military officers in OSD often find themselves in a position where they must moderate extreme ideological positions. To the political appointee who might come from the conservative wing of the political spectrum, the military members of the OSD will appear to be too liberal and too soft on military threats. On the other hand, the political appointees who come from the left will view the military people as right-wing Neanderthals. Of course, these military officers are the same folks, people who are somewhat right of center but generally quite sophisticated and suspicious of any simplistic ideological approach to complex national security issues.

Rather than give a full rundown of the functioning of the Office of the Secretary of Defense, let me list a few of the more interesting insights that I gained from my experience while working for and with OSD over many years. As a military assistant to the deputy secretary of defense I had the rare privilege of sitting in on many meetings with James Schlesinger and Donald Rumsfeld when they served as secretaries of defense during the Ford administration. The following is a list of phenomena that I found especially interesting or surprising when I worked in OSD that may be of interest to the reader, no matter what service, level, or agency

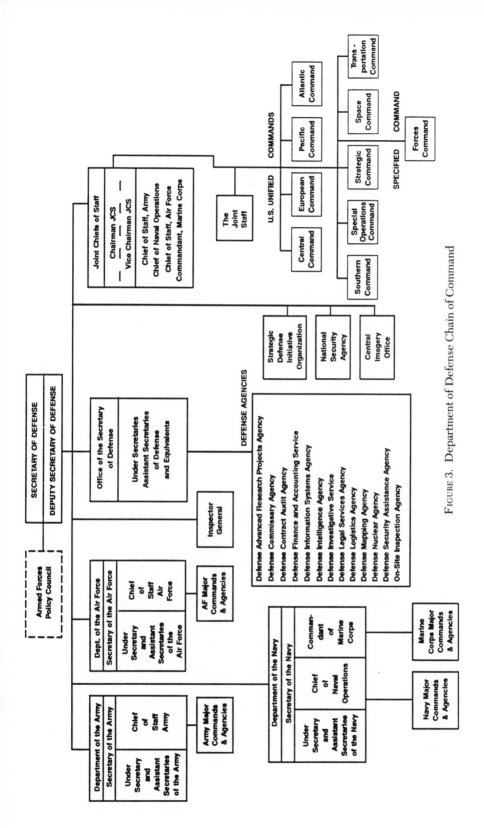

FIGURE 3. Department of Defense Chain of Command

you may be in. Before I give you my list, I must remind you that since each secretary establishes his own management approach, some of the situations that I describe below may not occur under certain secretaries.

Signing sessions. During the mid-1970s, about twice a week, the military assistants to the deputy secretary of defense would join him in his office where he would go through a large pile of action papers and sign his name just above his signature block. During the few seconds when he was signing, we would quickly explain what the package was about and why he should or should not sign the paper. Many of these actions were so routine that they required only 30 seconds of his attention—which is what they got. Others were quite important or controversial so we would stop the deputy secretary and say, "This is a tough one; the army is opposed as is one of your assistant secretaries for the following reasons. We thing you should sign but get ready for the irate phone calls," or "This is a stick of dynamite, you should read this and pay particular attention to the objections by the secretary of the Navy," or "The folks in X office are trying to slip this by you. We recommend you talk to assistant secretary of X before you buy this piece of garbage."

There are a number of points to be made about these signing sessions. First, the deputy secretary trusted the combined judgment of his military assistants (if we didn't agree among ourselves, he was quite interested in where we differed and why). If we agreed, he almost always supported us. Second, he made many decisions in less than a minute. Third, there could be no way that in a year or so, he would remember the details of something he decided so quickly. Although each defense secretary and deputy secretary handles the flow of paper in his own way, anyone who thinks that the deputy or the secretary reads every page of every package just doesn't understand the volume of the material that makes it to the desk of the secretary and deputy secretary.

Attention on the media. Most defense secretaries and deputy secretaries spend a great deal of their time dealing with the media.

Morning staff meetings are often dominated by what the news has reported in the past day or two, what news conferences and important speeches are coming up, and what questions and issues to anticipate. Articles in the early bird news summary, which most secretaries read in the chauffeured car on the way to work, trigger much of the discussion. The secretary and deputy secretary learn a lot about what is going on in the department from the press. In fact, the press is a much more broad-based source of information than all of the intelligence resources, the chain of command, and the inspector general system combined. The trouble with the in-house information systems is that they tend to be slow getting information to the secretary, and they tend to soften their stories for fear of overreaction in the chain of command or in the front office. I have often wondered if the media themselves realize how important a role they play in the formulation of defense policy. The media also play a preemptive role not well understood. Often a decision that is about to be made never happens because the secretary, deputy secretary, assistant secretary for public affairs, or one of the military assistants realizes how badly the decision will play in the media. This function of the media is a generally positive one until such time as the fear of the media response prevents important but controversial decisions from being made.

One of my most vivid memories of Don Rumsfeld when he was the defense secretary was the meeting on base closures in the spring of 1976. Rumsfeld opened the meeting by asking a series of questions.

"Was a base to be closed in Michigan?" ("Yes.")

"Was a base to be closed in Texas?" ("Yes.")

"Now how about Illinois?" ("No.")

His reaction: "Do you want me to be the only 'turkey' in the field?"

The point, of course, was clear: if the Department of Defense was going to close a number of bases, a base must close in the president's state (Michigan), in the secretary of defense's state (Illinois), and in the deputy secretary of defense's state (Texas), or the press would make a big case about favoritism in high office. It seemed clear to me at the time that if the press had not been a factor, Rumsfeld would have been less concerned that a base be closed in his home state.

Ineffective political appointees. It is quite common for a secretary of defense to have a number of political appointees working for him whom he would like to fire but cannot. Some of these people are so well connected politically and have contributed so much money to the party in power that the secretary has no power to fire them. He sometimes must take someone he doesn't want and keep someone he badly wants to unload. In some cases, a secretary may be unwilling to ease a political appointee out for fear that the next person that the White House sends will be even worse. Compare this situation with the chief of staff of a military service who has more authority to hire and fire (or at least move out), and you see why the secretary of defense is sometimes less effective in running his department than he might be. This problem also exists for the secretaries of the military departments, although the number of political appointees working for these three secretaries is quite small.

The scope of the criticism that the secretary of defense receives. Almost everyone knows and understands that the Pentagon receives lots of criticism from the media, but less well known is the secretary is criticized and second-guessed by a large number of players within the Building. The military departments and the Joint Staff are very critical of the secretary for some of his decisions. The State Department is often critical since many officials in State see the world from a different perspective than the Defense Department. The White House staff and the Office of Management and Budget are constantly criticizing the Pentagon for one transgression or another. Of course, Congress is one of the Pentagon's greatest and most diverse critics. With the much larger number of congressional staffers, the ability of Congress to probe and criticize in detail has increased significantly since the early 1970s. It is, therefore, easy to understand why secretaries of defense, like presidents and other Cabinet members in high-visibility positions, get worn down and sometimes develop siege mentalities in reaction to all this criticism from so many places.

Let me relate a true story to demonstrate the problem. In the mid-1970s, Deputy Secretary of Defense Clements felt he had to put some specific constraints on the configuration and cost of the brand new F-16 fighter aircraft so that the four European allies who were also building the F-16 could have some reliable planning factors for their factories, their budgets, and their programs. Clements did not want to write this guidance himself for fear that it would be unfair to the U.S. Air Force. Therefore, he asked me to work with the Air Force leadership to come up with the correct wording of the memorandum that he would sign back to the Air Force. I did so and the words were written by the Air Force R&D people and agreed to at the highest levels in the Air Force. All the words in the memo were Air Force words—none came out of OSD. When Clements signed the memo he asked me very directly, "Are you sure that this memo satisfies the Air Force?" I said, "Yes." Almost immediately he began to learn that there were many people in the Air Force who didn't know that the Air Staff had drafted this memorandum and criticized him for signing out such a dumb memo (curiously, the criticism focused on the lack of precision in the memorandum; yet that is exactly what the Air Staff was shooting for when the memo was written so there could be some flexibility when the time came to implement the guidance in the memo). I pointed out to some of the senior people in the Air Force that this kind of criticism was not helping to warm up the relationship between the deputy secretary and the Air Force and was, by the way, quite unfair. The criticism continued and the relationship (the Air Force secretary and chief with the deputy secretary), which was never a warm one, got even cooler when Clements realized that these two top Air Force leaders were unwilling or unable to turn off the criticism.

The strong personality differences at the higher levels. It should not be surprising that very strong, dedicated, and ambitious people with very different backgrounds would have, on occasion, strong personality conflicts. What was surprising to me was how long-lasting some of the personality differences were. I watched one secretary of a military department moved out of the Department of Defense to another job in another agency of government—one that he didn't want—because of the lack of respect a high official in OSD had for him. There are a number of "wells" that are "poisoned" not because of the incompetence or the poor judgment of officials, but because of the lack of chemistry between them and the secretary or deputy secretary. On one occasion I tried to intervene on behalf of an official for whom the military assistants had high regard, and I was told by the deputy secretary very firmly to stay out of the issue.

The role of the military assistants. Almost all the top officials in the Office of the Secretary of Defense have military assistants. Usually in the rank of colonel or captain to rear admiral or major general, they provide invaluable assistance to their bosses and are a source of good feedback to the staff, the military services, and others who have a legitimate interest in what is happening in the front office. Depending on the rapport that they have with their bosses, their ability to work cooperatively with a broad range of people, their stamina (the hours are very long since they must be in before the boss arrives and must remain after he leaves—hence 6:30 A.M. to 7:30 P.M. is about the norm), their substantive background, and their bureaucratic skills, they can be enormously influential or only modestly so. They usually sit in on all substantive meetings with their boss, take notes, and make sure that directions given are followed. They must be masters of nuance and know where the mine fields and critical points are on big and sensitive issues. They often have to approach senior members of the staff to prod them into doing what the boss ordered; they are called upon to hold the hands of high officials and others who need encouragement and help; and they are asked by their bosses on occasion to do things that the boss should do but would prefer not to.

If the military assistants do their jobs well, they often get in trouble with their own services since at times they must do things that are not in the narrow interest of their services. Those who stay in the job for an extended period of time are often not welcomed back to their services with great enthusiasm. This is particularly true if the boss that they served has left government and no longer has the leverage to ensure that they get a good job back in their parent services.

Some people see military assistants as pompous horse holders who confuse their rank with that of their boss. Unfortunately in some instances that is true; but, for the most part, military assistants are quite helpful to staff officers. Since they are personally selected by their boss, they usually reflect the management style of that boss. Military assistants have their own network within the Building that allows them to call, visit, or move papers and information rapidly up the parallel big boss chain of command, occasionally jumping over intermediate levels, if necessary. They usually have instant access to their boss and can get answers to questions or "chops" (coordination) on papers fast. Military assistants provide some of the oil that keeps the machinery in the Building running. They can be helpful to action officers and a source of lots of sage advice. If abused, like secretaries, they can hurt you. Since the passage of Goldwater–Nichols and the requirement that all future general officers must have served in a joint billet, the quality of the military assistants in OSD, which had always been quite high, has become even better. Many of the future leaders of the military services will have served for a couple of years in OSD as a military assistant or in another of the many important jobs on the third floor. (I should point out that although most OSD offices are on the third floor, there are a number of important OSD offices on other floors of the Building.)

It is a great learning experience, of course, and those who move on to high positions themselves carry with them a wealth of experience with both successes and failures and a deep understanding of where the levers of power are and how to use them without misusing them. A couple of examples that come to mind are two army generals, Colin Powell and Howard Graves. Both have had brilliant careers after having served as military assistants to the secretary of defense.

The power of the staff of the secretary of defense ebbs and flows depending largely on the management style of the secretary. For instance, under Robert McNamara the OSD staff was extremely powerful, while under Caspar Weinberger, who delegated broadly to the military departments and the Joint Chiefs of Staff, its power was quite modest. During Dick Cheney's tenure as secretary of defense, he relied on a handful of close advisers. This also reduced the power of many officials in OSD. The great advantage of an assignment in OSD is the perspective it gives on a broad spectrum of defense issues. This perspective has served many people well when they return to positions in the military departments. I would like to close this chapter with a personal story in that regard.

During the late 1970s, the military services were in terrible shape out in the field. I was commanding the fighter wing at Bitburg, and our pilots were getting only 11 hours of flying time per month in their new F-15s. Many support areas were starved for funds. We had been told so many times "to do more with less" that this phrase had become a cruel joke. Having worked in OSD only two years earlier, I decided to write a personal letter to the military assistant to the deputy secretary of defense. I wanted to lay out dramatically how bad the situation was, just in case the secretary and deputy secretary didn't fully appreciate the situation. Before I sent out the letter I showed it to my two-star boss and asked if he had any objections. He was also very frustrated by the severity of the budget cuts and told me to go ahead and send the letter. In the letter I asked the military assistant, who was a friend of long standing, to use the letter with great care. He showed the letter to both the secretary and the deputy secretary and it actually had some impact. Within a few months we began to receive some supplemental funds. I never would have written that letter if I hadn't worked in OSD and known how hard (and how important) it is for the top leaders to get unedited and unvarnished news directly from the field.

In this era of very restrictive budgets, the secretary of defense is going to have to knock some heads together so that more of the big decisions are made in the national interest rather than in the interest of a powerful individual or a military department. In this regard, the nadir was reached in the 1980s during the term of office of the secretary of one of the military departments. This very bright but arrogant individual operated largely on his own and pursued his own agenda. This secretary promoted his own cronies (both political appointees and flag officers) to high ranks, fought efforts made by some of the services to work with a greater sense of "jointness," and, in general, abused the great trust that Secretary Weinberger placed in him. It was sad to watch. It is unlikely that future secretaries of defense will give secretaries of the military departments as much latitude as did Mr. Weinberger. In many ways this is a shame, for trust and empowerment can help large organizations such as the Department of Defense operate more effectively and more compassionately.

Secretary Les Aspin is driven by a strong desire to deal with a new set of threats in the post–cold war era:

1. Regional threats such as a resurgent Iraq
2. New "non-deterrable" nuclear threats
3. Threats to economic security
4. Threats that may arise in Eastern Europe or the former Soviet Union if democratic reforms fail

Aspin is clearly committed to restructuring the Department of Defense so it can better meet these threats. Deputy Secretary of Defense Bill Perry and Under Secretary of Defense for Policy Frank Wisner are playing strong roles in the reform of the Defense Department. I am particularly pleased by the renewed interest in strategic planning.

13

The Complex Pattern of Rivalry and Competition

Tension within an organization is good—as long as its emotional content is low. When you are in an organization without tension, it is like watching a drunk—the muscles are flaccid, the coordination poor, and the "bundle of relations" is in danger of falling on its face.

—Harlan Cleveland

One of the prices that the United States has had to pay for the luxury of having four large and competent military services is the natural tendency for the services to engage in strong interservice competition. Much of this competition is good, for it helps to keep each service on its toes and working hard to maintain and demonstrate its capability to provide a major component of our military strength. Another advantage of competitive military services is that no single element of the military is so strong and powerful that it poses a threat to the democratic principle of civilian control of the military. The negative side to these rivalries is the extremes that the services take, at times, to defend their *essence*—their core roles and missions. But there is much more than just interservice

154

rivalries at work in the Building. Those who are new to the Pentagon need to understand the complex matrix of rivalries.

Interservice rivalries. These clearly are the most pervasive competitions, since each of the four services has its own separate history, culture, élan, uniforms, training establishment, staff college, bases and, with the exception of the Marine Corps, service academy and war college. These interservice rivalries are as old as the nation itself, but they have become more complex with the formation of the Air Force as a separate service in 1947. During the Truman administration, the roles and missions of the various services were worked out (the so-called Key West agreements) and these have remained relatively unchanged in the past 45 years. Interservice rivalries are, therefore, less focused on roles and missions and more on budgetary allocation among the services.

With the Joint Staff thrown into this hopper of interservice rivalry, there is a five-sided competition among military elements in the Building. The advantage of an odd number is obvious. A majority position normally emerges as three or more of the five players line up in support of a certain position. One of the strong bureaucratic reasons for not forming a fifth military service for space may be that this could lead to many three-three splits in the joint arena.

Intraservice competition. The branches of the U.S. Army (infantry, armor, artillery, aviation, etc.), the major command elements of the Air Force (combat, mobility, space support), the major components of the Navy (air, surface, subsurface), and the air and ground communities of the Marine Corps all provide subcultures within each service. These subcultures compete with each other within each service while remaining loyal to the service itself. One of the more interesting matters of discussion among knowledgeable officials is which subculture is gaining the upper hand within each service. Two important indicators are promotion lists (how many infantry people, fighter pilots, submariners, and so on, were on the latest promotion list?) and force structure decisions (if frigates are cut back and submarines are not, this may mean that the submariners are on the ascendency). Sometimes these subcultures cooperate across service boundaries. For instance, the fighter pilots of the three services sometimes join in temporary alliance in support of issues they hold dear, for example, fighter force structure and the need to keep competitive fighter production lines going.

At times, a subculture within a service will be dominant. Perhaps the best example was during the 1950s when the Strategic Air Command, under the leadership of General Curtis LeMay, had extraordinary power within the Air Force. The problem with a dominant subculture is that it tends to suboptimize. In other words, during the late 1950s and early 1960s, there was so much emphasis on the strategic systems that there was very little effort in the Air Force to develop new fighter and attack aircraft or conventional munitions for the tactical forces. If it had not been for the fine work of the U.S. Navy in developing such aircraft as the F-4 and the A-7 and in developing some advanced munitions for attack and fighter aircraft, the Air Force would have been in bad shape when the Vietnam war broke out. At the moment, there is no one dominant subculture in any of the military services, so suboptimization is not a significant problem, but it is something that could occur again in any of the military services.

Intra-intraservice rivalries. This competition is usually (but not always) rather lighthearted between certain elements within a branch of a service. For instance, the helicopter people in the Army are divided into a number of subgroups. The attack helicopters use lethal firepower to attack enemy targets, the transport helicopters carry troops to and from combat areas, and the surveillance helicopters provide reconnaissance and intelligence to army commanders. These three elements of Army aviation compete among one another for resources and priority. In the Navy, there are many such rivalries including the natural competition between the attack submarine community and the ballistic missile submarine people. In the Air Force, there is competition between the large and powerful fighter community (F-16, F-15, F-22) and the smaller and less influential attack community (A-10, A-7) that takes place within the overall tactical aviation community. The natural competition among these subgroups (and among many others) that takes place in the field carries over to the Pentagon.

Some of these communities feel they have permanent second-class status. The tactical airlift people in the Air Force (C-130) feel that the strategic airlift people (C-17, C-5, C-141) always get top priority within the airlift community. The bomber pilots feel that they receive fewer opportunities for high-level promotions than do their fighter pilot colleagues in the Air Combat Command of the U.S. Air Force.

Intra-intraservice rivalries are more prominent in the field than in the Pentagon, but they do come into play occasionally in Washington. For instance, when a service can buy only one new weapons system within a mission area and must choose between a new attack submarine or a new missile-launching submarine or between an air-to-air fighter or an attack aircraft, these rivalries surface strongly. If you find someone pushing a new weapons system hard, you might ask yourself what subcommunity that individual comes from and whether some objectivity has been lost on the part of the individual because of a great affection for a certain subelement of a military service.

Service staff–military department rivalries. Military service staffs find themselves, at times, in competition with the staff of a secretary of the military department. For instance, when I was the director of plans in the Air Staff, I had more problems with an assistant secretary of the Air Force than with any other individual in the Building. Because they are larger and have an easier access to the field, the staffs that work for each chief of staff are more influential than the staffs of the secretaries. The staffs of the secretaries of the military departments have some clear advantages, however. They are more aware of activities on Capitol Hill, and they have a better institutional memory since they have a higher percentage of long-term Pentagon people. One of the aims of Goldwater–Nichols was to reduce the rivalry between these two staffs. The consolidation of the acquisition functions, the comptroller, and the inspector general under the secretary of the military departments was mandated to reduce manpower requirements in the Pentagon as well as to reduce this tension.

Deputate rivalries within each military service staff. Since each of the staffs of the individual service chiefs is very large, it is quite natural that there are ongoing rivalries within these staffs. Some of the more permanent rivalries are between planners and programmers, between personnel and manpower people, between operators and planners, between logisticians and programmers, between the comptroller and almost everyone, and between the inspector general and the world. There are also lots of natural alliances. For instance, logisticians and operators, who argue a lot in the field, come together nicely on many issues in the service staffs. The R&D officials and planners find lots of areas of common interest since they both look to the longer-range future and tend to place high priority on programs that are in development.

Rivalries between OSD and the Joint Staff. Although the secretary of defense works hard to ensure that the Pentagon speaks with one voice when it deals with other executive branch departments and Congress, the views of the Joint Staff and the OSD staff are not always the same. On many interagency committees in Washington, both the Joint Staff and the OSD staff are represented, and the representatives from these two bodies occasionally take somewhat different positions. Various departments in the executive branch and committees of Congress sometimes try to take advantage of these differences. Let me give an example. When I was a colonel in the Pentagon, I was asked by the chief of staff of the Air Force to attend a hearing on arms control where the secretary of defense was testifying. My task was to report back to my chief on what the secretary said and how he responded to questions. Senator "Scoop" Jackson, the subcommittee chairman, personally asked me to leave the hearing. Clearly he wanted to ascertain if there were any differences in view between the secretary of defense and the service chiefs and didn't want to be part of any effort to coordinate the testimony of the chiefs and the secretary of defense.

When all of these rivalries are working at the same time on some complex issue, it takes a very sophisticated and knowledgeable individual to be able to sort out all the agendas and biases at play. It can be a fascinating business. It is vital that experienced individuals teach new people about these complex rivalries, while at the same time encouraging them to avoid dysfunctional parochialism. One of the most important responsibilities of officials who work in the Building is to cut through these many rivalries and serve the national interest rather than some narrow service or subservice interest.

14

THE PLANNING, PROGRAMMING, AND BUDGETING SYSTEM

The future is not ordained by anybody but us.

—SIR MICHAEL HOWARD

There is a saying that is heard fairly often in the various offices in the Pentagon: "Show me your budgets and I will show you your strategy." Ever since Robert McNamara came bursting through the front door at the River Entrance in early 1961, the Planning, Programming, and Budgeting System (PPBS) has dominated the life of most Pentagon officials. Although this system has been modified many times since the 1960s, the basic structure and rationale remain intact. Conceptually the system is quite sound and can best be described by outlining a number of sequential events (please excuse the oversimplification).

1. Develop a military strategy that is based on a national overall strategy.
2. Do some long- and medium-range planning to support the strategy.
3. Give the military departments some fiscal guidance for the upcoming six-year period.
4. Have each of these three departments build a six-year program

that best meets the military strategy and best serves the goals and priorities of the plans.

5. Have the military departments submit these six-year programs to the secretary of defense every other year.
6. Conduct an honest debate about the merits and demerits of these programs with the military departments, the Joint Staff, the OSD staff, the defense agencies, and the Office of Management and Budget properly represented. Be sure to have a strong input from the commanders of the Unified and Specified Commands in the field.
7. Have the secretary of defense make his final decisions on the defense budget.
8. Submit the DoD budget to the White House for inclusion in the president's budget, which, in turn, is presented to Congress in January or February.
9. Have Congress approve the budget with appropriate modifications, hopefully before the new fiscal year begins in the fall of each year.
10. Carry out the budget during the fiscal year that commences on the first of October.
11. When unexpected expenses arise during this fiscal year, submit proposals to Congress for supplemental funds.
12. Have Congress approve these requests for supplemental funds so that at the end of the fiscal year the books of the military departments are reasonably well balanced.

This sequence of events has occurred each year since the early 1960s. But this tells only a part of a much larger and more complex story, and it does not explain what changes have taken place in recent years. Given the nature of the Planning, Programming, and Budgeting System, three budgets are being worked on simultaneously. Since this can be quite confusing, let me explain what each of these budgets accomplish and by what rules the military departments, the secretary of defense, the White House, and Congress play. First, the current budget is being executed and there are usually a number of attempts on the part of the military departments to obtain supplemental funds during the year to pay for unexpected costs. However, the secretary of defense or the Office of Management and Budget often will turn down these requests, since each one of these supplementals increases the size of the federal deficit. Even if these supplementals are approved within the executive branch, the Congress will often turn them down. If a supplemental cannot be obtained, the military departments have another option: they can attempt to reprogram funds from one program to another. This also requires approval at the OSD, OMB, and congressional levels, but since these actions do not add to the federal deficit, they are more likely to be approved at each level.

While all these supplemental and reprogramming actions are going on for the current budgetary year, even more work is being done in preparation for the upcoming budgetary year. The upcoming budget (usually referred to as the president's budget) is being considered on Capitol Hill. Pentagon officials are streaming back and forth to the Hill to testify in support of the budget that the president formally presented to the Congress early in the calendar year (normally late January or February).

It is, however, the third budgetary cycle (the POM cycle) that generates most of the work in the Pentagon. The military department's Program Objective Memorandums (the POMs) are developed in the winter months and submitted to the secretary of defense in the spring. The issue cycle takes place in the summer, and the budget details are worked out in the autumn. In the late fall, the Defense Department budget is submitted to the president. By the late 1990s, this budget will amount to less than 15 percent (during the Eisenhower presidency it was more than 50 percent) of the overall federal budget that the president presents to Congress.

Things get more complicated when an administration changes, a major budget-cutting exercise occurs, or a major international crisis with big budgetary implications takes place. No matter how hard the senior officials try, most get caught up in the details of the program as well as in the budget making and in budget changing. Therefore, they generally fail to do much planning. The PPBS, as it actually works, may be best shown graphically as follows: planning, PROGRAMMING, and Budgeting System. It is generally conceded that the programmers within each military department have the greatest amount of power since they capture a disproportionate amount of the time of the top bosses. Having good access and the information that the big bosses need gives the programmers a great deal of influence. As the old saying goes, "If it ain't in the POM, it ain't." To give a very specific example, as the Air Staff planner I saw my chief about twice a week and my secretary about once a week throughout the year. The Air Staff programmer saw both top leaders a couple of times a week, and when the POM was being finalized, he saw them nearly every day.

By the late 1980s, some people began referring to the PPBS as the BPPES, with the *B* standing for biennial and the *E* for evaluation. The two-year budget cycle, which was initiated in the late 1980s, made a modest improvement in the PPBS, for it allowed more time for planning. However, it will be a number of years before the full impact of this new cycle will be fully understood. Much depends on if and how Congress changes its approach. Another trend worth watching is the idea of doing an evaluation (*E*) of the POMs during the year when a full POM development exercise is not required in this two-year cycle. Many feel that the attempt to move to a two-year budgetary cycle has failed since Congress did not go along with such an approach. If the Department of Defense returns to a one-year cycle as many predict, the time to plan and the time to evaluate how well the budget meets the requirements will be reduced. Only time will tell.

The Planning, Programming, and Budgeting System is orchestrated by the secretary of defense and his staff and is one of his major tools for managing the Department of Defense. Through such important documents as the *Defense Planning Guidance,* he establishes the military strategy, goals, priorities, fiscal guidelines, and deadlines that the military departments, defense agencies, commanders in the field, and the Joint Staff must follow. The defense agencies have grown in number to 16 by the early 1990s. The majority are headed by two- or three-star active duty officers while the others are headed by very senior civilians. Most of these agencies work in relative obscurity until some event occurs that brings them to the public's attention. For instance, the shootdown by the Soviets in 1983 of the Korean airliner 007 brought the National Security Agency to the fore, and the Pentagon procurement scandal of 1988 brought attention to the Defense Investigative Service and the Defense Contract Audit Agency. These agencies employ about 100,000 people, most of whom are professional civil servants. The agencies are as follows:

- Defense Information Systems Agency (DISA)
- Defense Nuclear Agency (DNA)
- Defense Contract Audit Agency (DCAA)
- Defense Intelligence Agency (DIA)
- Defense Logistics Agency (DLA)
- Defense Advanced–Research Projects Agency (DARPA)
- Defense Investigative Service (DIS)
- Defense Legal Services Agency (DLSA)
- Defense Mapping Agency (DMA)
- Defense Security Assistance Agency (DSAA)
- National Security Agency (NSA)
- Strategic Defense Initiative Organization (SDIO)
- Defense Finance and Accounting Service (DFAS)
- Central Imagery Office (CIO)
- On-Site Inspection Agency (OSIA)
- Defense Commissary Agency (DCA)

To manage the department the secretary uses a number of very powerful boards and committees. Let me explain two. The Defense Planning and Resources Board (DPRB), which is chaired by the deputy secretary of defense, includes almost every heavy hitter in the Building with the exception of the secretary of defense himself. In general terms, it includes the secretaries of the three military departments, the chairman of the JCS, the two under secretaries of defense, the director of defense research and engineering, the comptroller, and the head of the OSD analysis shop (the assistant secretary for programs, analysis, and evaluation). A high official from OMB and a few others fill up the room. The service chiefs are normally invited and usually attend. Also, the commanders of the Unified and Specified Commands are invited on occasion. The DPRB reviews the various POMs and budget submissions and ensures that fiscal guidance is followed. It provides recommendations to the secretary of defense on important issues.

The Defense Acquisition Board (DAB) is another powerful group. One of its major functions is to review major weapons systems in development and to provide recommendations to the Defense Acquisition Executive (DAE), who is the under secretary of defense for acquisition and chair of this committee. The vice chairman of the Joint Chiefs of Staff is the vice chairman of this board. This is very important for it gives the chairman of the JCS a very powerful role in the acquisition business, a role he did not have prior to the Goldwater–Nichols revolution.

Interacting quite directly with the PPBS is the Joint Strategic Planning System (JSPS), which is orchestrated by the Joint Staff. A key document in the JSPS is the National Military Strategy Document (NMSD). Published biennially, and based on the results of the joint strategy review and the chairman's guidance, it provides the chairman's advice to the NCA regarding the recommended national military strategy and fiscally constrained force structure required to support the attainment of the national security objectives during the defense planning period covered by the next defense planning guidance. There are a number of other important documents discussed in CJCS MOP no. 7, Joint Strategic Planning System. In addition, all of these documents are explained quite well in the *Joint Staff Officer's Guide.*

What is missing within these planning structures, however, is any serious effort at strategic (long-range) planning within either the Office of the Secretary of Defense or the Joint Staff. There is some lip service paid to strategic planning in OSD and the Joint Staff, there is a long-range planning annex in the National Military Strategy Document (NMSD), and there are some individuals who honestly think some useful systematic long-range planning is going on within these two organizations; but they are wrong (at least through 1993). The military services do some strategic planning, but their efforts at long-range planning have not been well institutionalized. The services are also limited in how well they can do long-range planning with OSD and the Joint Staff doing so little. With no overarching Department of Defense long-range plan or long-range planning system, the services tend to plan in isolation. They all, however, should be complimented for making an honest effort at long-range planning.

It is my fervent hope that sometime soon a secretary of defense or a chairman of the Joint Chiefs of Staff will establish something that all large organizations should have—that is, an institutionalized long-range planning system in which the top leaders have regular access to a small group of dedicated strategic planners. In that way, the Pentagon will establish the long-range priorities and goals that will give the Department of Defense a vision for the future so that when day-to-day decisions are made, they can be made in the context of these long-range goals and priorities. The comparison between the French military and the German military during the period between World War I and World War II comes to mind. Whereas the German military took full advantage of the technological developments of the interwar period (especially the tank, the attack aircraft, and the developments in two-way radio communications), the French military did not. If the United States is going to avoid becoming like the French military of the 1930s, it would be very helpful if it institutionalized some coherent long-range planning to take full advantage of potential developments in technology, doctrine, and concepts. Creative long-range planning can help to avoid the natural tendency toward gradual obsolescence, and the proclivity of all large organizations to get stuck in the present (or some cases, the past) and not to anticipate and plan for the future.

With the end of the cold war, chaos can be expected in many regions of the world. As ethnic, religious, and racial groups do battle with each other, the need for coherent strategic planning within the various organizations of the Department of Defense is compelling.

15

WORKING WITH DEFENSE CONTRACTORS

*We are attempting to develop major new systems with
ten-year technology, eight-year programs, a five-year
plan, three-year people and one-year dollars.*

—NORM AUGUSTINE

There is a major problem that exists for Pentagon employees in
dealing with defense contractors that should be thought through
by anyone working in the Building and by those thousands of contractors who market their wares and their ideas with the Department of Defense. Although President Eisenhower warned against
the dangers of the military-industrial complex, if there weren't
such a complex, someone would have to invent it *fast*. The days
when most of our weapons were produced in government-owned
plants, shipyards, and munitions factories are long gone. There is
no way that the Department of Defense can have the items that it
needs unless it buys most of them from private industry. In addition, the only way the Department of Defense can obtain all the
analytical support it needs is to tap the intellectual resources of the
private and non-profit research firms. With over 50,000 contracts
being signed every day, the Department of Defense is a major
player in the American economy and, to an increasing extent, in
the economies of many other nations.

Philosophically, it is important to recall that our system of entre-

167

preneurial capitalism has served this nation well for many years. The freedom to innovate, invest, take risks, and engage in competition for business is inherent in this system. Our capitalistic system has produced weapons systems that, in general, have been superior to those of our adversaries and our allies throughout this century. Inherent in this process, of course, are the concepts of risk, margin, profit, and return to shareholders. Of course, competition for defense business has always been different from and somewhat more muted than private-sector competition. However, it is useful to remind ourselves of three points. There is a fairly large element of competition in America's defense business, the profit margins in recent years have been quite small, and despite significant problems through the years, the level of integrity within the system has been quite admirable.

Senator Harry Truman gained a reputation for objectivity and toughness during World War II when he examined war production. His Special Committee Investigating National Defense exposed many examples of corruption, graft, waste, and product deficiencies. Since that time, there have been many success stories in weapons development, production, and deployment (Minuteman, Polaris, Sidewinder, Tomahawk, H-60, C-130, C-141, F-15, F-117, to name a few) and quite a number of capability shortfalls or cost overruns (C-5A, the B-1 ECM suite, Divad, and others—as well as overpriced coffee makers, toilet seats, and claw hammers). Trying to find the proper balance between safeguards against corruption, cost overruns, and capability shortfalls, and the rapid development and fielding of needed military systems has been an ongoing dilemma for the Department of Defense. If you safeguard too much, you deploy a new system too late or never deploy it at all; if you push hard for deployment of a new system, there are lots of risks of graft, cost overruns, reliability problems, or shortfalls in capability.

Without question, there is, within the Building, a deep suspicion of defense industry and the complex network of consultants that hurts what should be a positive relationship of close cooperation between groups of people who need each other badly. Let me explain one experience that I had that colored my thinking about defense contractors for a while. I can remember vividly when, as a

brigadier general, I was the head of the Force Structure Committee in the Air Staff. One day, a vice president of a major aerospace
company came to visit me in my Pentagon office. After I reacted
rather negatively to his briefing and his appeal to keep an aircraft
production line open for a few more years, he said, "Listen, General, if you don't support my position, I will see that you never get
promoted again." I replied, "Fine, and I will be sure that you and I
never have the opportunity to speak together again." This kind of
overt pressure is very rare indeed but it certainly caused me to
have negative feelings about that defense contractor for some time
after this incident. (I am happy to report that the line closed down,
I was promoted, and I never saw "Mr. Intimidation" again.)

The rules and regulations about contact with defense contractors are appropriately quite tight. It is important that all officials in
the Pentagon who have any dealings with contractors understand
their role in the process. Contractors have a legitimate need for
information; so do Pentagon officials. Pentagon officials have a responsibility to articulate clearly service and joint requirements. If
this nation is to acquire systems that genuinely satisfy military
needs, a timely exchange of information between the Pentagon
and industry must take place. Corporations must be aware of future plans and programs. Pentagon officials must also be aware of
what industry can provide. Let me outline some rules of thumb
that may be helpful to those of you who will deal with defense contractors.

Maintain a professional relationship. This is an absolute requirement even though some of the people you are dealing with may be
old friends. Government regulations are stringent on this point as
are the regulations of most of the corporations themselves. The
contractors expect you to observe the rules and normally find it
much easier to deal with you if you understand the regulations and
abide by them.

When faced with unethical behavior by a contractor, report it. As
the old adage says, don't let a few bad apples spoil the whole barrel. Unethical individuals who attempt to abuse the system should

be purged from business. If you look the other way and tolerate a certain level of unethical behavior, you will encourage others to play this game and things will slide downhill fast. The same rule applies to unethical behavior by government employees. If an official in the government seems to favor a contractor even though another contractor has the better system, start asking some very tough questions. If you don't like the answers you receive, start blowing some whistles.

Treat all defense contractors equally and honestly. Know the implications associated with competitive procurements but also understand contractor requirements for information and data. Don't forget that if the competition is going to lead to the best possible product, the competitors must know what you need with lots of specifics. Also, remember it is not fair to let one contractor get more information than another. Finally, during the period when active competition is underway, don't subvert that competition in any way. For instance, don't share the proprietary information from one contractor with another contractor.

Do not accept gratuities. Government officials at all levels must be sure not to accept gratuities, free lunches or dinners, or free trips to the Bahamas because of the chance that these gifts will put them in compromising positions when it is their responsibility to give objective advice on upcoming contracts. When the bill for the lunch, the golf game, or the dinner arrives, be very quick with your wallet so that you pay your full share. It is best if you use a credit card so that you will have a record that you fully paid your way. Even the appearance of impropriety must be avoided. Be squeaky clean at all times and in all places.

Do periodic "integrity checks." Sniff the wind often and if anything looks or smells bad, seek some help. The staff of the general counsel, the inspector general, and professional contracting officers can give you good advice if you have any questions or concerns in this area. Don't hesitate to check with them.

The challenges of the 1990s will require conceptual innovation, technological creativity, efficient production lines, and close cooperation between business and government. How well we meet the national security challenges in an era of extended budgetary austerity will depend in large part on our ability to husband our resources. We will be even more dependent on defense contractors in the future than in the past. we will also expect and demand more from defense industry. This is only fair. We must, however, avoid making dealing with the pentagon so difficult and unprofitable that some of our best defense contractors decide against competing for defense business. Keeping the important relationship between the pentagon and defense industry in proper perspective will be one of the great challenges of the 1990s.

16

SOME OF THE FUDGE FACTORY'S DEFICIENCIES

The physician can bury his mistakes, but the architect can only advise his client to plant vines.

— FRANK LLLOYD WRIGHT

Let's fact it. There are aspects of the Pentagon that are rather unattractive. This short chapter is written to alert the reader to these areas so that they will not be such a big surprise when they are encountered for the first time. Let me start my discussion with the Building itself. Those who have never visited the Pentagon and observed its physical condition both inside and out are in for a considerable shock.

The building style has often been described as "early ugly." The corridors, with the exception of tastefully decorated corridors such as those dedicated to distinguished Americans such as Marshall and Eisenhower, are painted in dull and uninteresting colors. There are packing boxes and furniture piled up in various hallways and the windows, which are washed about once a year, seldom sparkle. Most of the offices have no rugs on the floor, are quite overcrowded, and with printers and photocopiers running constantly, are quite noisy. The rest rooms are plentiful but rather unattractive and usually have a sink and a few toilets that are not functioning. There are many clocks dispersed around the corridors; most of them tell the right time only twice a day. A civilian

172

landscaper has made many improvements to the grounds, and the amount of trash lying around has decreased somewhat. However, the Building remains generally unattractive both inside and out. Most of the top people are so busy that after a while they fail to notice the run-down condition of the Building. The happy news is that the maintenance work force no longer works for the General Services Administration. The maintenance workers now work for the "mayor of the Pentagon," Doc Cooke, and the quality of the maintenance is slowly improving, since he has hire-and-fire authority.

The cafeterias serve food that can best be described as ordinary. There are lots of places to grab a bite to eat and that is what most people do—grab a bite. The leisurely, elegant, two-hour lunch has never existed anywhere in the Building. About the only place where meals are served with style and grace are in the messes of the secretary of defense, the chairman of the Joint Chiefs of Staff, and the secretarial and general officer messes of the three military departments. However, these messes are only available to the top officials in the Building. There is an executive dining room on the third floor (tenth corridor) where lower-ranking people can have a meal served by waiters and waitresses. In addition to regular walk-in service, you can reserve one of four small dining rooms for private breakfasts and lunches. This is also where you might attend a prayer breakfast or a luncheon for outside visitors or conferees. This dining room also provides a catering service where you can order plates of food for office parties and other functions.

Another less attractive aspect of life in the Pentagon has to be the parking situation. With the vast majority of the people who work in the Building arriving each day by car, the size of the parking lots is huge. If you are an assistant secretary, a member of the senior executive service, or a flag officer, you will not have to join a car pool and your parking place will be fairly close in. If you are a member of a four-person car pool, you will also receive priority parking and the walking distance to your office will normally be less than half a mile. However, if you are a member of a three-person or a two-person car pool, the parking space you have will be a long way from a Pentagon entrance. If you drive to work on your own, be prepared to pay for your parking and for a long walk from the far end of North Parking each morning and afternoon. A mile walk from parking space to office is not unusual (half that distance can be within the building itself), and you must allow as much as 20 minutes each way on top of your long commute. On nice days, these walks can be quite pleasurable, but when the Potomac is frozen and the wind is blowing 25 knots from the north, be sure to wear your earmuffs and warm gloves. Certain key officials below the flag officer rank have authorized private parking spaces. However, getting one of these assigned can be extraordinarily frustrating for new arrivals. It sometimes takes months, and in the meantime you have to pay for parking at the far end of the North parking lot.

Another unhappy situation is the Pentagon official car system: if you have important business around town and if you are of high enough rank, your secretary can order a car, and it will be waiting for you at such convenient spots as the River or Mall Entrance. Unfortunately, the reliability of this system has never been great, particularly on the other end of the trip when you are to be picked up on Capitol Hill, at the State Department, or somewhere else around town. Sometimes the car doesn't show up on time or is waiting at the wrong place and you can't find it. My recommendation, if you have access to this service, is to allow lots of time and bring something along to read while you wait. Also have back-up plans if the car doesn't show up. Taxis can be used as an alternative means of transportation if you know exactly where you are going and how to get there. Many of the D.C. taxi drivers are new to the city, use English as a second language, and don't know their way around town very well. The shuttle bus service is somewhat more reliable and is available to anyone with an ID card who is on official business. The schedules for these small shuttle buses are listed in the back of the DoD phone book.

Another less than satisfactory aspect of Pentagon life is that invaluable phone book. Although it is useful in helping you operate effectively in the Building, it is *never* up to date as far as names of individuals are concerned. This is largely due to the constant turnover of personnel as people rotate through the Pentagon and people change jobs within the Building. It does contain a wealth of information, particularly related to the organizations within the Building and in the local area. It contains over 80,000 names of Department of Defense people in the Washington area, hence it is officially called the *Department of Defense Telephone Directory*, rather than the Pentagon phone book as it is usually known.

After a while, you will become used to the deficiencies of the Building, but I would suggest that you not spend a lot of time trying to correct them. You are not likely to succeed and the nonsuccess can be frustrating. When I worked in the front office of OSD, we tried hard to correct a number of deficiencies, and our performance record was not impressive.

17

SOME PENTAGON FREEBIES AND PLEASURES TO INVESTIGATE

You must learn day by day, year by year, to broaden your horizon. The more things you love, the more you are interested in, the more you enjoy, the more you are indignant about—the more you have left when anything happens.

—ETHEL BARRYMORE

There are a number of aspects of Pentagon life that are both enjoyable and completely free. Some are absolutely unique and others are rather mundane but all are well worth investigating as you settle into Pentagon life.

The informal share-a-ride system. Would you believe that there are lots of people who ride to and from the Pentagon each day without driving, taking a bus, or taking the Metro? Would you also believe that they do this at absolutely no cost? Yes, in the marvelous world of the Northern Virginia suburbs there is a share-a-ride (also called *scab-a-ride* or *slug-a-ride*) system that works and works well without bureaucracy, organization, regulations, or directives. In fact, it is one answer to the comment, "There ain't no free lunch."

176

There may not be a free lunch, but there are lots of free rides. Here is how it works. Because there are faster-moving car pool (known as HOV, or high-occupancy vehicle) lanes available on the Shirley Highway, there are two ways to get to and from the Pentagon from the southwest: very quickly, using the car pool lanes, or very slowly, using the regular lanes. It is to the great advantage of most drivers living in the outlying suburban areas to the southwest of the Pentagon to have enough passengers on board during the rush hours to be able to use the high-occupancy vehicle lanes that run down the center of I-395 and zip into the Pentagon. Using the same lanes during the evening rush hours, these drivers and their passengers can get home quickly. Therefore, if you stand at certain spots in the Manassas, Woodbridge, Lake Ridge, Springfield, West Springfield, and Burke areas, cars will swing by and a driver will shout out, "Pentagon!" You can pile on board and off you go. In the evening, the place to stand is at the share-a-ride shelters opposite South Parking. Cars will swing by and take you near home. The lines form starting a few minutes before 4 P.M. each weekday; the cars swing by to pick up those extra passengers until just before the car-pool-lane period is over in the evening.

This system provides a fine way to observe the driving habits of many Washington drivers (always be sure to buckle your seat belt) and to meet lots of interesting people both going and coming. If you don't like the way a certain driver handles a vehicle, just make a mental note to never pile into that car again. This is no problem since there will be many more drivers to choose from.

Remember this option when your car is in the shop or on the fritz, your car pool has left you behind, or you have just run out of ideas on how to get home some evening. It is also a fine option when you are driving and need an extra passenger or two. Some riders let buses go by because they are so sure that soon they will get a free ride and race into the Pentagon (or get home) faster and cheaper than by taking the bus.

Nowhere in this country is there such a widespread use of such a free share-a-ride system. It says a lot about the willingness of Pentagon employees to trust each other. Having commuted into New York City for a couple of years from New Jersey, I cannot imagine a system like this working there. Where are the ad hoc pickup points? In downtown Springfield in front of the Fish and Chips restaurant on Old Keene Mill road, at the Rolling Valley Mall bus stop (just this side of Burke), and at most bus stops in Springfield, Burke, Woodbridge, Lake Ridge, and Potomac Mills.

The center court. Another pleasure worth looking into are strolls around the interior grounds of the Pentagon. This center court or inner court area is quite attractive in the springtime, summer, and fall. The outdoor snack bar opens in the late spring and many people spend their lunch break or a few quiet minutes during the day strolling around center court. Weekly band concerts are held during the summer and walkathons, stretcher races, and other activities are held on occasion.

Walking and jogging. Head out past the Pentagon Officers' Athletic Club (POAC) for a brisk walk. If you are fortunate you will run into the Pentagon's own wonder woman as she carries out her daily exercises. The best walks are through the Lyndon Baines Johnson Memorial Grove on the east side of North Parking. This is also a nice place to enjoy your lunch. If a walk is not your style and you are an avid jogger, pull on your togs and take a trip up the Potomac to the north, across the Memorial Bridge, down Ohio Drive, and back across the 14th Street Bridge. Want a couple more miles? Go around the Tidal Basin and check out the Jefferson Memorial on the way to the 14th Street Bridge.

Ceremonies at the River Entrance. Keep an eye on the schedule, and you will have a chance to observe some of the ceremonies held in front of the River Entrance for various visiting dignitaries. The honor guards from one or more of the services put on a splendid show; usually there's no difficulty finding a good spot to watch. Just wander out the River Entrance a few minutes ahead of time and observe from the sidelines.

Strolling the Concourse. During the winter, the Concourse is the place to stroll when you have a few spare minutes. Band concerts, choral groups, and dance groups are featured quite often. The performances are always free. It is impossible to walk up and down the Concourse a couple of times without running into friends, colleagues, or other interesting people. People who are visiting the Pentagon from all over the world often take a few minutes to hit the Concourse. You can often spend a few useful minutes meeting friends who are visiting the Building and getting filled in on what is happening out in the real world of posts, ships, and airplanes.

Shopping and banking are quite convenient. Let me list the various names and telephone numbers of the concessions along the Concourse for your convenience.

Bank (NationsBank)	697-0000
Barber shop	695-2470
Beauty salon	697-1644
Bookstore/Newsstand	695-0870
Camera shop	695-5208
Department store (Woodward and Lothrop)	695-3775
Drug store	695-6009
Dry cleaning and laundry	695-5047
Florist	695-0800
Jewelry and watch repair	695-6215
Optometrist	695-6016
Pastry shop	920-8070
Post office	695-6835
Shoe shine and shoe repair	695-2440

So it is someone's birthday and all of a sudden you remember that you have no flowers, no card—no nothing. The Concourse has saved many busy folks through the years.

Feeling ill? Don't forget that there is a military clinic at the south end of the Concourse. Observe someone pass out or experience a heart attack? Call 7111, describe the problem and your location quickly, and a professional team will be on the way. Many lives have been saved through the years with this service. There is also a convenient civilian medical clinic in the Building: Room 1E356 (telephone 74778).

18
INTERVIEWING

*I am not interested in whether a man is ambitious: the
question is whether he is ambitious to do something or
ambitious to be somebody.*

—JEAN MONNET

A number of you will be interviewed for a job before you arrive in
the Building. Many more will be interviewed after you have
worked there for some time. Having been interviewed by a secretary of defense, a deputy secretary of defense, and having watched
a deputy secretary interview dozens of candidates for assistant secretary of defense and assistant secretary of the military departments, for three- and four-star promotions, for military assistants,
executive assistants, and executive secretaries, I have learned a lot
about this business. I have included excerpts from the memorandum for record that I dictated the afternoon of my interview with
Secretary of Defense Jim Schlesinger in 1974 to give the reader a
very specific idea of how an interview might go. Here are some
tips for the person that gets the word that very soon he or she is to
be interviewed by a top boss.

Don't covet the job too much. If you come across in the interview
as someone who loves his or her present job and is not terribly
anxious to climb the greasy pole to fame and fortune, you will often
be given top grades by those who interview you. Top leaders in the

Pentagon are inherently suspicious of hyperambitious individuals. If you give that appearance, it may hurt you.

Try to avoid seeming like someone's crony. Chances are that you would not be being interviewed unless someone was pushing you pretty hard. That can be a negative factor if the person sponsoring you is not liked or admired. If, for instance, the person interviewing thinks that your mentor is trying to push you into a job so that the mentor can have a spy in the front office, be prepared for a rough interview.

Read a couple of recent books on defense matters before the interview. Some interviewers love to ask people what books they have been reading lately. If they get a dumb stare in return, they may get the impression that your in box is about all you can handle and this next big job may be too much for you. Having read nothing lately may be a sign of lack of intellectual curiosity as well as overall lethargy.

Be willing to discuss objectively your strengths and weaknesses. If you have a hard time coming up with a list of strengths and weaknesses, you may come across as not really understanding yourself. This can be fatal in an interview since you may give the impression of being non-introspective, excessively arrogant, or excessively modest. As the Greeks said, "Know thyself." Be sure you also know how to articulate who and what you are and what values you hold dear.

Don't try to give the "expected answer." I watched the deputy secretary of defense set up people with leading questions like, "What do you think of the managerial ability of my fellow Texan, Mr. Blank?" Some interviewees would bite and praise the individual to the heavens. Little did they know that the deputy secretary held Mr. Blank in great contempt. I always thought this technique to be too slick and too sneaky, but it seemed to work for the deputy secretary, who didn't want "yes" men or sycophants working for him.

If this interviewer doesn't ask the skeleton-in-the-closet question, answer it anyway. By this I mean if there is something in your background that the big boss really needs to know and he hasn't pulled it out of you, tell him about it. A good time to do this is at the end of the interview when you will probably be asked if there is anything you would like to add. I watched one man answer this question with, "I am an alcoholic." He got hired, I think largely because he was willing to volunteer this fact and because he had been recovering for over a year. In my interview with Dr. Schlesinger, I told him at the end of the interview about the controversial book I had written about the Air Force and that some senior officers felt I was a bit disloyal. I felt he needed a full deck of cards when he made the decision about whether to hire me.

Be prepared for the power stare. If the interviewer tries to stare you down, hold his or her eyes and don't look down. Although I personally find this interviewing technique distasteful, I have seen it used in the Pentagon, so be ready.

The following are excerpts from the memorandum I wrote on 9 July 1974 about my interview for the position of military assistant to the secretary of defense—a job I did not get. Although some of the stuff in it is dated, it should give a feel for the kind of issues that are raised in an interview like this.

MEMO FOR THE RECORD   9 July 1974

SUBJECT: Discussion with Dr. Schlesinger.

On 8 July, I had a 45-minute discussion with Dr. Schlesinger in conjunction with an interview relating to the position of military assistant to the SECDEF. The discussion was wide-ranging, and he expressed some very strong opinions on a number of matters relating directly or indirectly to the Air Force.
The following topics were discussed.
—*Air Force Leadership*
He feels the Air Force suffered from poor leadership from

about 1953 onward. He feels the Air Force was the most progressive and innovative service in the late 1940s but somehow lost its way and reverted to a stereotype, which impeded progress and innovation.

— *Strategic Arms*

He is unhappy with what the JCS is sending him on SALT issues. He feels it demands that we build too many very expensive weapons systems. He specifically mentioned the Trident. In addition, he was not complimentary of the B-1. He recently asked an Air Force general what the most important requirement for the Air Force was and the general answered the B-1. Mr. Schlesinger did not like that answer.

— *Purple Suiters*

He was extremely outspoken on this issue. He said that if I came to work for him I must wear purple underwear.

— *Lightweight Fighter*

He wanted to know how the Air Force felt about the LWF. I told him that the Air Staff fully supports the LWF and is most anxious to procure it for the active inventory. He said that the lightweight fighter was a bloody issue, that the Air Force did some dumb things to try to ensure that the F-15 was procured in quantity, and he was happy that the Air Force finally came around to supporting the LWF.

As far as his comments in general, he feels that the Navy systems are oversold, overpriced, and undercapable. He is generally more pleased with the Air Force but sprinkled criticism about us rather freely. He feels we play fairly in the bureaucratic arena except on the issue of expecting our purple suiters to remain blue suiters. The Army was never mentioned. Since most of his comments were critical, the Army seems to be highly regarded as an institution.

He stated that there were two theses about the JCS process and asked me which one I agreed with. One is that anything that goes through as much staffing, coordination, compromising, and waffling must be garbage and should be ignored. The other theory is that the staffing and coordination produces a good product and the advice of the JCS should therefore be followed by OSD. I told him that I generally subscribed to the second theory and that the role of OSD was not to throw out everything that the JCS sent but to cull the occasional bad advice.

My impression of him is that he is extremely capable and intelligent, enjoys debating issues, does not like or respect yes men or sycophants, and chafes under the criticism he is getting from the press, especially on SALT-related matters. He has little respect for academic critics who he feels are part of the problem when they should be providing answers to our national security problems.

19

HOW TO GIVE AND RECEIVE BRIEFINGS IN THE PENTAGON

Use soft words and hard arguments.

—ENGLISH PROVERB

Giving a briefing to higher-level officials is not unlike orally defending a Ph.D. dissertation. You, the briefer, normally know a lot more about the specifics of the subject than the top officials you are briefing. On the other hand, their depth of experience, collective intellectual capabilities, and vast experience in receiving and criticizing briefings make them a formidable group. The first times I briefed my service chief and my secretary were when I was at Udorn, Thailand, in the late 1960s. On each occasion, I had just landed from a five-hour night combat mission in F-4s where I had been shot at a lot over Laos, and they had not engaged in combat in many years. Fielding their questions was easy compared to dodging 37mm and 23mm rounds from the North Vietnamese, and I found I not only had solid credibility but also was not intimidated by the presence of senior officials. Whenever I had a chance to brief high-level officials again, I often would remind myself of those briefings. So much depends on your credibility, your knowledge of the subject, and your confidence level.

But let's get back to the Pentagon. If you have done your homework well, practiced in front of your colleagues, have coordinated your ideas widely, know where support and opposition exist within the room, and have brainstormed with your colleagues about the kinds of questions you might expect, your briefing should go quite well.

First rule of briefings: never apologize. Too many briefers make the mistake of starting the briefing off with one or more apologies.

- "I didn't have time to build good slides."
- "My analysis is not complete."
- "I haven't coordinated this briefing with all of your offices."

This apologetic approach reduces your credibility with the audience and erodes the impact of your briefing. The normal reaction of a busy official is, "Why am I here if that clown at the podium is not ready to brief me?" Officials will normally not say this, but I can almost guarantee that some of them will be thinking it.

Creating slides. Construction of viewgraphs or slides is an art that is well worth cultivating. Some slides confuse, others divert, while others clarify, educate, and gain support for your recommendations. If you use too many slides, you may not get to the end of the briefing before some of the key players have to race off to the next meeting. If you use too few you may not be able to make your points well enough for your ideas to stick in the craniums of the listeners. In general terms, you should not use slides that contain long sentences or paragraphs. However, if your slides do contain a series of phrases, you should give the listener a chance to read each slide. In any case, be sure the slides can be read by everyone in the room, including the people with bad eyesight who might be in the back of the room. *Make sure all words are spelled correctly,* and the data displayed is, in fact, accurate and up to date. If someone else constructs your slides for you, be absolutely sure that you can explain each slide in detail. You should have your backup slides organized in a way that you can call for them (or get to them) very quickly.

The key slide is the last one. If the briefing is a decision briefing then you should leave the last slide on the board until the meeting is over. This slide should have no more than five points outlined. You, or your principal, should keep referring back to the last slide to make sure that the group actually comes to a decision on each of the key issues. If you don't use this technique in decision meetings, these decisions may not be made and you may have to call additional meetings.

Giving a briefing. Before a briefing, the action officer should *always* check out the room, the slide or overhead projector (including the availability of extra bulbs—of the right type), number of seats needed and available, and the time constraints for the key participants. Briefings should start and finish with a short description of the purpose of the briefing (information, update, decision, looking for reactions) as well as expected outcomes, if any. The briefer should never assume that the participants have read the "read ahead" materials provided. Briefers should also avoid the use of hidden agendas, misleading data, single-factor analysis, half truths, or any other tricks. These techniques can reduce briefers' credibility with participants, some of whom will be clever enough to realize that they are being manipulated. Briefers should always keep in mind that the participants will be making various judgments about them.

- How well prepared are they?
- Are they trying to mislead or manipulate?
- How honest are they with the data they display and the options they present?
- Does the briefer have the interest of the country at heart, or is he or she pushing a parochial point of view?

Action officers and other briefers should keep in mind that one of the great frustrations of senior officials is a briefing that uses 58 minutes of a 60-minute meeting, allowing almost no time for discussion after the briefing is completed. Insecure or manipulative briefers often are guilty of trying to use too many slides. All briefers should be aware that they are unlikely to gain the respect and the support they are looking for if they are guilty of this common mistake. In addition, briefers should avoid talking down to audiences and being patronizing toward senior officials. Other traits to be avoided are using an excess number of obscure acronyms, displaying overly complex slides or view graphs, or using unfamiliar or esoteric terminology. Briefers should try to remember two fundamental rules. First, approach your audience with neither condescension nor awe. Second, remember that first and foremost you are trying to communicate. Ask yourself, "Will this briefing allow me to communicate with my audience well?"

The quickie briefing. All briefers should be prepared to take their carefully crafted 40-minute briefing and condense it into a three-minute briefing. Usually, the summary slide will be all that you have time to use, and often you will have to give your three-minute briefing walking down the hall with some high official and you will not be able to use any slides at all. In three minutes you will have time to cover the five or six major points or issues, your four or five major recommendations, and a quick summary of any opposing views. You should be ready to answer the standard questions that come up at the end of these quickie briefings:

- What is your "fall-back" position?
- Are there any other good options?
- Does this need to be decided right away?
- Is this a change from what has been advocated before?
- How does the chief (or some other big boss) feel about this?

Receiving a briefing. Receiving a briefing properly is also an important skill. Those who serve as the principal, to whom the briefing is primarily addressed, should keep in mind the need to maximize the value of the briefing and the time being spent by the important and busy officials in the room. They should set basic parameters for briefings (length, number of slides, attendees) so the action officers can prepare themselves properly. The principal should also discipline both the briefer and the participants if they become engaged in time-wasting activities. A useful rule of thumb that works in most (but certainly not all) briefings is to have the briefer complete the full briefing without interruption; a question-and-answer and discussion period can follow. If the senior official allows lots of interruptions, the coherency of the briefing breaks down, and many points that would be better made later in the briefing are made when the questions are raised. If the "no questions until the end" rule is too rigid for the principal or the audience involved, an alternative approach is to establish a rule that only the principals sitting at the table can raise questions during the briefing. The people who sit along the side walls must give a note to their principal if they want a question asked. I have used this technique with some success. This "limited questioner" rule reduces the chaos. It is best if the briefer numbers the slides so that the audience can read the number of each slide easily. Then the questioners can refer to the specific slide for which there was a question.

It is very helpful if the senior official actually introduces the briefing and the briefer with a short (one or two minutes) rundown of how the briefing will be conducted and how much time is available for questions, as well as outlining the purpose and desired outcomes of the briefing. The senior official should let the group know how long the meeting will last and what constraints there may be on the time of key participants. At the end of the discussion period, it is helpful if the senior official gives an oral summary of the briefing, any decisions that have been made, and where the briefing should next be given. Too many meetings end with most people wondering what happened, where the issue is headed, and how the principals feel about the issue or issues.

Good leadership can reduce many of these problems. Let me give a specific example. The late General Jerry O'Malley, when he took over as the vice chief of staff of the U.S. Air Force in the early 1980s, announced that there was too much time wasted in long briefings and meetings. He mandated that no briefing to top executive committees of the Air Staff would have more than 20 slides. What a wonderful change that was. Four-hour meetings with as many as 200 slides had become quite common. Those of us on these top committees found out quickly that we could accomplish in a hour or so what was taking much longer. In fact, because we normally finished the new briefings in about half an hour, we actually had more time to discuss the major substantive issues. What was lost was lots of very detailed information that we didn't use and soon forgot anyway.

For those who receive lots of briefings, let me suggest a useful technique if you happen to have a little extra time at the end of a briefing. Say to the briefer, "Now run quickly through your backup slides." Often there are some fascinating slides that will provide you and the rest of the audience with additional insights. Occasionally these slides were removed from the briefing by some intermediate-level boss who said, "We don't want to show the boss *that* stuff," when *that* stuff is just what you need to see!

Many critics of the Pentagon feel that there is too much time devoted to preparing, giving, and receiving briefings. This is true (I was amazed when I served in a NATO headquarters how much we were able to accomplish with very few briefings). Yet briefings do serve a number of useful purposes and will remain an important aspect of life in the Building. Those who can give polished, punchy, and persuasive briefings can be very effective in the decision-making process. Those who receive briefings with open but well-disciplined minds can maximize the value of this pervasive aspect of Pentagon life.

Finally, a very senior retired officer who reviewed my manuscript asked me to make a plea for occasional stand-up breaks to reduce the "snooze" factor. It is quite disappointing to a briefer who has worked so hard to put together a really first-rate presentation to have the audience use the briefing as an opportunity to "pick up some Zs."

20
PHRASES TO AVOID

If you your lips would keep from slips,
five things observe with care.
To whom you speak, of whom you speak,
and how and when and where.

    —W. E. NORRIS

There are lots of phrases that are tossed around so often in the Pentagon that they often begin to be accepted as gospel. It may be useful to take a hard look at some of the most common phrases since they often indicate a mindset that may be unfortunate or counterproductive. If you find that you are using these phrases, you might ask yourself if they are sending out the kind of messages that you wish to convey.

Let's throw money at the problem. The trouble with this phrase is that it indicates an attitude that is damaging in substance and in form. Throwing money at problems seldom works well, may lead to funds being wasted, and sends bad signals to lots of people in the Defense Department. In addition, it appears to the outside observer who hears this phrase that the Pentagon is once again taking a cavalier attitude about the spending of hard-earned tax dollars.

There must be a hidden agenda somewhere. This attitude leads to suspicion and mistrust that do nothing to help break down the barriers to good coordination and cooperation. If you are so suspicious

192

of everyone's motivation that you are constantly looking for hidden agendas, it may be time for you to ask for reassignment outside the Building. I do not want to carry this point too far, however. Street-smart Pentagon people must be able to ferret out hidden agendas where they do exist and give their various bosses a full deck of cards to play with as far as the motivations of others.

If the Navy (Army, Air Force, Marines, Joint Staff, OSD, etc.) is pushing that issue, it can't be in our interest. This "zero sum game" mentality contributes to the unproductive nature of many of the rivalries in the Building. Most interactions in the Pentagon can and should be "win-win" not "win-lose." A better approach to take is: The Army is pushing that issue; how can we both benefit from the idea?

My bosses are not smart enough to support my idea so I am going to push it over on the Hill. I have seen action officers who are sure that they have found the silver bullet. If they can't get support within their service they will advocate the idea in the field commands, in the Joint Staff, in the Office of the Secretary of Defense, the White House, or on Capitol Hill. One of the great strengths of the U.S. military is its discipline and its loyalty. When this breaks down badly because of rogue elephants running all over Washington, the ability of the senior leaders to manage their programs is seriously diminished as is the credibility of the services and the Department of Defense.

I don't get mad—I get even. This kind of talk, especially by people in leadership positions, establishes a pattern of intimidation that breaks down the trust and cooperation that helps make life in the Pentagon reasonably pleasant. There are certainly times when someone does something so flagrant that it is necessary to take very strong action in retaliation. But magnanimity works much better than threats and intimidation in most cases. If you become known as an embattled street fighter who is always trying to get even with someone or some agency, people will not enjoy working with you or for you, and your effectiveness will diminish over time.

To get along you must go along. This is a commonly used phrase on Capitol Hill. People who work in the Pentagon should not expect to get 100 percent of what they want, but the dangers of going along must be faced. Going along with lowest common denominator solutions when better solutions can be found is wrong. Going along with positions that violate personal and institutional integrity is even worse. The "fight to the death" mindset is bad; the "go along to get along" mindset should also be avoided.

21
A SCHOLAR'S VIEW
OF THE PENTAGON

*The nation that will insist on drawing a broad line of
demarcation between the fighting man and the thinking
man is liable to find its fighting done by fools and its
thinking done by cowards.*

—SIR WILLIAM BUTLER

This chapter was specifically designed for the scholar who may
wish to conduct research, test hypotheses, or develop or modify
theories on management of complex bureaucratic organizations. It
was also designed to help explain the bureaucracy and the politics
of the Building in more scholarly terms than the rather breezy approach and style of the rest of this book. Readers who don't feel
comfortable plowing through a more scholarly discussion may
wish to skim this chapter or perhaps skip it altogether.

For students of public administration, political science, management, sociology, bureaucratic politics, defense policy, and economics of national security, the Pentagon is a veritable gold mine
of case studies and insights. However, there are many difficulties
involved in conducting serious research in the Building. One of
the greatest problems with conducting scholarly work is the inability or unwillingness of most researchers and scholars to get the
necessary security clearances to be able to do a thorough study or
analysis. In addition, the lack of access to key decision makers and

the general lack of institutional memory in the Building are major impediments. An even more fundamental problem is the generally suspicious nature of Pentagon inhabitants toward scholars; these officials assume that scholars are more interested in being critical than objective. I would hope this book, and more specifically, this chapter can help those who would like to "break the code" on gaining substantive access to the Building and understanding how the place operates.

Before I worked my first day in the Pentagon, I had written a book on U.S. military planning and had taught defense policy as a faculty member at both the Air Force Academy and the National War College. I had also graduated from a service academy, served in the Air Force for 17 years, flown 180 combat missions (over Laos and North Vietnam), and conducted research for my dissertation in the Pentagon. A few days before I reported in for my first job in the Building, I met a Pentagon flag officer who told me with great conviction that no one knows *anything* about the Pentagon unless he has actually worked there. This mentality on the part of the battered veterans of the Potomac Puzzle Palace is very common and makes the task of the scholar even more difficult. Many Pentagon officials refuse to give up any of their valuable time to an outsider. They feel that no matter how hard outsiders try, they will not be able to understand and explain with accuracy and insight what goes on.

However, the situation is certainly not hopeless. Many people with vast experience in the Pentagon, particularly those in the retired ranks, are very willing to "tell it like it is" to a probing scholar. At the end of this chapter, I will provide some specific ideas on how to find help.

The bureaucratic politics model. The best academic model for explaining the workings of the Pentagon is probably the bureaucratic politics model. Entrenched bureaucracies, fighting hard to enhance (or at least maintain) their policy and budgetary positions, are the norm. The major bureaucratic players are the military services, the Joint Staff, the OSD staff, and the major defense agencies. The secretaries of the military departments are also significant actors and their influence has been enhanced somewhat as a result of the changes mandated by the Goldwater–Nichols Act.

Since the budgets of the military departments are very large and the results of deterrence and defense policies are difficult to quantifiably measure, there are literally hundreds of ways to weigh military capability and performance and to slice up the defense pie. Systems analysis has matured considerably since the 1960s, and the use of decision analysis in the form of Mission Area Analysis (MAA) has progressed significantly in recent years. One of the big advantages of decision analysis over systems analysis is that it can give the decision maker an answer to his or her "what if" questions in a day or two, whereas most systems analysis requires many weeks or months.

Despite the maturation of these analytical techniques, there are still many unknowns and uncertainties that prevent analysis from providing definitive answers. With the demise of the Soviet Union, trying to figure out which nations or organizations will seriously threaten our national interests will be quite difficult. In addition, trying to ascertain what action will deter these nations or movements from taking aggressive action and what weapons systems can best defeat them in war will remain a tough job indeed.

As far as the bureaucratic politics model is concerned, it is useful to discuss briefly the key players and what motivates and constrains them. The *service chiefs* are four-star officers who serve for four consecutive years in the top military job in their respective services. The chiefs must serve many constituencies, and their flexibility is constrained significantly as they try to steer a steady course through the mine fields of everyday policy making. Each chief must serve his active duty forces, reserve forces, military families, retired service members, and their families. He also has responsibilities to the U.S. Congress, particularly the key committees that concentrate on defense issues. Each chief has major responsibilities to the chiefs of his comparable service in the allied nations that look to him for assistance and support. Of course, each chief must lend support to the chairman of the JCS, the commanders in chief in the field, and the secretary and deputy secretary of defense. Where a service chief stands depends on where he sits, and self-abnegation is not a quality that chiefs are either picked for or excel at. For instance, even if a chief wishes to take a major initiative in divestiture, he finds it extremely difficult to do so.

Following is a specific and little-known example. A few years before President Carter canceled the B-1 bomber, the chief of staff of the Air Force was facing an enormous squeeze on resources as a result of post-Vietnam budgetary cutbacks. This chief decided that it would be prudent to consider the cancellation of the B-1 so that he could preserve most of the other force structure and R&D programs of the U.S. Air Force. At the time, the B-1 was still under development but was clearly running into performance shortfalls, and various cost factors were going up dramatically. A secret and very sensitive meeting took place in the Pentagon. The chief presented the idea of the cancellation of the B-1 to the assembled four-star officers of the Air Force, who urged him not to cancel the B-1. They argued that the manned bomber was the very essence of an independent Air Force and to cancel it would significantly reduce the ability of the Air Force to carry out its most important mission. The chief of staff, not wishing to provoke the ire of the entire senior military leadership of the U.S. Air Force, decided to proceed with the development of the B-1.

Since the passage of the Goldwater–Nichols Act, the *chairman of the Joint Chiefs of Staff* has become the most important and influential military leader in the United States. He serves a two-year term, but it is quite common for a chairman to serve for more than one term. He, too, serves many constituencies and is torn on many issues between the strong and legitimate needs of one constituency that is opposed to similarly strong and legitimate needs of another. His staff has become the most talented staff in the Pentagon, but it is still considerably smaller than the staffs of the military services in Washington (the Marine Corps is an exception). In addition, whenever the services wish to call upon the help of experts in the field, it is easy to do so, since each service has tens of thousands of officers and professional civil servants in the field. When the services decide to combine forces against the Joint Staff, the opposition can be very powerful. Although all of the officers on the Joint Staff are supposed to be "purple suiters" and give their full loyalty to the Joint Staff and the chairman, some cannot and others do not. A fundamental dilemma that the Goldwater–Nichols Act addresses only in part is that all Joint Staff officers (except those close to retirement) have to look to their services for the next assignment, their next job beyond that, and their next promotion. Hence, the chairman faces a problem of divided loyalties on his own staff; divided loyalties are generally not a problem for the chiefs of staff of the four services.

The *secretary of defense* also has a strong and talented staff and has the luxury that many other key players do not have; that is, he has a high percentage of professional civilians with long experience in the Building. However, his staff is not as large as the staffs of the service chiefs. In addition, some of his staff is military and some of these serve as conduits for insider information back to their services. So he has a modest loyalty problem that he shares with the chairman but does not share with the service chiefs.

The *defense agencies* have a large number of permanent civil servants who give good continuity to policy and a fine institutional memory to these agencies. However, the heads of these defense agencies pay a price for this large professional long-term staff: They find it very difficult to move an agency in any major new directions during the two or three years they are in charge.

The *military services* maintain the preeminent position of power and influence among all the Pentagon bureaucracies, but this strong position is offset somewhat by the strong rivalries between and among themselves. When the services can agree and simultaneously coordinate their efforts, they have enormous power even in the face of major opposition. The example of the Panama Canal Treaty during the Carter presidency comes to mind. The frequent polls indicated that a majority of the American people were opposed to the treaty, but since the chiefs were unanimous in their support and were willing to say so publicly, the treaty received the additional votes in the Senate needed to achieve ratification. If even one chief had opposed, it is highly unlikely that the treaty would have received the consent of the Senate.

The biggest change that has taken place recently in the power equation in the Pentagon was with the passage of the Goldwater–Nichols Act of 1986. Congress, in general, has been very suspicious of any consolidation of power in the Pentagon since the creation of the Department of Defense in 1947. In addition, members of Congress have enjoyed the opportunity to play one service off against another in hearings and during the budgetary process. Strong interservice rivalries not only enhance the power of Congress, they also contribute to the continuance of strong civilian control of the military. However, by the late 1970s, many members of Congress began to see disadvantages in the weak position of the *chairman of the Joint Chiefs of Staff* and the somewhat substandard caliber of the officers who were assigned to joint billets (as compared to the quality of the officers on the service staffs). With a strong push by some key congressmen and senators and an aggressive group of staffers on the Hill, and with strong support from experienced individuals like retired General David Jones (who had served as a member of the JCS longer than anyone in history), the Goldwater–Nichols bill was passed in the fall of 1986.

The chairman's position has been enhanced considerably and although he will still have to use the power of persuasion as his principal weapon in the bureaucratic wars, he enters each discussion from a stronger position, by far, than that of any previous chairman. Much now depends on the competence, vision, and leadership ability of chairmen over the next decade or two. The Joint Staff is evolving into the most competent staff in the Pentagon. The chairman now has a strong vice chairman, and if in the years ahead a number of vice chairmen move up to be chairmen, that will certainly enhance the power and prestige of the subsequent vice chairmen. Any new chairman who has just moved up from vice chairman will hit the ground running and no power will slip away during the transition period.

In addition to organizational changes, however, attitudes and loyalties are important. The military services will remain the primary area of personal commitment and loyalty for uniformed officers. However, subtle changes are taking place and there is a chance for greater service cooperation as more officers gain experience in the joint arena. Having spent a considerable part of my career in joint and international positions in which I felt obliged to take positions that were not in the narrow interests of my own service, I returned to my service with a broader and less parochial viewpoint. Although not necessarily career enhancing in the past, this pattern is becoming the trend for the future.

Obtaining research assistance. The Defense Technical Information Center (DTIC), located in Building 5 of nearby Cameron Station, has a marvelous file of books, articles, studies, analyses, and databases that serious scholars will find quite useful. Many of the files are classified, but many are not. For instance, almost all the research at the various war colleges is unclassified and available through DTIC.

Scholars who wish to pursue issues relating to national security and who do not know how to gain access to the right people should contact retired senior-level DoD policy makers for ideas on how best to approach the problem. In many cases, these recently retired officials are not only extremely knowledgeable but also feel less constrained by time and bureaucratic factors than people who are still working in the Building. The social science and political science departments at the service academies also keep in close touch with activities in the Building as do the various war college and staff college faculties.

Research groups and think tanks are also good sources of information since they are constantly competing for, winning, and fulfilling contracts. In addition, many think tanks do research that is not funded by the government. There are too many to name, but they range from the left-leaning Center for Defense Information to a number of right-leaning groups such as the Heritage Foundation and the American Enterprise Institute.

The Institute for Defense Analysis, RAND, the Center for Naval Analyses, and the Concepts Analysis Agency serve the Office of the Secretary of Defense, the Air Force, the Navy, and the Army, respectively, but some of these branch out and provide service to other clients (for instance, RAND does a lot of work for the Army).

SAIC, SRA, TASC, BDM, PRC, JAYCOR, NSA (National Security Analysts), and many other commercial companies provide important research as well as analytical and technical support to various parts of the Department of Defense. Within each organization are people who not only have considerable talent and expertise but also stay in touch with current affairs in the Building. A number of universities around the country do substantive research for the Pentagon. Being able to call upon some of the best minds in the country is quite an asset for the Department of Defense. Hence, an inquiring scholar can often find considerable expertise within his or her own academic community.

Dr. Lewis Sorley, who came up with the idea of being a "study doctor," has made significant contributions to a number of departments and agencies and is as well tuned into defense issues as anyone that I know. Sorley, who has always had a great interest in stage productions, was aware of the so-called play doctors who are called in when a play is doing poorly in tryouts in New Haven or Boston. The role of the play doctor is to fix the play in short order—and usually anonymously—so that when it opens on Broadway it will get good reviews and be a success. Sorley does the same thing for many different clients, both in and out of government. If the study is in terrible shape and can't be fixed in time to meet a fixed deadline, Sorley recommends euthanasia. If, however, he can fix it, he works closely with the study team, advises them to collect some additional information, and using his considerable intellectual and writing skills, restructures and rewrites the study. As you would expect, he gets lots of business.

There are also groups in the Washington area who will do fast analysis. One such group will do an analytical study in two weeks. Since this group has an excellent database and superb people, it can often give a client almost as good a study as it could get elsewhere in six months' time.

In addition, there are many experts who are working on their own and serve as consultants to industry, research groups, and to the military services and agencies themselves. There is an informal and complex internetting system and there are some people who are involved in myriad activities. Any scholar with the time and the inclination can tap into these nets. A good place to start is with the various colleges and research groups of the National Defense University.

22
MILITARY ETHICS
IN THE PENTAGON

Our government cannot function cloaked in secrecy. It cannot function unless officials tell the truth. The Constitution only works when the . . . branches of government trust one another and cooperate.

—CONGRESSMAN LEE H. HAMILTON

The events surrounding the Iran–contra affair of 1986–87 and the Pentagon procurement scandal of 1988 raised many questions about the ethical climate in Washington as well as the role of the military as it tries to operate in the bureaucratic and political jungle of the Pentagon, the White House, and Congress.

Although I have touched upon issues relating to personal and institutional integrity throughout this book, I would like to devote this chapter to discussing some of the ethical dilemmas that face our military officials. As long as military budgets are large and as long as there are many active-duty and reserve officers and non-commissioned officers working in Washington, the military's presence here will remain high. The military's interaction with Congress and with the various departments within the executive branch will continue to be complex and important.

The military ethic of a strong institutional and personal commitment to duty, honor, and country has served this nation well in war and peace for over 200 years. The concept of civilian control of the military is deeply ingrained in our national culture and is one of the great strengths of our constitutional system. Unlike so many other nations, we have not had to face a real problem with a "man on horseback" with desires or plans for a military coup. This great democracy has been blessed by a long line of military leaders who respected and followed the very basic democratic tenet of civilian control. The "Bonapartist" phenomena is unknown in the American political culture.

But let's face it—Washington is a tough political town and there are pressures from various sources that make it difficult for military men and women at all levels to stay true to the traditional military ethical concepts of duty, honor, and country. It may be useful to break down the Washington scene into a couple of segments: the interaction of the military with Congress, and the interaction of military officials with various parts of the executive branch of our government.

Military interaction with Congress. Perhaps most interesting is the military relationship with Congress. There is a constant, daily stream of military people going to Capitol Hill to brief staffers, to meet with individual congressmen, and to give testimony in open and closed hearings to subcommittees and committees of both houses.

Senators and Representatives have strong local interests and often take positions that serve their constituencies but do not necessarily serve the national interest. For instance, if there are military bases in their districts or if there is a defense contractor or subcontractor with a production facility in their district, they are very unlikely to vote in favor of closing the base or canceling the weapons system (or subsystem) being built in their district. In fact, they are likely to work very hard against any position of the Department of Defense that might put some of their constituents out of a job. Congress is a place where deals are made, votes are traded, and political "log rolling" takes place. Rational decision making, where the best choice among a number of viable options is picked irrespective of political considerations, is not the name of the game. It is awfully easy for a military person to become cynical about this process and to begin to see Congress first as incompetent, then as an impediment to progress, and finally as the enemy.

Although the process of making laws and passing appropriation bills to fund these laws is a messy one, the interests of many groups are being heard; the result, though far from perfect, is representative government at work. Since this whole process is clearly part of the system that underlies our constitutional form of government, it is incumbent upon those who have sworn allegiance to the Constitution to work with a high sense of purpose and integrity in full cooperation with congressmen and staffers.

Having testified many times to many committees and subcommittees of both houses of Congress, I have noticed how parochial interests tend to balance themselves out. In most cases, Congress makes good decisions, if not perfect ones. What also has impressed me is the lack of leaks by members of Congress and staffers. I have briefed committees of Congress on a number of very sensitive, compartmentalized programs, and not one of these programs has ever been leaked by any of the members or staffers that I briefed.

One of the cardinal rules for military people in dealing with Congress is never to lie. It is wrong, and it is clearly a violation of a military person's constitutional responsibility. Much less important, but certainly of interest, is the fact that if you lie you will be caught and you will never have any credibility in Congress *for the rest of your life.* It is amazing how long memories are on the Hill. Most congressmen and key staffers stay for decades. You can go away for years, come back and find most of the *same* people in the *same* committees facing you in the *same* hearing room. It is important for military people, no matter what position they hold, not to assume that their wisdom is greater than the collective wisdom of the Congress and the people they represent. This mistake is made often. I am appalled at the arrogance of some military people who think that they are always right and the Congress is always wrong when it will not support their position.

A final point about Congress: what if you are told by your boss that he or she wants you to "cook the numbers" or not tell the whole story in your upcoming testimony? May I suggest the following course of action. Reply by saying, "If you want me to testify,

I must have the authority to tell the truth; I just can't go to the Hill and lie." If you don't think this approach will work, may I suggest that you go to the Hill anyway, tell the truth, and accept whatever consequences result.

Ethics within the executive branch of government. Switching to the subject of ethics within the executive branch, the problems are many. In the interest of protecting your boss, defending your service, or serving your ambitions (and for lots of other reasons), it is very easy to sell your soul incrementally. If the goals you and your service are pursuing are good and honest ones, you may feel the pressure to lie as a means to carry out those goals. One thing is worth remembering in this regard: duty, honor, country should not and does not apply just to ends, it also applies to *means*. Military women and men should not follow those tenets of Machiavelli that advocated unethical behavior; the American democracy in the later part of the twentieth century is not the Italy of the sixteenth century and we should not follow the rules outlined for Machiavelli's prince.

Too many people in the Pentagon see another service, the Joint Staff, or the Office of the Secretary of Defense as the enemy and are willing to act unethically if necessary to win the bureaucratic wars. So often the rationale is along the following lines, "If we don't 'game' the POM (the overall departmental program for the upcoming six years), OSD will kill some of our most important programs." Or more subtly, "If we show weakness toward this program, OSD or Congress will kill it." Military services must, of course, understand the bureaucratic and political rules of the game, but they can still live within the framework of high institutional and personal integrity. If standing up for a principle costs you a promotion, a great new job, or forced retirement, so be it. Happily, what often happens when a person maintains his integrity is that the boss backs down when he or she understands how strongly the subordinate feels. The boss may be mad at you at first but learns to respect and treasure you as a person who always tells the truth. It is the responsibility of everyone in the chain of command to take a stand on issues of integrity. If the integrity level of the boss is not too high, you can often raise it by taking a stand.

There are those who think that nothing of importance can be accomplished in the bureaucratic quagmire of Washington without bending the rules, "cooking the numbers," or misleading the enemy, but, of course, they are wrong. Let me trace some recent history. From the time of the invasion of Afghanistan on Christmas eve of 1979 until 1986 much was accomplished under two presidents to strengthen our defenses and to deal with international crises without serious violations of integrity. There have been some problems with integrity in the 1986–1988 period, but these problems have been the exception, not the norm. It is not when we have told the truth that our policies have failed; it is when we have lied and misled people in the executive branch and in Congress that the United States has stumbled badly.

I would hope that in the years ahead the military can lead the way in raising the level of integrity throughout our government by setting good examples and by maintaining a sense of outrage when uncovering legal or ethical violations. For those who operate in the corridors of power both now and in the future, a useful model for them to emulate is George C. Marshall—a leader, a man of great vision and, most important, a man of towering integrity throughout his long and distinguished career of public service. In the brilliant book, *Commander in Chief,* Eric Larabee tells the story of Brigadier General Marshall in 1938, when he strongly disagreed with President Franklin Roosevelt on an important issue. Marshall clearly felt that FDR was wrong and that someone had to tell the president the truth directly and forthrightly. A year later Roosevelt chose Marshall to be the new chief of staff of the Army. When you look at what Marshall accomplished as Army chief of staff, as secretary of state, and as secretary of defense, it is easy to come to the conclusion that when Roosevelt picked this honest man for a position of great influence it was the most important personnel decision of his 12-year presidency.

Finally, a word about the integrity of political appointees in the Pentagon. The Pentagon procurement scandal of 1988 clearly demonstrates how political appointees can tarnish the reputation of the Department of Defense and everyone who works in the Pentagon. It is incumbent on all civilian officials in the Pentagon to establish and maintain a position of integrity that is as high or higher than that of the military services. This responsibility is absolutely fundamental. Those senior civilian leaders in government (or anyone else) who would politicize the military and who would reward the bureaucratic street fighters rather than the people of substance and honesty do a terrible disservice to our great democracy. In addition, those who accept money or other compensation from defense contractors or consultants are as much of a threat to our system of government as any foreign enemy.

The name of the game in the Pentagon for the future, for both military and civilian officials, must be subordinates who demonstrate a deeper commitment to personal and institutional integrity than to their personal ambitions and bosses who respect, support, and reinforce that commitment.

23

FUTURE SHOCK:
PENTAGON CHANGES
THROUGH THE YEAR 2000

I am interested in the future because that is where I
intend to spend the rest of my life.

—ANONYMOUS

Many feel that the Pentagon is like a giant log floating slowly down a turbulent river. This log has lots of ants running around on top who stick their legs into the water on occasion to try to steer the log in some direction or the other. Some of these ants have somewhat longer legs than others, some seem to avoid ever sticking their legs in the water, while some others fall or are pushed off the log. Most seem to be in a great hurry as they run from one side of the log to the other. Some shout a lot, and others are rather quiet. In recent years the ants have bought lots of computers, word processors, photocopiers, and overhead projectors, but these technological innovations do not seem to have much impact on the log itself, which continues its voyage largely unaffected by what the ants seem to do.

This steering-the-log metaphor has much validity. In fact, a brilliant unpublished paper written more than 20 years ago by a lieutenant colonel named Beavers entitled "Steering the Log" is still worth reading today. However, the river, the log, and the ants on top will undergo some major changes over the next 10 or 15 years. The river will bend slowly as America looks more to the west and south and less to the east and across the north pole. The log will grow much smaller as military manpower, force structure, and oversseas deployments diminish in the face of continued budgetary austerity under presidents from both political parties. A few of the ants will grow quite large and will be sporting some rather long legs. The log will be not only smaller but also a little more steerable.

How will the Pentagon change in the years ahead? Let me make a few predictions.

The electronic office. The electronic office is slowly becoming a significant reality in the 1990s after many stops and starts and many broken promises. With computers, advanced word processors, better software packages, modems, and laser printers in combination with a very large number of people who can make this equipment sing, life is becoming a bit easier for many. Even today, in many offices there is an opportunity for the coordination of routine packages through electronic mail and electronic coordination. The amount of time saved in the simple but time-consuming coordination of papers will by the late 1990s be rather impressive. By the turn of the century, the use of automatic dictation machines will make an impact. When the day comes when action officers can routinely talk into a smart machine and out will come a staff summary sheet, a message, or an action paper, life in the Building will change dramatically. Some agencies and services will get this technology in place faster than others. Those that do so will perform at a higher level than others moving more slowly. Some folks will find that giving dictation to a smart machine will be difficult, and the chronic mumblers may have some problems. However, for most, the learning process will be speedy and those who already know how to dictate well will make the transition easily.

Built into these machines will be some artificial intelligence, including spelling and syntax checkers as well as formatted software that, on command, will print out the words onto the correct form. Whereas in the past an action officer would have to go to some analyst for help with a complex problem, many action officers now have programs on their office computers that allow them to do quite sophisticated analysis, answer their bosses' "what if" questions, and accomplish various analytical exercises easily.

There is something being lost, however, with the reduced need to race up and down the hall to get information, find some analytical help, and coordinate papers and packages. People must make a greater effort to get out of their offices to make sure they stay up to speed on all the latest issues and rumors. However, there will always be plenty of meetings. The electronic office will not appreciably reduce the social need for folks to get together for meetings. There will, however, be a bit less traffic from outside Washington since teleconferencing will finally be feasible. Not as many people will have to fly all the way from Europe, Asia, and around the United States to attend meetings. Teleconferencing will, however, present problems because of time-zone differences around the world. Lots of meetings will be scheduled around the noon hour in Washington so the people in Europe, Washington, and elsewhere in the United States can all tune in without a great deal of scheduling hardship. The folks in Hawaii will find themselves reverting to the pre-World War II (and pre-air conditioning) pattern of coming in very early, not to beat the heat, but to join a teleconference that started at noon, Washington time. Those who serve in Asia will be most disadvantaged by the trend toward teleconferencing, since it will mean midnight meetings for some.

"Black" programs turning "white." A fascinating phenomenon is taking place in the field and the fleet during the 1990s. The many compartmentalized programs that were born in the 1980s behind "green doors" all over the Building have become operational. They are undergoing the slow and often painful transition from black to grey to white. Some of the defense critics of the 1980s will be less vocal as they see these programs emerge from the compartmentalized world. A few will even admit that had they known about these programs earlier, they would have been less critical about how the military was spending its R&D money.

Unloading the dogs. Systematic divestiture activity will take place in each of the military departments in the 1990s. Planners are attacking the problem of coherent divestiture of obsolescent weapons systems, organizations, and doctrines as they develop better analytical techniques, models, war games, and simulations to address the capabilities and costs of military systems. These analytical techniques will more systematically identify the dogs and, despite some resistance from the war lords in the field, divestiture will become a bit easier and more systematic. Serious base-closure initiatives, both in the United States and overseas, will continue to occur throughout the 1990s, and many of our more obsolete bases and posts will close. Although the closing of these bases will be costly in the short run, the long-term savings will be considerable.

A diminishing defense budget. Whereas the real growth in the defense budget from the late 1950s through the late 1980s was a modest 1 percent per year (GNP growth was 2.5 percent per year), the defense budget throughout the 1990s will decrease dramatically. By the end of the twentieth century, the percentage of the gross national product spent on defense will drift down to 3 percent or less. As a result of this period of extended budgetary austerity, the size of the U.S. military will decrease to fewer than 1.2 million active-duty forces. There will also be a major reduction of U.S. forces stationed overseas, and our complex alliance structure that has served the free world so well will show more serious signs of weakness. The defense budget should stabilize at somewhat less than $230 billion (1995 dollars) through the late 1990s.

The vital role of the vice chairman. If there are two people to watch in the next few years, it is the chairman and vice chairman of the Joint Chiefs of Staff. How the successors to Colin Powell and David Jeremiah accomplish their key tasks and how quickly the position of vice chairman becomes institutionalized will help determine the relative influence of the Joint Staff and the relative power of the concept of jointness. With the chairman on the road a great deal, the vice chairman serves as the chairman on many occasions. This two-person team has provided the continuity of advice to the president and the secretary of defense, as well as the continuity of direction to the Joint Staff that was so sadly lacking in the pre-Goldwater–Nichols period. The vice chairmen have the full executive authority of the chairman and they have not hesitated to use this authority on many occasions. The vice chairman attends most of the Tank and executive sessions with the chiefs and therefore does not miss a beat when he chairs these meetings in the chairman's absence. As vice chairman of the Defense Acquisition Board, he is a heavy hitter in the whole weapons development and procurement business. As chairman of the Joint Requirements Oversight Council, he can exercise pressure on the services when he observes them developing duplicative weapons systems or not supporting joint programs. Despite the fact that the vice chairman serves on 18 separate committees and is therefore spread very thin, I fully expect that this position will grow in importance, therefore enhancing the influence and effectiveness of the chairman and the Joint Staff.

Competition among the services. In this period of negative growth, the normal expectation would be that the services would be less cooperative toward each other as they fight hard for scarce defense dollars. I think this will be the case but this conflict may be somewhat muted because of the changing sociology that has resulted from the Goldwater–Nichols Act.

The power of the Joint Staff. By the late 1990s, the Joint Staff, in my judgment, will have become the most talented and powerful staff in the entire federal government. The military services will find themselves working closely together, especially when the Joint Staff tries to push an imprudent idea through. Let me suggest a couple of modest analogies. For many years in Europe, there was tough competition and doctrinal disagreement between the two allied tactical air forces in the central region of Europe. The Second Allied Tactical Air Force, with its headquarters in Rheindahlen in northern Germany has, since its creation, been dominated by the British. The Fourth Allied Tactical Air Force, stationed a couple hundred miles to the south in Heidelberg, Germany, has always been dominated by the Americans. In the early 1970s, a new headquarters (Allied Air Forces Central Europe—AAFCE) was formed at Ramstein, Germany, and both of these allied tactical air forces were put under its control. These two air forces soon found themselves cooperating more as they found the new headquarters proposing some strange ideas and initiatives. The same thing happened when the National Defense University was formed in the mid-1970s, and the two war colleges (the National War College and the Industrial College of the Armed Forces) found it useful to cooperate more than they had before. Hence, because of the increasing power of the Joint Staff, interservice competition will at times become more muted. Whereas in the past the Air Staff usually considered the biggest adversary in the Pentagon to be the Navy Staff and vice versa, the Joint Staff could begin to play the role of the common adversary.

How Joint Staff officials handle their enhanced power may be the most important internal question in the Building of the 1990s. If the Joint Staff truly operates in the national interest and if it avoids the natural proclivity of staffs to take actions that serve narrow bureaucratic interests, the nation will be well served indeed.

To those who will serve on the Joint Staff in the 1990s, I would ask that you make a passionate commitment to serving your nation in the broadest context and waste no time in turf battles, power accumulation, or service bashing. To the rest of you who serve this country in the Building in the 1990s, I would appeal to you to look forward not backward and to build the military strategy, force structure, doctrines, and organizations that will serve us well for the first few decades of the twenty-first century.

To those who work *with* the Building but do not work *in* the Building, I would ask that you try to understand and be sympathetic to the pressures and the problems of these fine public servants; don't put pressure on them to do dumb, illegal, or unethical things. The Pentagon official has many more important things to do than waste time answering unimportant requests or demands from Congress, the White House, other federal departments and agencies, defense contractors, the media, or anyone else.

One final note for those who will work in the Pentagon. It is quite useful to remind yourself periodically that there is an authentic nobility in dedicating yourself to a nation that is the beacon of hope for much of the world. There is much less nobility when you dedicate yourself to the goals of your service or your subservice when its goals do not further the goals of the nation. The nobility of public service is badly tarnished by the zealots with their poverty of judgment and their unwillingness to pursue the greater good.

May the example of George Marshall inspire us all. He gave up his personal ambitions on many occasions; he pursued not the narrow goals and priorities of the U.S. Army or the U.S. military but the goals of the nation and the Western alliance. His willingness to take the time to do strategic planning, his careful mentoring of the innovators, and his abiding commitment to personal and institutional ethics stand as a beacon for all who will serve in the Pentagon throughout the 1990s and beyond.

APPENDIX A.
ANNOTATED
BIBLIOGRAPHY

The following is a short, selective list of books that I highly recommend. I have also included a list of books that I would suggest you either not read at all or read only in part.

RECOMMENDED BOOKS

The recommended books are listed in order of importance. In other words, if you do not have time to read them all start from the top.

Joseph Kruzel, ed., *American Defense Annual* (Lexington, Mass.: Lexington Books).

This annual, produced at the Mershon Center at the Ohio State University, includes numerous articles by some legitimate experts on national defense. Be sure to order the most current edition.

Annual Report to the Congress (Washington, D.C.: Government Printing Office).

This annual report of the Secretary of Defense has a wealth of useful information and lots of interesting charts and graphs. To get the current copy, just drop a note to the Superintendent of Documents, U.S. Government Printing Office, Washington, D.C. 20402-9325, with a check for the cost. GPO pays for the mailing costs.

Amos A. Jordan, et al., *American National Security: Policy and Process* (Baltimore: The Johns Hopkins Press, 1993).

Somewhat academic but well worthwhile.

Bob Woodward, *The Commanders* (New York: Simon and Schuster, 1991).

Woodward captures the story of the decision making for the Gulf War well; however, his use of quotes is fundamentally dishonest. So read this book with caution.

Margaret Truman, *Murder at the Pentagon* (New York: Random House, 1992).

Not a great novel, but a fun read that highlights some aspects of Pentagon life.

Henri Gault and Christian Millau, *The Best of Washington, D.C.* (Englewood Cliffs, N.J.: Prentice Hall, 1987).

This is the best guidebook of Washington on the market. Be sure to get the most recent edition.

Alfred Goldberg, *The Pentagon: The First Fifty Years* (Washington, D.C.: Government Printing Office, 1992).

Representatives Les Aspin and William Dickinson, *Defense for a New Era: Lessons of the Persian Gulf War* (McLean, Va.: Brassey's (US), 1992).

BOOKS THAT I DON'T RECOMMEND

Allen Drury, *Pentagon* (New York: Doubleday, 1986).

The first 11 pages are very well written. The rest is a long, rambling novel that has a first lieutenant in a powerful decision-making position (a lieutenant colonel perhaps, a lieutenant—never) and the chairman of the Joint Chiefs hopping in and out of bed with lots of prominent ladies of Washington (when would he ever have the time or the energy?). In addition, Drury has the jobs and the locations within the Building terribly confused. Also, he seems to be in some kind of time warp; he uses the language of the 1950s, not the 1980s—quite distracting.

   Diana Resor, *The Pentagon Underground* (New York: Times Books, 1985).

This book drips with paranoia and outrage. Occasionally it hits the mark with its criticism, but it is hardly worth the three or four hours it will take you to plow through it.

   John Lehman, former secretary of the Navy, writes books on defense issues. Unfortunately, his books provide little in the way of insight or objectivity.

Appendix B.
Sample Welcome
Letter

Those offices that send out the bland, two-paragraph welcome letter or that fail to send out a welcome letter at all are missing a great opportunity. The time between when someone learns of a Pentagon assignment and the arrival date should not be wasted. If you want to have well-prepared people, both in background and attitude, a warm, substantive welcome letter can assist quite appreciably.

Dear Major/Commander/Mr./Ms. A:

It is my great pleasure to welcome you to the X directorate on the Y staff here in the Pentagon. I have been personally involved in the selection process, and I am most pleased that my wishes have been honored and that you will be coming to the Pentagon to work in this important area. I have been in my job for over Z months and would like to explain to you the aspects of this work that I have found most interesting.

Our job here is quite simple: to develop the very best plans, programs, and policy that we can, not only to serve our nation well in the years ahead but also to serve the interests of our many allies who count on us so heavily. From my experience here, I have found that there are two areas that are quite difficult for us all. One is the ability to reach out into the future and to form a vision for our institution to move toward. Second, it is important to take a broad national view on issues and not slip into the trap of being interested only in our own speciality or individual service.

Both of these areas are so vital that I hope you will think about them before you come and that you will make a commitment to them both during your time with us.

You should be hearing from your sponsor shortly. Please do not hesitate to ask for advice and assistance. I can remember well when I first reported in to the Pentagon. Although it was an awesome experience in some ways, the learning experience was remarkable. I can still remember the thoughtful people who helped me during those first few months. I trust that you will get the same type of assistance as I did.

If for some reason you do not hear from your sponsor soon, please give my executive officer a call (telephone 000-111-2222) so we can ensure that you get the full welcome packet. In order to help you make the transition to this environment, I would like to suggest two books; I have read them both and have found them very helpful. Both are relatively short, available in paperback, and should be in your local library or bookstore. These books should not only teach you some useful things, they should also help you get into a mindset that will serve you well while you are here.

- *American Defense Annual* edited by Joseph Kruzel
- *Annual Report to the Congress* by the Secretary of Defense (be sure to get the latest edition—if you can't find it locally, contact the Government Printing Office for a copy).

In conclusion, I hope that you are as pleased with this assignment as I am. I feel very fortunate knowing that someone of your background and talent will be joining our team. We all look forward to working with you and getting to know you in the months ahead. Since there are only *xxx* people working for me, I am sure that you and I will get to know each other quite well in the months and years ahead.

Sincerely,

Appendix C.
Transition into the
Pentagon Checklist

Let's assume that you have this book in hand a month or so before you report to your first job in the Pentagon. These are the steps that I recommend that you take in the next few weeks.

1. *Read two or three books from my recommended list of books.* This short guide is not enough. If you are going to a joint job, make the *Joint Staff Officer's Guide* your first priority (be sure to get the latest edition). If you do not have much high-level staff experience, put *Tongue and Quill* at the top of the list. If you are going into a high-level plans or policy job, read *Thinking in Time.* See my annotated bibliography for a more complete list of books to read.

2. *Spend an afternoon with a friend who is an old Pentagon hand.* During this session do a lot of listening and try to keep the discussion from turning into a "good old times" session. Ask such probing questions as, What was your biggest setback? Who has been fired lately and why? Who are the people I should not trust? One caution—try to pick someone who is not a cynic.

3. *On a weekend, try out the commute with the whole family in the car.* This will teach family members how to get to and from the Building. Later, when you are stuck with no wheels and the buses aren't running, a member of your family can come to pick you up and have a reasonably good chance of finding the Pentagon and the spot where you are waiting.

4. *Get a Department of Defense Telephone Directory* (the Govern-

ment Printing Office sells them) and go through it carefully. It will teach you how the place is organized and lots of good information is contained between the covers. Being able to use that book quickly is one of the secrets to success for all Pentagon folks. Be sure to look through the bus schedule in the back, so you will know how to get to key locations around town easily and at no cost. By buying one, you'll have one at home.

5. *Check out the schools with your kids.* This will help their transition and help you understand better their lives and their commuting problems over the next few years.

6. *Check out the local medical, commissary, and PX/BX facilities with your family.* Life in the Washington area has become very expensive so it is useful to know where the bargains are as far as shopping and medical care.

7. *Take an objective look at the mechanical condition of your automobiles.* A breakdown or flat tire on the ramp to one of the superhighways can ruin your whole week, especially if the breakdown causes you to miss that key morning meeting with your flag officer boss. An older car makes a fine commuting vehicle if it has good tires and the engine, transmission, battery, and generator are in good condition. Also, check out your spouse's car; both cars must be able to operate efficiently in the increasing agony of heavy traffic.

8. *Take a hard look at yourself.* If you are overweight, a heavy smoker, or someone who doesn't exercise, it may be time to turn over a new leaf in your life. Your health in the Pentagon can deteriorate rapidly under the heavy pressure of the workload, short suspenses, and long hours in combination with bad personal habits. I have watched individuals age by ten years in less than three as they put on more weight, smoked even more heavily, and failed to exercise regularly. The high number of heart attacks that are handled by the Pentagon clinic each year is an indicator that the Pentagon can be as fatal to you as it has been for some others through the years, especially if you let bad habits get worse.

9. *Join the Army and Air Force Mutual Aid Society or the Navy Mutual Aid.* Every once in a while in life you stumble across something that is such a good deal, you want to tell all your friends about it. When General Custer and his troops were killed by the Indians, there was no one to take care of all the

widows and families left behind. Soon after, a society was formed to provide a whole range of service to Army officers and their families. Now all the services are covered and the deal is a great one for all officers. These two societies are superb. It sure is nice to have peace of mind as far as family benefits are concerned.

Appendix D.
Interview Checklist:
Some Questions
to Expect

Let me list the kind of questions that you are likely to be asked. At the end I will throw in a few others that I have used to test the quickness of mind and the vision of the candidate.

1. Do you really want this job and if so why?
2. What strengths and weaknesses will you bring to this job?
3. What are your long-range plans? Where would you like to be five years from now?
4. What has been your biggest setback? What did you learn from the experience?
5. If you don't get this job, whom would you recommend for it?
6. Is there anything in your professional or personal life that I should know about before I hire you?
7. What do you think are the three most important issues facing the Department of Defense today?
8. If I should call in some of your subordinates and ask for candid off-the-record evaluations of you, what would they tell me?
9. What good books have you read in the last five years? Which ones would you recommend to me? What professional journals do you find most helpful in keeping up with defense issues?
10. What questions would you have wished I had asked and didn't?
11. What questions do you have of me?

224

Bonus questions for the finalists for some big jobs

12. What two or three major events in your life helped make you the person you are today?

13. It is now the year 2025, there is a black tie dinner for 3,000 being held in New York. The president of the United States is there to give the annual George C. Marshall Award for distinguished lifelong public service in the national security field. You are the recipient. What did you do to deserve this award?

APPENDIX E.
THE HEARTBREAK
OF HOUSE HUNTING

This is a time for objective pessimism, but also a time for subjective optimism.

—WILLIAM BUCKLEY

When you get the word that you are headed for the Pentagon, two of the very first questions you ask yourself are, "Where will I live?" and "How can I afford it?" Unfortunately, time is often short, and you may need to make a decision within a few days or a few weeks. The realities of escalating housing costs since the mid-1970s come home to the house hunter very quickly. It can be very tough, but not impossible, to find a home that is near the Pentagon, near job opportunities for your spouse, with good schools nearby, and one that is reasonably priced. Let me share with you my insights. Having lived in West Springfield, McLean, Bolling Air Force Base, Fort McNair, and northwest Washington, and having talked to many who have struggled with the real estate market quite recently, I may have a useful idea or two for you.

Realities of the real estate market. In the history of the real estate market in the Washington area since World War II, there have been some interesting cycles of growth, downturn, and no growth. When interest rates get very high, the real estate market stagnates, and it's very hard to sell your home. Potential buyers find that the monthly house payments are just too high. What happens during

226

these periods is that many people coming in to the area rent houses. If, later on, the interest rates go down considerably, they will often buy a house and move out of the house they are renting. On occasion, there is significant downturn in the real estate market, and the value of houses actually goes down (in 1989–1992, for example). This does not happen often, but when it does the impact can be devastating. In recent years there have also been times when the value of homes in the area has stagnated (the early 1980s, for example). Although the acceleration of home prices has benefited those who bought in the 1960s, 1970s, and early 1980s, high prices make it tough on those arriving in the area in the mid- and late 1990s.

The basic considerations. When you come to Washington, you'll have three basic choices: buy, rent, or apply for government housing. If you apply for government housing you may have to wait 12 months or more. In the meantime, you may have to leave the family where they are or rent in the area until housing at Ft. Belvoir, Bolling Air Force Base, Quantico, or wherever becomes available.

One of the factors to consider when you make a choice between buying and renting is whether you will want to keep the house when you leave. The differential between your house payment and what the house may rent for could get you into a negative cash flow situation for many years. For instance, if your monthly house payments are $1,800 and you could rent the house for only about $1,100, you might find yourself unable to handle this negative cash flow situation and have to sell the house when you are reassigned. If you choose to buy, here is my advice.

Be a long-term planner. If you possibly can, try to find the house that you'll be happy with now and on subsequent Washington tours over the next 15 years. If you decide to keep the house as an investment, you will have a home to move back into when you return for the next Washington assignment. Pick a house that will serve you well with kids still at home but will also be fine later when the kids have gone off to college or to work. Pick a school district that has high-quality schools nearby. When you finally sell the house and leave the Washington area for the last time, the school district will still be an important factor to many of the people house hunting.

Take a look at traffic patterns. Try to ascertain what the rush-hour traffic situation is today and whether it will stay about the same or get worse in the years ahead. For instance, the completion of Route 66 in the late 1970s relieved traffic from the McLean and Great Falls area since much of the traffic that used to use the George Washington Parkway from the north shifted over to Route 66. Of course, most commuting routes have become steadily worse with each passing year. However, if the Washington bypasses are completed (and all through truck traffic is routed around Washington during rush hours), if double car pool lanes are put in on Route 66 outside the Beltway, if the Dulles tollroad is extended to Leesburg (with HOV lanes included), and if the double car pool lanes on I-95 are built all the way to Fredericksburg, the commuting problems could ease somewhat from some locations.

Before you begin to explore the area, be sure to buy a copy of the *Washington, D.C. and Vicinity Street Map* (see D.C.-area map on pages 256–257. Published by ADC of Alexandria, these street maps—with indexed streets, place names, postal zones, and other features—are absolutely indispensable! Be sure you buy the one that covers your neighborhood; you can pick one up at convenience, drug, office supply, or book stores and at newsstands everywhere. Your best bet is to buy a copy for every car you own, or one day, while you're desperately lost, you'll discover a family member has "borrowed" your map book *again!!* Many of my friends keep copies in their offices. They really help when you're running late getting the boss to that meeting across town.

Make your choice based on a complete analysis of options. A few years ago, Dr. Steve Knode of the National Defense University developed a decision matrix and a computer program that was designed to help make these tough housing decisions on a rational basis. This program was not a great success, for it forced people to make explicit value judgments that they preferred to make only implicitly. Just for fun, however, you might want to sit down with your family and list in order the most important priorities that you have.

- Quality of schools for kids
    - private versus public
    - small versus large (some kids get lost in the megaschools with 2,000 kids or more)
    - quality and morale of the teachers
    - diversity of course offerings
    - special programs for the gifted or the learning impaired
    - sports and extracurricular activities
    - drugs on school grounds
    - discipline in classroom
    - academic motivation of the children
- Proximity of house to spouse's work place
- Proximity of house to Pentagon
- Preference to buy
- Preference to rent
- Preference for house
- Preference for townhouse
- Preference for apartment
- Size of house desired
- Size of house needed

After listing as many relevant factors as you can think of, weigh each with a numerical score; you may be surprised with the results. If there are major differences in viewpoints among family members, it is useful to know them ahead of time. If you can resolve these differences, your house-hunting chores can be easier. Remember, you will sleep there; your family will *live* there.

Be careful when you pick a real estate agent. Probably the best approach is to ask around among friends and colleagues. Pick a real estate agent who comes strongly recommended. Try to avoid someone who just got a real estate license last month. Before you commit to any real estate agent, be sure that this person has time to devote to your house search. (If this person is about to take off on a three-week vacation and wants to hand you off to the newest agent in the office, you should go elsewhere.) Avoid real estate people who have rigid mindsets (you *must* buy, you *must* rent, Fairfax County is the *only* place to live, etc.)

Living in close. If, by chance, you are independently wealthy, have no children, and your spouse is sure of finding a high-paying job, your search for housing close to the Pentagon will be rather easy. In this case, you can find a fine apartment in the nearby Rosslyn or Crystal City areas. You can be within close Metro distance to the Pentagon and many of the good employment opportunities for spouses. Although apartments in these two nearby areas are expensive either to rent or buy, they are really quite reasonable when compared to other American cities. For between $1,200 and $2,500 a month, you can rent some nice two-bedroom apartments.

If you want to buy in close, there are a number of older homes (40 to 70 years old) and newer townhouses inside the Beltway and within a 15-minute drive to the Building in the $200,000 to $350,000 range. If you want to live in close and have school-age children, you might consider private schools.

The outer suburbs. If you have school-age kids (and you prefer public schools) and yours is a one-income family, you may wish to check out the outer suburbs (five miles or more beyond the Beltway and 15 miles or more from the Pentagon). The tendency over the past 20 years or so is for families to live farther away and endure the long commute to the Pentagon in order to find good public schools and reasonable house payments. These two important considerations drive many to the outer suburbs where an hour's commute (or more) each way is the norm. There are lots of advantages to the outer suburbs, including reasonably priced houses and townhouses, bigger lots, newer homes, nice neighborhoods, and good public schools. The biggest disadvantage is the long commute, but many find it relatively easy to adjust to the long drive or have work hours that enable them to miss the worst of the rush hour traffic.

However, many recent arrivals are refusing to spend so much of their time commuting and are choosing older homes. These homes at first glance seem very small, out of date, and somewhat run-down, but they have great potential for upgrading. This option is certainly worth pursuing since some of the older neighborhoods are making nice comebacks, and the purchase of an older home that you could upgrade could be one of the better investments of the 1990s.

If you decide to buy, select your lender with care. There are many reputable lenders in the area. The Pentagon Credit Union and the Navy Federal Credit Union may be able to beat the competition and should be considered along with lenders that your real estate agent might recommend. In order to qualify for a loan, you will need credit information, income and tax information, and a balance in your checking or savings account large enough to cover the down payment. The more of this you have available, the quicker you can act when you find the home of your choice.

Don't forget the advantages of living near the Metro (see map on page 258). Most old-timers will tell you that houses in the areas that are within walking distance of Metro stations are accelerating in value. As traffic gets worse and worse and as insurance rates rise for automobiles used for commuting, the Metro option will become more attractive to many. Commuting time on the Metro can be more productive than time in traffic. You will learn more reading the paper or a good book than you will learn by listening to the radio in traffic.

Let me give some specific examples of areas on the way up that are near Metro stops. First, the area immediately to the west of Crystal City has lots of smaller homes that were built in the 1920s. At first glance, these houses seem expensive for their age and size, but the area is bound to boom and it may not be too late to find a home which you could fix up. Being near Crystal City, Pentagon City, the Army–Navy Country Club, and the Pentagon makes this area quite an attractive location.

The areas to the west of Rosslyn that are within walking distance of the Ballston, Virginia Square, Clarendon, and Court

House Metro stations all have great potential. Stores, restaurants, office buildings are all moving into these areas. What had become rather unattractive neighborhoods are coming back strongly. The Metrobus is an excellent option, also.

It may be hard to pay big bucks for a small 70-year-old house that cost less than $6,000 to build and has only 1,200 square feet of floor space. But the possibilities are endless for turning houses like these into great homes with high resale value. Some of the remodeling you may wish to do yourself; for the bigger renovations, there are many companies in the area that specialize in renovations of older homes. If you do decide to go this route and you are looking for remodeling firms, be sure to get at least three estimates, and before you make your final choice, check out the reliability of the contractor that you favor. Many have been burned by picking the lowest bidder, making a down payment, and finding out later that the firm is bankrupt and the owner just skipped town.

The hottest new factor: Rail service from Fredericksburg and Manassas. At long last, the Virginia Railway Express became a reality in Northern Virginia in 1992. One line runs from Fredericksburg through Brooke, Quantico, Featherstone, Woodbridge, Springfield, and Alexandria. The other runs from Manassas through Clifton, Fairfax Station, Burke, Springfield, and Alexandria. Both lines terminate at Union Station in the District of Columbia (see map, page 259). You may never ride one of these trains, but this new service will clearly impact on land values, housing values, and commuting patterns. If you do decide to use the trains, you will want to get off in Alexandria and change to the Metro in order to get to the Pentagon. The cost will be from $5.00 to $10.00 a day, but the savings will be less wear and tear on your car and your nerves, reduced car insurance, and a chance to do some reading to and from work.

The option of renting. If you decide to rent, there is much less need to do long-range planning. If you think this will be the only time you will be assigned to the Washington area, if you can afford to rent a nice home but can't afford to buy that same home, if you don't want to sink too much of your savings into a big down payment, renting can be the best decision. In general terms, you will have more discretionary income if you rent than if you buy since that big check you must write at the first of each month will be less. However, don't forget that you will need to write a check for one month's rent plus a security deposit when you apply to rent. Also remember that rentals are generally available to see only two to four weeks before occupancy, so if you don't plan to move to Washington until three months in the future, you are a little early to start your quest for that rental home. There are many sources for rentals, including friends, the suburban papers, the Pentagon bulletin board, and the major Washington newspapers.

Pets can be a real factor if you are trying to find a place to rent. If, for instance, your dog weighs more than 40 pounds, you may not be accepted. Many places have a strict no-pets rule, while others will accept a cat but not a dog. Be sure to ask the pet question early, before you fall in love with that rental home or apartment. Please keep in mind one caution about renting: If your landlord is a military or government employee and returns to the area in the middle of your Pentagon assignment, you can get booted out and have to make a disruptive move at your expense.

Recent trends. With the incredible acceleration of housing values within the last couple of years, the trend among new arrivals to the Pentagon is toward renting rather than buying. Just before this book went to press, I interviewed an action officer who is renting and is in a car pool with four others, all of whom rent. This is quite a change from the past when it was rather unusual to find someone who had a family and was serving on a full four-year tour who had not purchased a house somewhere in the area. As long as there is a considerable differential between the rent and the house payments on the same home, this trend should continue. Since the 1986 omnibus tax law still gives the home owner a significant tax break, buying a home certainly has its advantages. But the choice is now a very close one, and the renting option clearly is a prudent one for many.

Final caution. Crime has accelerated dramatically in recent years in the District of Columbia, Prince George's County, Maryland, and in Arlington and Alexandria in Virginia. The situation will deteriorate even further, especially in the District, as the quality and morale of the District's police force continue to decline. Those who may be inclined to live in these areas should weigh the crime situation in their decision making.

APPENDIX F.
FAMILY, CULTURAL, ACADEMIC, AND JOB OPPORTUNITIES

We are like trees; we must create new leaves, new directions in order to grow.

—ANONYMOUS

Living in Washington in the last decade of the twentieth century is like living in London in the nineteenth century, Paris in the eighteenth century, Madrid in the seventeenth century, Florence or Venice in the sixteenth century.

It is not only the nation's capital; it is the center of the world. The city of Washington is lovely with its marvelous design, its restrictive covenants governing the height of buildings, its glorious architecture, its liberal use of white marble, and its relative dearth of industrial pollution. Many of the sights can be seen free of charge, and except during the busy tourist seasons, the sights are quite accessible.

A walk or a jog around the Tidal Basin will take you past the Jefferson, Lincoln, and Washington memorials; an early morning trip in late March when the cherry blossoms are in full bloom and before the hordes of tourists have arrived is a very special pleasure. There may be no more beautiful large city in the world than Washington in the springtime. The National Capital Park region each year plants 70 large flower beds with 280,000 flowers, including

235

145,000 tulips and 25,000 daffodils. The sea of color around the Mall, the Tidal Basin, and the area to the north and east of the Pentagon is spectacular. When someone suggests that you should take some time and smell the flowers, you will have plenty of places to do just that.

Once you get settled into your home, you will find that many out-of-town friends will let you know they are coming to Washington for a visit. Showing them around can be a special pleasure. At the end of this chapter, I have made some suggestions of my favorite places in the area, in case the many suggestions in the guidebooks of Washington boggle your mind.

For anyone involved in school work at any level from junior high to postdoctoral work, the research facilities available are truly impressive. The Library of Congress is accessible by Metro, and all the major departments and agencies of the executive branch of our government have impressive libraries. The library of the National Defense University at Ft. McNair is a pleasant place to do research and parking there is normally not a problem; the Pentagon Library itself is excellent, although it is not open at night or on the weekends.

Although a cultural wasteland until recently, Washington now takes pride in the Kennedy Center, Arena Stage, the National Theater, Ford's Theater, and Wolf Trap in the summer, to name just a few of the theaters. First-rate opera, musicals, drama, and concerts are available throughout the year. The museums are superb (there are 56 at last count). In addition to its National Air and Space Museum, the Smithsonian provides a rich offering, indeed. The National Portrait Gallery, the Hirshhorn Museum and Sculpture Garden, and the Corcoran Gallery of Art are a few of the world-class museums that beckon to us all.

An area of great cultural and ethnic diversity, Washington has restaurants that reflect an extraordinary blend of culinary tastes and ethnic and national backgrounds. The best restaurants are in northwest Washington, Georgetown, Bethesda, and Old Town Alexandria, but there are many fine restaurants in the outer suburbs. The *Washingtonian* magazine rates the restaurants on a regular basis; its ratings as far as quality of food, service, ambience, and price are quite accurate and up to date.

Washington has two major newspapers: the *Washington Post* is slightly left of center (although its editorial page is quite well balanced) and the *Washington Times* to the right. Both newspapers have excellent weekend sections that tell the reader on Thursday or Friday what is happening over the coming weekend. You can get home delivery of the *New York Times,* the *Wall Street Journal, USA Today,* the two Washington papers as well as suburban papers like the *Journal.* The papers usually arrive quite early (before 6:00 A.M.), which is awfully nice for folks who must leave very early for work.

Job opportunities for spouses are reasonably good, in part because there is a large turnover of people each year as government employees and their families come and go. The federal government now employs less than half of the work force in the area, so there are not only opportunities for jobs in the executive branch and on Capitol Hill, but there are also many openings in the private sector. Washington has become a high-tech town in the last few years, and if your spouse has a background in computer programming, computer repair, software development, database management, or artificial intelligence, jobs are rather plentiful. Real estate is a popular field for employment, and with the prices of houses, townhouses, and condominiums so high and with the 6 percent real estate fee the norm, the opportunity to make big bucks in this business is quite good. Employment opportunities in education are good from the pre-school level to the fine universities in the area. Retail marketing is also a growing field. There are some jobs available in the many high-quality department stores that sprinkle the area. The arrival of Nordstrom from the West Coast in the late 1980s has brought high-quality service to the customer back to Washington, and many of the other stores are working hard to mirror the grand example that Nordstrom has set. There are a number of large malls and the competition that they provide each other is very healthy. At one time, Tysons Corner (just outside the Beltway in Fairfax County, Virginia) was the best place to shop, but as parking there became difficult and as the Springfield, Fair Oaks, Potomac Mills, and other malls opened, Tysons Corner's reputation slid downhill. The management of Tysons finally woke up, put in more parking, brought in Nordstrom, modernized some facilities, and Tysons—in combination with the new Tysons II—is coming back strongly. However, the hottest area for the 1990s is Pentagon City, which of course is very convenient to those who are able to live close to the Building.

The colleges and universities in the area provide a rich diversity of programs and courses. George Mason University in Fairfax, Virginia, is the most aggressive university in the area. George Johnson, the dynamic president of George Mason, did wonders by bringing a small, second-rate school into national prominence in the 1980s. By hiring excellent professors, opening new research centers, and getting the financial backing of the Northern Virginia business community, George Mason now has much to offer the newcomer. George Washington, Georgetown, and American universities are all fine institutions and each seems to improve every year. Being located in northwest Washington has many advantages, but these three schools are less accessible than George Mason to those many Pentagon people who live in the outer suburbs of Virginia. The University of Maryland is quite convenient for those who live in Maryland and in the District and has a number of very strong departments (the public affairs department—political science, public administration, government—is very impressive).

The University of South California and Central Michigan University have excellent programs, which are tailored for the Pentagon people and employees in other federal departments and agencies. To give a specific example, the master's program in administrative management from Central Michigan University offers a master's-level course every month. For someone with the time and energy, it is possible to complete all the course work, finish the master's project, and obtain the degree in one year. Most, however, wisely take more time and obtain the degree in 18 months or so. This Central Michigan University program is particularly attractive to those who have graduated from the U.S. Army schools at Fort Leavenworth, since Central Michigan allows constructive credit for some of the professional courses taken there. I have had the pleasure of lecturing in graduate programs at American, George Mason, George Washington, and Central Michigan and was quite impressed with the quality of both the courses and the students at all of these schools.

When the boxes are unpacked and you have a little time to begin to explore the area, I think you will find that the best guidebook is Gault and Millau's *The Best of Washington, D.C.* Subtitled "the only guide that distinguishes the truly superlative from the merely overrated," it is on target in most areas. Its only major weakness is its second-rate maps.

Since all of the Washington guidebooks give so much information, it is a little hard to know where to start. Hence, I would like to close this chapter with a list of recommended things to do and see in the area. This is not based on a systematic analysis, but is an impressionistic list from someone who has lived in Washington off and on for 40 years and who has sampled many parts of the scene.

DINING

Recommended informal restaurant	R. T.'s in Arlington
Recommended more formal restaurant	Chez François L'Aubèrge in Great Falls
Recommended elegant restaurant	Prime Rib in Washington, D.C.
Recommended restaurant overlooking the Potomac River	The Potowmack Landing
Recommended luncheon restaurant	Le Rivage in Washington, D.C.
Recommended carry-out chicken	Crisp and Juicy in Arlington
Recommended Italian restaurant	The Alpine in Arlington

Recommended after-theater restaurant	Dominique's in Washington, D.C.
Recommended tavern	Middleton Tavern in Annapolis

ENTERTAINMENT AND RELAXATION

Recommended theater seat	First row in the balcony at Ford's Theater
Recommended theater in summer	Wolf Trap (Vienna)
Recommended movie house	Uptown Theater on Connecticut Avenue
Recommended movie about Washington	*Mr. Smith Goes to Washington* (starring Jimmy Stewart)
Recommended spot to watch fireworks	Ft. McNair during Riverfest in June
Recommended place to take children	National Zoo
Recommended park	T. R. Roosevelt Island in the Potomac
Recommended tennis courts	The outdoor courts at Fort McNair
Recommended museum	National Portrait Gallery
Recommended jogging areas	Around the Tidal Basin, around Hains Point, a tour around the Lincoln, Washington, and Jefferson memorials
Recommended bike path	Along the George Washington Parkway
Recommended place for a weekend	Maryland Inn in Annapolis
Recommended day trip	To Gettysburg (read *Killer Angels* first)

SHOPPING

Recommended department store	Nordstrom

Recommended discount men's store	Today's Man (Bailey's Crossroads)
Recommended commissary/PX/gas station complex	Bolling AFB
Recommended shopping centers	Tysons I and II in McLean

MISCELLANEOUS

Recommended book about Washington	David Brinkley's *Washington Goes to War*
Recommended speaker	Congressman Newt Gingrich
Recommended leadership program	GWU's Contemporary Executive Development Program
Recommended auditorium	Arnold Auditorium at the National War College
Recommended professors	Bard O'Neill (National War College), Jim Pfiffner (George Mason)
Recommended library	Army library in the Pentagon
Recommended foot race	Army ten-miler in October, Marine Corps marathon in November
Recommended airlines	*Out of National:* Delta *Out of Dulles:* United
Recommended departure point from Washington	The magnificently restructured Union (train) Station near the Capitol
Recommended magazine about Washington	The *Washingtonian*

Appendix G.
Glossary

AAW	Antiair Warfare
AAWS	Airborne Adverse Weather Weapons Systems
ABM	Antiballistic Missile
AC	Active Component
ACCS	Army Command and Control System
ACM	Advanced Cruise Missile
ACMR	Air Combat Maneuvering Range
ACIP	Aviation Career Incentive Pay
Ada	DoD Computer Programming Language
ADATS	Air Defense/Antitank System
ADCAP	Advanced Capability (torpedo)
ADDS	Army Data Distribution System
ADI	Air Defense Initiative
ADP	Automated Data Processing
AE	Assault Echelon
AFV	Armored Family of Vehicles
AGR	Active Guard and Reserve
AID	Agency for International Development
AIDS	Acquired Immune Deficiency Syndrome
AIM	Air-Intercept Missile
AIS	Automated Information System

242

ALCM	Air-Launched Cruise Missile
ALMV	Air-Launched Miniature Vehicle
ALS	Advanced Launch System
AMRAAM	Advanced Medium-Range Air-to-Air Missile
ANG	Air National Guard
ANZUS	Australia-New Zealand-United States (Treaty)
AOCP	Aviation Officer Continuation Pay
AOE	Multipurpose Stores Ship
ASAT	Antisatellite
ASDS	Advanced SCM Delivery System
ASW	Antisubmarine Warfare
ATA	Advanced Tactical Aircraft
ATACMS	Army Tactical Missile System
ATAS	Air-to-Air Stinger
ATARS	Advanced Tactical Air Reconnaissance System
ATB	Advanced Technology Bomber
ATF	Advanced Tactical Fighter
ATM	Antitactical Missile
ATSD(IO)	Assistant to the Secretary of Defense (Intelligence Oversight)
AWACS	Airborne Warning and Control System
BA	Budget Authority
BAMC	Brooke Army Medical Center
BFV	Bradley Fighting Vehicle
BM/C^3	Battle Management/Command, Control, and Communications
BMEWS	Ballistic Missile Early Warning System
BSTS	Boost Surveillance and Tracking System
BTI	Balanced Technology Initiative
C^3	Command, Control, and Communications

C^3CM	Command, Control, and Communications Countermeasures
C^3I	Command, Control, Communications, and Intelligence
CBR	Chemical, Biological, Radiological
CDI	Conventional Defense Improvements
CHAMPUS	Civilian Health and Medical Program of the Uniformed Services
CINC	Commander in Chief
COCOM	Coordinating Committee for Multilateral Export Controls
COMSEC	Communications Security
CONUS	Continental United States
CRAF	Civil Reserve Air Fleet
CS	Competitive Strategies
CSI	Competitive Strategies Initiative
CSOC	Consolidated Space Operations Center
CV	Aircraft Carrier
CVN	Aircraft Carrier, Nuclear Powered
CY	Calendar Year or Current Year
DAB	Defense Acquisition Board
DARE	Drug Abuse Resistance Education
DARPA	Defense Advanced Research Projects Agency
DCAA	Defense Contract Audit Agency
DCIMI	Defense Council on Integrity and Management Improvement
DDDR&E(T&E)	Deputy Director, Defense Research, Engineering, Test, and Evaluation
DDG	Guided Missile Destroyer
DDN	Defense Data Network
DDS	Dry Deck Shelters

DDT&E	Director, Defense Test and Evaluation
DEPMEDS	Deployable Medical Systems
DEW	Directed-Energy Weapons, Distant Early Warning
DIA	Defense Intelligence Agency
DINET	Defense Industrial Network
DLA	Defense Logistics Agency
DMA	Defense Mapping Agency
DNA	Defense Nuclear Agency
DoD	Department of Defense
DoE	Department of Energy
DOT&E	Director, Operational Test and Evaluation
DPC	Defense Planning Committee
DPRB	Defense Planning and Resources Board
DRG	Diagnosis Related Group
DSB	Defense Science Board
DSCS	Defense Satellite Communications System
DSN	Defense Switched Network
DST	Defense and Space Talks
DTSA	Defense Technology Security Administration
EC	Electronic Combat
ECI	Employment Cost Index
ECM	Electronic Countermeasures
ELF	Extremely Low Frequency
ELV	Expendable Launch Vehicles
EMP	Electromagnetic Pulse
ENSCE	Enemy Situation Correlation Element
ERIS	Exoatmospheric Reentry Vehicle Interceptor System
ESF	Economic Support Fund

ESM	Electronic Support Measures
EW	Electronic Warfare
FAADS	Forward-Area Air Defense System
FFG	Guided Missile Frigate
FLOT	Forward Line of Troops
FMS	Foreign Military Sales
FMSCR	Foreign Military Sales Credit (Financing)
FOFA	Follow-On Forces Attack
FORSCOM	Forces Command
FY	Fiscal Year
FYDP	Future Years Defense Program
GAO	General Accounting Office
GLCM	Ground-Launched Cruise Missile
GNP	Gross National Product
GOCO	Government-Owned Contractor Operated
GPS	Global Positioning System
G-R-H	Gramm-Rudman-Hollings
GS	General Schedule
GSTS	Ground-Based Surveillance and Tracking System
GWEN	Ground Wave Emergency Network
HARM	High-Speed Antiradiation Missile
HCS	Helicopter Combat Support Special Squadron
HEDI	High Endo-Atmospheric Defense
HHG	Household Goods
HIV	Human Immunodeficiency Virus
HNS	Host Nation Support
ICBM	Intercontinental Ballistic Missile
IFF	Identification Friend or Foe

IG	Inspector General
IHPTET	Integrated High Performance Turbine Engine Technology
IIR	Imaging Infrared
IMA	Individual Mobilization Augmentees
IMET	International Military Education and Training
IMC	Internal Management Control
IMIP	Industrial Modernization Incentives Program
INDCONS	Industrial Alert Conditions
INF	Intermediate-Range Nuclear Forces
INFOSEC	Information Security
ING	Inactive National Guard
IR	Infrared
IRR	Individual Ready Reserve
IRS	Internal Revenue Service
IUSS	Integrated Undersea Surveillance System
JCS	Joint Chiefs of Staff
JMMC	Joint Military Medical Command
JSTARS	Joint Surveillance/Target Attack Radar System
JRMB	Joint Requirements and Management Board
JROC	Joint Requirements Oversight Council
JT&E	Joint Test and Evaluation
JTFME	Joint Task Force Middle East
JTIDS	Joint Tactical Information Distribution System
KEW	Kinetic Energy Weapons
LAMP	Land-Air Maritime Patrol
LANTIRN	Low-Altitude Navigation and Targeting Infrared System for Night
LCAC	Landing Craft, Air Cushion
LDCs	Lesser Developed Countries

LEDET	Law Enforcement Detachment
LF	Low Frequency
LHX	Light Helicopter Experimental
LIC	Low-Intensity Conflict
LOS-F-H	Line-of-Sight Forward-Heavy
LOS-R	Line-of-Sight Rear
LRAACA	Long-Range Air ASW Capability Aircraft
LRINF	Longer Range Intermediate-Range Nuclear Forces
LVT	Assault Amphibian Vehicle
MAB	Marine Amphibious Brigade
MAD	Mutual Assured Destruction
MAF	Marine Amphibious Force
MAP	Military Assistance Program
MAW	Marine Aircraft Wing
MIDEASTFOR	Middle East Force
MiG	Mikoyan-Gurevich (Soviet aircraft)
MILCON	Military Construction
Milstar	Military Strategic and Tactical Relay System
MIMIC	Microwave/Millimeter Wave Integrated Circuit
MIP	Model Installation Program, Management Improvement Plan
MIRV	Multiple Independently-Targetable Reentry Vehicle
MLRS	Multiple-Launch Rocket System
MMP	Master Mobilization Plan
MOA	Memorandum of Agreement
MOU	Memorandum of Understanding
MPS	Maritime Prepositioning Ship
MPTS	Manpower, Personnel, Training, and Safety

MRT	Miniature Receive Terminal
MRTFB	Major Range Test Facility Base
MSE	Mobile Subscriber Equipment
MYP	Multiyear Procurement
MWR	Morale, Welfare, and Recreation
NASP	National Aerospace Plane
NATO	North Atlantic Treaty Organization
Navstar	Navigation Satellite Timing and Ranging
NCA	National Command Authorities
NCMS	National Center for Manufacturing Sciences
NEACP	National Emergency Airborne Command Post
NFIP	National Foreign Intelligence Program
NLOS	Non-Line-of-Sight System
NMCC	National Military Command Center
NORAD	North American Aerospace Defense Command
NPG	Nuclear Planning Group
NRRCs	Nuclear Risk Reduction Centers
NSA	National Security Agency
NSDD	National Security Decision Directive
NSNF	Nonstrategic Nuclear Forces
NWS	North Warning System
OCONUS	Outside of the Continental United States
O&M	Operation and Maintenance
OJCS	Organization of the Joint Chiefs of Staff
OMB	Office of Management and Budget
OPTEMPO	Operating Tempo
OSD	Office of the Secretary of Defense
OT&E	Operational Test and Evaluation
OTH	Over-the-Horizon

OTH-B	Over-the-Horizon Backscatter (radar)
PAVE PAWS	Phased-Array Radars
PBA	Production Base Analyses
PCS	Permanent Change of Station
PECI	Productivity Enhancing Capital Investment
PGM	Precision Guided Munitions
PIF	Productivity Investment Fund
PIOB	President's Intelligence Oversight Board
PKO	Peacekeeping Operations
PLRS	Position, Location, and Reporting System
POL	Petroleum, Oil, and Lubricants
POMCUS	Prepositioning of Materiel Configured to Unit Sets
P&Q	Productivity and Quality Team
PPBS	Planning, Programming, and Budgeting System
PPI	Planned Product Improvements
PRC	People's Republic of China
R&D	Research and Development
RC	Reserve Component
RDT&E	Research, Development, Test, and Evaluation
REFORGER	Return of Forces to Germany
ROK	Republic of Korea
RO/RO	Roll-on/Roll-off
ROTHR	Relocatable Over-the-Horizon Radar
RPV	Remotely Piloted Vehicle
RRF	Ready Reserve Force
RV	Reentry Vehicle
S&T	Science and Technology
SADARM	Search and Destroy Armor

SALT	Strategic Arms Limitation Treaty, Strategic Arms Limitation Talks
SAM	Surface-to-Air Missile, Sea Air Mariner
SASC	Senate Armed Services Committee
SATKA	Surveillance, Acquisition, Tracking, and Kill Assessment
SBI	Space-Based Interceptor
SDI	Strategic Defense Initiative
SDIO	Strategic Defense Initiative Organization
SDS	Strategic Defense System
SEAL	Sea-Air-Land
SEMATECH	Semiconductor Manufacturing Technology Institute
SFS	Surface Effect Fast Sealift
SHORAD C^2	Short-Range Air Defense Command and Control
SICBM	Small ICBM
SINCGARS	Single-Channel Ground and Airborne System
SINCGARS-V	Single-Channel Ground and Airborne System, VHF
SLBM	Submarine-Launched Ballistic Missile
SLCM	Submarine-Launched Cruise Missile
SLEP	Service Life Extension Program
SLKT	Survivability, Lethality, and Key Technologies
SM	Standard Missile
SLOC	Sea Line of Communications
SNA	Soviet Naval Aviation
SNF	Short-Range Nuclear Forces
SOF	Special Operations Forces
SRAM	Short-Range Attack Missile
SSBN	Ballistic Missile Submarine, Nuclear-Powered

SSGN	Cruise Missile Attack Submarine, Nuclear-Powered
SSN	Attack Submarine, Nuclear-Powered
SSTC	Space Systems Test Capabilities
SSTS	Space-Based Surveillance and Tracking System
START	Strategic Arms Reduction Talks
Su	Sukhoi (aircraft)
SWA	Southwest Asia
SWCM	Special Warfare Craft, Medium
SWS	Special Warfare Systems
T&E	Test and Evaluation
TACS	Auxiliary Crane Ship
TASM	Tactical Air-to-Surface Missile
TEC	Test and Evaluation Committee
TGSM	Terminally Guided Submunitions
TIARA	Tactical Intelligence and Related Activities
TLAM	Tomahawk Land Attack Missile
TOA	Total Obligational Authority
TOW	Tube-Launched, Optically Tracked, Wire-Guided (antitank missile)
TRI-TAC	Joint Tactical Communications Program
TRSS	Tactical Remote Sensor System
UHF	Ultrahigh Frequency
URI	University Research Initiative
USCENTCOM	United States Central Command
USCINCCENT	United States Commander in Chief, Central Command
USCINCEUR	United States Commander in Chief, Europe
USCINCLANT	United States Commander in Chief, Atlantic Command

USCINCNORAD	United States Commander in Chief, North American Aerospace Defense Command
USCINCPAC	United States Commander in Chief, Pacific Command
USCINCSO	United States Commander in Chief, Southern Command
USCINCSPACE	United States Commander in Chief, Space
USCINCSOC	United States Commander in Chief, Special Operations Command
USCINCSOUTH	United States Commander in Chief, Southern Command
USCINCSTRAT	United States Commander in Chief, Strategic Command
USCINCTRANS	United States Commander in Chief, Transportation Command
USD(A)	Under Secretary of Defense (Acquisition)
USD(P)	Under Secretary of Defense (Policy)
USSOCOM	United States Special Operations Command
USSR	Union of Soviet Socialist Republics
USSOUTHCOM	United States Southern Command
USTRANSCOM	United States Transportation Command

VA	Veterans Administration
VE	Value Engineering
VHA	Variable Housing Allowance
VHF	Very High Frequency
VHSIC	Very High Speed Integrated Circuit
VLF	Very Low Frequency
VLS	Vertical Launch System
VLSI	Very Large Scale Integration
V/STOL	Vertical/Short Take-Off and Landing

WARMAPS	Wartime Manpower Planning System
WHNS	Wartime Host Nation Support
WIMS	Worldwide Intratheater Mobility Study
WIS	WWMCCS Information Systems
WWMCCS	Worldwide Military Command and Control System

APPENDIX H.
MAPS

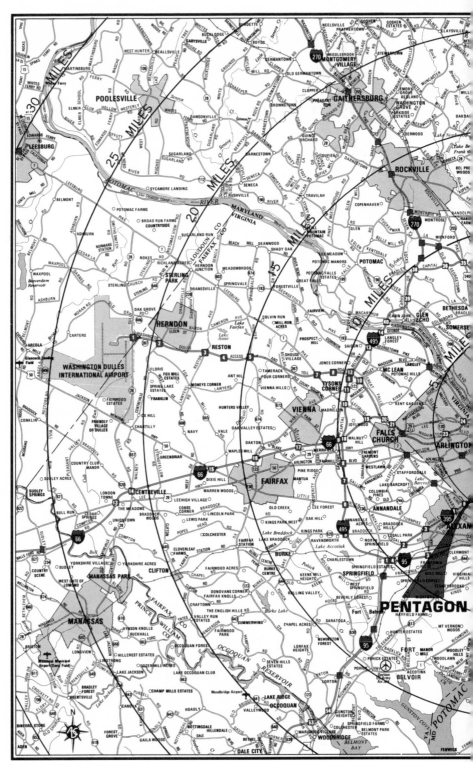

STOCK NO 30200

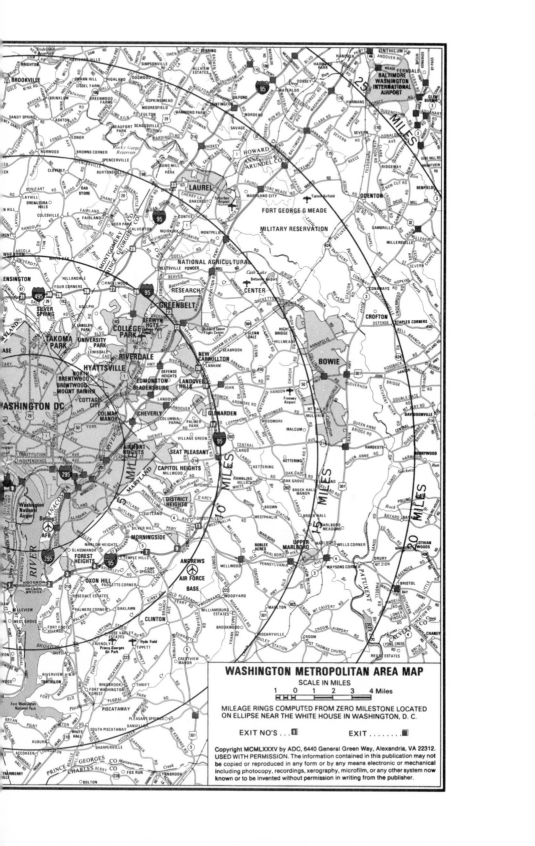

WASHINGTON METROPOLITAN AREA MAP

SCALE IN MILES

1　0　1　2　3　4 Miles

MILEAGE RINGS COMPUTED FROM ZERO MILESTONE LOCATED
ON ELLIPSE NEAR THE WHITE HOUSE IN WASHINGTON, D. C.

EXIT NO'S . . . 🔲　　　　EXIT . . . . 🔲

Copyright MCMLXXXV by ADC, 6440 General Green Way, Alexandria, VA 22312.
USED WITH PERMISSION. The information contained in this publication may not
be copied or reproduced in any form or by any means electronic or mechanical
including photocopy, recordings, xerography, microfilm, or any other system now
known or to be invented without permission in writing from the publisher.

METRORAIL SYSTEM MAP

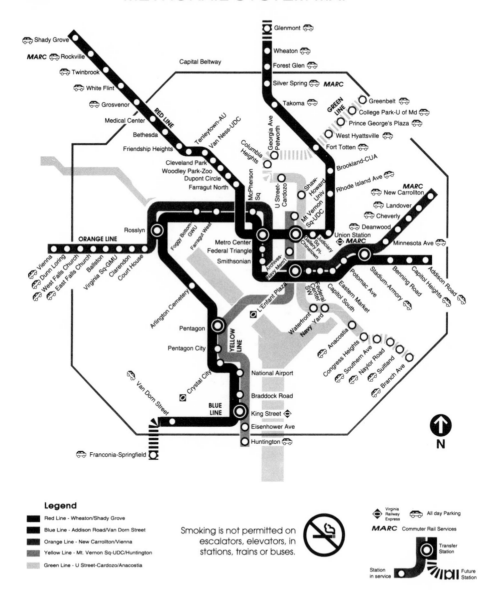

Legend

- Red Line - Wheaton/Shady Grove
- Blue Line - Addison Road/Van Dorn Street
- Orange Line - New Carrollton/Vienna
- Yellow Line - Mt. Vernon Sq-UDC/Huntington
- Green Line - U Street-Cardozo/Anacostia

Smoking is not permitted on
escalators, elevators, in
stations, trains or buses.

Virginia Railway Express

All day Parking

MARC Commuter Rail Services

Transfer Station

Station in service

Future Station

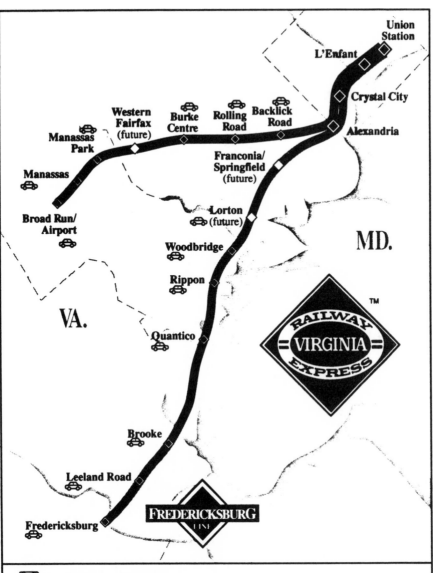

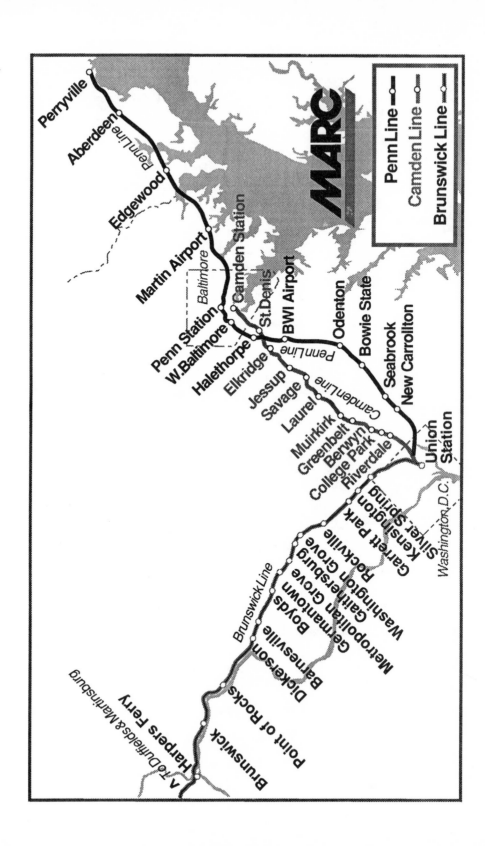

INDEX

ABOUT THE
AUTHOR

Perry Smith worked for many years in the Pentagon. During his first tour of duty he served as a branch chief, a division chief, a JCS planner, and as a military assistant to the deputy secretary of defense. On his second tour, he served as the director of plans for the Air Force.

A graduate of the class of 1956 at the U.S. Military Academy, Major General Smith earned his doctorate in international relations from Columbia University in 1967. He taught at the U.S. Air Force Academy and was a faculty member, and later commandant, at the National War College.

He has an extensive operational and leadership background. During the Vietnam War, he flew 180 combat missions in the F-4D in Southeast Asia, including 50 over North Vietnam. Later, he commanded the F-15 Wing in Bitburg, Germany. Smith retired in 1986 as a major general with over 30 years of commissioned service. During the Persian Gulf War of 1991, he was a military analyst for CNN and the "MacNeil-Lehrer News Hour" and appeared on camera more than 100 times during that six-week war. He is also a special consultant to CNN.

Since his retirement, General Smith has written *Taking Charge: Making the Right Choices* and *How CNN Fought the War*. His practical guidebook for leaders, *Taking Charge*, with more than 100,000 copies in print, is being used by dozens of leadership development programs. He has also produced a four-cassette audio tape series on leadership for Nightingale-Conant, entitled *Taking Charge: How to Make Things Happen in Your Organization.*

He is the president of Visionary Leadership, Ltd., of Augusta, Ga. He lectures to and teaches seminars for military and business audiences on leadership, strategic planning, ethics, and strategy. His address is P.O. Box 15666, Augusta, Ga. 30919 (telephone 706-738-9133).